DANCE WHILE—YOU CAN

BY SHIRLEY MACLAINE

"Don't Fall off the Mountain"
You Can Get There From Here
Out on a Limb
Dancing in the Light
It's All in the Playing
Going Within
Dance While You Can

DANCE WHILE YOU CAN

—Shirley MacLaine

BANTAM BOOKS

NEW YORK • TORONTO • LONDON • SYDNEY • AUCKLAND

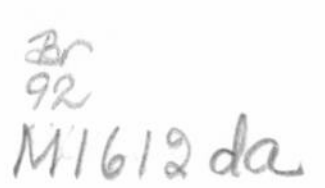

UNLESS OTHERWISE CREDITED, ALL PHOTOGRAPHS ARE COURTESY OF SHIRLEY MACLAINE'S PERSONAL COLLECTION.

DANCE WHILE YOU CAN
A Bantam Book / November 1991

Book design by Terry Karydes.

For information address: Bantam Books.

Library of Congress Cataloging-in-Publication Data

MacLaine, Shirley, 1934–
Dance while you can / Shirley MacLaine.
p. cm.
ISBN 0-553-07607-8
1. MacLaine, Shirley, 1934–
2. Entertainers—United States—Biography.
3. Spiritualists—United States—Biography.
I. Title.
PN2287.M18A3 1991
791.43'028'092—dc20
[B] 91-13527
CIP

Published simultaneously in the United States and Canada

Bantam Books are published by Bantam Books, a division of Bantam Doubleday Dell Publishing Group, Inc. Its trademark, consisting of the words "Bantam Books" and the portrayal of a rooster, is Registered in U.S. Patent and Trademark Office and in other countries. Marca Registrada. Bantam Books, 666 Fifth Avenue, New York, New York 10103.

PRINTED IN THE UNITED STATES OF AMERICA

RRH 0 9 8 7 6 5 4 3 2 1

For Dr. Leroy Perry

If we can genuinely honor our mother and father
we are not only at peace with ourselves
but we can then give birth to our future.

~ Contents

DANCE WHILE —YOU CAN

Part One

~ MOTHER MOVIE

Chapter 1

~ Hollywood Freeway

I SAT IN MY CAR ON THE Ventura Freeway going to work at five o'clock in the morning in order to beat the traffic. Everyone else in town seemed to be doing the same thing. The usual speed limit observed was sixty-five or seventy miles an hour. We were doing two.

I looked out of my window. A creeping civilization on wheels surrounded me. To the left a man ate yogurt out of a container, anxiously stirring some kind of fruit from the bottom. I thought of the dancer's guilt I used to feel when I went over my calorie quota by doing the same thing. I would have been better off with plain yogurt. Denial was necessary to success somehow.

To the right of me a woman had her window down and

a smile on her face. Puccini came from the front seat in glorious stereo. She had the right idea. If this was going to take eons, she'd spend it listening to *Madame Butterfly*.

I moved around in my seat trying to give myself a back adjustment. This was going to take a certain kind of centeredness.

For thirty-five years I had negotiated these freeways in early morning soggy mist on my way to the movie studios. I had adjusted to them as a gradual lesson in patience. Or had I settled? Was I like the fish that had learned to survive on the pollution of Lake Erie? I was appalled.

I looked up and over the cars ahead of me. I had to imagine what the skyline of Burbank looked like, because I couldn't see through the smog. I couldn't see the mountains either. I felt suspended in time in a polluted morning soup. California had been so glorious when I first came in 1954. This freeway hadn't even been constructed. It was, instead, a main thoroughfare that allowed Khrushchev, after his visit to our *Can-Can* set, to see the future of the San Fernando Valley and how it worked. I remembered he had said something about our not needing to be afraid of him and the Soviets: "You will bury yourselves from within." Is this what he meant?

I chuckled to myself and thought of the scene around the table in *The Magnificent Ambersons* when Orson Welles, as a fictitious Henry Ford, described a litany of potential disasters that might result from his new idea. Perhaps the car was not the best invention for man. At that moment, I imagined what it would be like if the "Big One" hit right now. In the event of an earthquake, I'd be inundated by yogurt, Puccini, carbon monoxide, and air that I could feel more than I could breathe.

My stomach turned over with a very slight little quake of its own. It must have been the fruit I ate, I thought to myself. Or was it nerves?

I was inching my way along to Warner Brothers, a studio

where I had never before worked, to be part of a film that had high-powered talent, high-priced actors, a budget one could easily come in under, and a schedule that would be as luxurious as the catering table.

Beginning a new film was always a new adventure for me, but as production time passed, it usually became a kind of boring, tedious exercise, sprinkled with the sporadic thrills of the scenes that went particularly well. The long waits between setups got on everyone's nerves; it was always hurry up and wait, particularly in the morning. I never liked getting up early in the morning: I was a night person, seeming to come alive after the sun went down. "Moon energy," someone told me once. "Moon energy is female." Women sparkle at night.

I took a deep breath, a kind of a deep memory sigh. I couldn't smell anything, not even the fumes. I had lost my sense of smell the previous January with some strange Asian brand of the California flu. "I probably created this to endure the freeway," I thought. I remembered just a few weeks ago being in an elevator where five guys with pinkie rings were smoking fat stogies, and it hadn't bothered me one iota. Previously I could smell a person with a cigar a mile away, particularly one with a pinkie ring. Having no sense of smell has its advantages. But I missed being able to smell the sea air and the pungency of seaweed when I walked out on the balcony at Malibu. The ocean sustained me in California. I could feel my blood run smoothly from the twenty-five postures of yoga I had done on the balcony as the sun rose. It was worth the price I paid in the loss of an extra hour of sleep.

I turned on the radio, AM980 on my dial, all the news all the time. "You give us twenty minutes, we'll give you the world," it continually reminded me. Another hostage had been taken, more corruption in government, a drug bust to the tune of twenty million dollars, a new report that said cholesterol was not bad for me. And Gorbachev had made yet another extraordinary advance in the cause of democracy behind the Iron Curtain. Would the Soviet Union ultimately reap the same fruits of democracy that seemed to be our inheritance on this particular day of freedom in the land of prosperity and openness?

I sighed again with a kind of hope and pleasure that I had somehow survived it all, and had yet another good job, and was still here, as the song I would sing later on in the film triumphantly insisted.

Yet movies had not been really interesting to me for some time now. I didn't like the small talk in between setups: "Where did you eat last night?" "I've seen a new store with a great bargain in shoes." "I found ribs with a sauce that doesn't have any sugar in it." Blah, Blah, Blah. I seemed to be the only one interested in meaningful talk these days, which was guaranteed to cause people to either vague out or be intimidated. The "vague glaze" was always followed by the instant need for a coffee or a smoke. I played a game with myself deciding who would vague out and who would be interested by talk about the way the world was going.

In any case, we could never become involved in a deep discussion, because at any moment we might be called to work. The hurry-up-and-wait syndrome could play havoc with "bonding" with anyone on a movie set. To arrive early or on time and not be used for hours didn't seem fair to me. It seemed to be a waste of time, and it was on that level that I found being on a film emotionally draining.

I reached into my tote bag and pulled out the pages of the scene we would shoot on this first day. I had a nearly three-page monologue. Maybe that was why my stomach was upset. Up until last year, I had not spent much time learning lines. Somehow I could always manage when I got to work. But lately either the gray matter was going, the attention to specifics reduced, or I was suffering from what I jokingly called "Actor's Alzheimer's." I also knew that the director was a stickler for having every word correct. I picked up the pages, finding it not at all difficult to read them as I was driving. I didn't know which was slower, my memory or the traffic.

I had been gifted with what we call in the business "a part and a half." It was fabulous. In fact, I guess you could say it was reminiscent of some of my own life. I was playing a movie star who was still hanging in there, still working, with a daughter who was also talented.

The day before, we had rehearsed in the home of the movie star on whom my character was based. I was completely unprepared for what I faced when I walked into the living room of her "Beverly Hills House." There on the walls, peppered with museumlike memories, were pictures of the real me taken from magazine covers, portrait sittings, movie stills, premieres, awards ceremonies, live performances, from my childhood and adolescence—even a shot of me from the chorus of the subway circuit of *Oklahoma!* when I was sixteen years old that I had forgotten existed. *I* had suddenly been translated into the character I was playing, while my mind was flooded with memories of my own real career in the theater and films.

My eyes had filled up with the overwhelming impact of this pictorial reminder of my own show business past, and although I have no problem looking at events in many past lives, here I was overcome with reminiscences of this life. I had gotten to the rehearsal early and wandered through the rooms of Doris Mann's home, allowing myself to wallow in the emotional feelings of certain red-letter events that beckoned to me from the past. I was in some kind of time warp as the images triggered fast-frame memories of my experiences.

I looked at a cover of myself and Clint Eastwood and

remembered the day on location in Mexico under a tree, 116 degrees in the shade, when he had become impatient with his horse and belted the animal in the nose. At first I was shocked, but then I remembered thinking, What can you expect from a Republican? I had mellowed since then, not only about Clint, but about Republicans.

I saw a shot of me and Dean Martin and remembered the day of the comedic fight in *All in a Night's Work,* which tore the silver ranch mink coat I wore. I asked wardrobe to give it to me at the end of the shoot. The producer refused. No matter. If I wore a mink coat these days, I'd be stoned.

There was a picture of me at eighteen years wearing false eyelashes, thick, not only with mascara, but with old-fashioned stage beading. They could have turned me upside down and swept the floor with those lashes. My lips were outlined like Joan Crawford's and glistened with lip gloss that looked as though it might drip off any minute. That had been my eighteen-year-old interpretation of "sexy." I even remembered the turquoise earrings I wore in that portrait sitting. I wondered where they were now. I had always had such an emotional attachment to personal adornments. It wasn't the value of the possessions that had meaning to me; it was the reason for their existence that kept me attached. All the nostalgic things we cling to, or even yearn for, really because they are memory triggers.

In fact, I was still haunted by a pair of green glass earrings that I had seen once when I was sixteen years old in a shop in the Village in New York. They were something like $19.95, far too much for me to afford, so I had bypassed them. I had been looking for those earrings ever since in whatever antique or costume jewelry shop I passed. To this day I wondered why they meant so much to me; but more than that, I wondered why, if they had meant that much to me, I hadn't splurged and bought them anyway.

DANCE WHILE YOU CAN

A picture on the wall reminded me of the day I had my ears pierced, going straight to ballet school, and having Madame Perioslavic of the Ballet Theatre School grab me by the ear and toss me across the room because I had been inept in a step I had done. I always wondered if she knew that I had just had my ears pierced. Or had it been some personal sign to me that working with discipline superseded vanity.

As I wandered through the rooms with my life staring back at me, I realized that I was remembering predominantly two things: one, whatever man I happened to be involved with at the time; and two, how much I weighed. I remembered—to the pound—how much I weighed in each of the pictures. Fascinating, once a dancer always a dancer.

Being a dancer meant body priority. Being a dancer meant discipline. Being a dancer meant the show must go on. Being a dancer meant you nearly always thought about food. But mostly, being a dancer meant the awareness of physical health and the alignment of your mental attitude. I could never really do anything if I was not moderately happy with it. If I was really unhappy with something, I was prone to leave it, regardless of the consequences.

As I puttered through the rooms of Doris Mann's house, I knew that I really understood this character, was happy with her, and had indeed been happy, or reasonably so, with my own life. What was it then that was gnawing away at me? Why the question, What was the point anymore?

And now, sitting in my car on the Ventura Freeway, I had that same sense of angst. I was happy to be going to work. I was grateful to have the job. I was proud of my talent. I was comfortable and confident of my experience and contribution, but there was that certain something that picked and pricked away at my soul saying, basically, that there was more. Much more. So what was missing? And how did I, with all I had in my life, and all that I had been able to accomplish, have the right to such a vain and arrogant anxiety?

Probably it hadn't that much to do with me but more to do with the world and where I fit in and, indeed, where we all fit in. Things seemed to be deteriorating rapidly—just look at the adjustment necessary simply to get to work in the morning.

I found that I wasn't enjoying socializing so much anymore. There was an inherent desperation in the interplay and values of people so much centered around money, as though money could shore up confidence in an otherwise bleak future.

Since I was away traveling so much, I wasn't often invited to small "pace-setting" dinner parties anymore. People didn't bother because they usually thought that I was at some wine tasting festival in Romania or involved with a coup d'état in Tibet. But, even on the off chance that I was invited, I usually found myself in the corner talking deeply with one person all night about something that really mattered to me, or I might leave early, preferring to sit and think or watch the waves crash at the edge of the Pacific.

Was old age setting in? Was I becoming concrete in my habits? Or did I want everything all my way? In fact, I thought as I drove along, would it even be possible for me at this stage in my life to ever have a committed and "unified" relationship again? It had been some time since I experienced that, and I wasn't at all unhappy in my freedom. I never got lonely, although I spent a lot of time alone. I seemed to need the aloneness. But was I being selfish, I wondered, in not giving a relationship a chance? Or, more to the point, was I too intimidating to men? I looked at some of the problems and some of the pleasures that friends of mine were experiencing in their relationships, and, for myself, anyway, decided none of it was worth the hassle.

He travels fastest who travels alone, I remembered thinking when I was a teenager. Was I really interested in traveling fast? Where was it I really wanted to go? And what was I really doing on the path to that destination? The moment, I thought. Live in the moment. I know that's where real and deep happiness lay. Perhaps I was in that transitional no-man's-land of realizing something intellectually but not having integrated it emotionally.

Was I indeed becoming like this traffic? Slow and congested? If so, I should simply accept it, enjoy it, and recognize that there was much happiness to be had in the enforced slowdown of the outrageous speed with which I had conducted my life.

I remembered how often my mother had commented on the fast pace she said I had set for myself. "I don't know how you do it, Shirl," she'd say. "You should slow down sometimes. You look tired."

The "tired" line always irritated me. I thought she accused me of looking tired so that *she* could take care of me again. It would give her a resurrected role to play if I were tired and needed her. I understood the need, but I longed for her to go out into the world and do something else, something really for herself. There she was, sitting in her wicker chair, wide-eyed at my latest escapade, questioning me with genuine interest, yet somehow simultaneously editorializing that I was just doing too much.

And now in her old age (eighty-seven) I'd return home from an exciting round-the-world tour filled with stories and happenings to find her waiting for me as though she had put her own life on hold until I returned to instill energy into her again. *She* had been the one convinced that she was too tired to live.

Through my mother, I realized the profound importance

of living life for myself. She never did. She lived her life for me, for my brother, Warren, and for her husband. She was the emotional support system for the family. She was the thread of continuity. She was who we came home to. She was the reason we ventured out again. And as I was reflecting so much lately on my own life and adventures, I began to realize, with specific deepness, how much I had been motivated by living out the dreams my mother never fulfilled for herself.

She had been a "dramatics" teacher and actress, reciting lines of poetry with rounded musical tones at my bedside when I couldn't sleep. She'd mix aspirins and jelly into a teaspoon in the kitchen; and with a book of poetry under her arm, she'd administer the "jelly meddy" and then recite to me until I fell asleep. She was wonderful at it. I think she could have had a career in the dramatic arts.

I wondered now if she ever beat her pillows in frustration that she never really took her own creativity out of the house. I remembered a few little theater productions she had been a part of, but her participation was usually compromised by my dad complaining that he never got a hot meal anymore, and there was dust accumulating on the mantelpiece. Dutifully Mother returned to hearth and home to live out her creative dreams through her children.

Had this been her destiny? Had the seeds for my success been sown and nurtured in the small middle-class rooms of a home that housed potential creative giants, married to one another in an unspoken bond of frustration, with a hidden agenda to never live out their own dreams?

Every day of my childhood, and even later, I must have felt I was the chattel of their repressed creativity, molded by a society that demanded that a father be the breadwinner and the mother be the housekeeper. And now I realized more than ever that whatever I was in the world, or indeed in my inner life, was a direct result of those two people who sculpted and conditioned my feelings, both consciously and unconsciously.

Say what I would about the influence of the world around me—my teachers, friends, and life itself—my parents were the root of my identity: all the selves within me that I was attempting to bring into some kind of balance with the world in which I functioned today. And Mother was, because of her constant attendance, the eyes through which I had learned to view life.

She was my female parent. I was her female child. The values of the feminine then were the energies I was grappling with. Did I have the patience that she did? The tolerance, the talent for nurturing? Did I have the capacity to be less self-centered and more giving to others as my mother had? Certainly I would be more understanding of others the more I understood myself. But I had approached life and the pursuit of excellence and creativity from such a masculine point of view. My masculine assertiveness had not been a problem for me. But my feminine talent for surrender had not been one of my strong suits. What did the act of surrender feel like?

I remembered the night Mother had seen me in *Madame Sousatzka*. She had begun to cry ten minutes into my portrayal of a possessive, demanding, committed, and passionate music teacher; and she never stopped. She was wracked with silent sobs.

When it was over, she said, "Oh, Shirl. That was your destiny—not mine. I always wanted to be a star, but this was for you to do—not me. I realize that now. I could never have given a portrayal like that."

I couldn't speak after her confession. I guess I had been waiting for it for forty years. I would never have had the emotional honesty or courage to voice such a painful surrender. I never loved her more. I wondered how different our lives would have been if she had lived more for herself. Would I have been diminished?

I remembered the day she asked me to teach her to meditate. She settled in her chair with taut urgency. When I spoke of relaxation, I saw her shoulders slump in release, but her face retained its determination to relax. I laughed to myself. Her determination was alive and well in me now. She could afford to give some of it up. Mother could walk through a room with such determination that she collided with the furniture. She was of tough Canadian stock, this patient, tolerant woman who continually surrendered to the will of others. Ah, but the surrender carried an emotional price tag that we all had to pay. She never let us forget that everything she did was for *us*.

I gently placed my hand on Mother's brow, as I guided her through a meditation. Her neck was stiff and unyielding. She felt her own rigidity.

"Just relax," I said gently, "and try to find the God within yourself."

She opened her eyes. "The God within myself?" she questioned.

"Yes," I answered. "God is within you. When you pray, you speak to God. When you meditate, you listen to God."

Her eyes filled with tears. "Oh, Shirl," she said. "Don't say that."

"Don't say what?"

"Don't say God is within me."

"Why?" I asked.

"Because," she said, "I know that when I pray to God outside of myself that he is really there. If you say God is within me, then I don't trust it, and therefore I have no one to pray to and no one to listen to."

I was stunned at the implication of what she said. Could it be that the level of her self-esteem was so low that she couldn't countenance the idea that God could be within her? Was I an arrogant, self-centered know-it-all because it made sense to me? If I saw God within myself, wouldn't I then see God in everyone else?

The meditation didn't work. We both realized we couldn't even begin.

"Oh, Mother," I thought, as I inched along the freeway. "Am I going to work today because of you? Do I act because of you? Am I me because you couldn't find a way to be you?"

The traffic began to pick up. My thoughts flashed to money. Mother never felt comfortable that there was enough money. "Don't spend money on bringing me to California," she'd say. "We'll just wait until later when we can afford it."

"But I can afford it now."

"Really? Are you sure?" she'd say. "You work so hard for your money."

"I know," I'd say. "But nothing is more important than being together when we can."

"Oh, Shirl," she'd go on. "We have to save our money. You never know what might happen."

Oh, yes, I knew that. I'd heard that fear expressed so many times from the beginning of my childhood. I thought now about my own relationship to money. The car I was driving was rented. I didn't want to own one.

My values were becoming more simple as time passed. Was I rebelling against my mother's fear? I didn't really want to own much of anything anymore. I found myself desiring to give away half my wardrobe. I remembered how she used to lovingly make most of my clothing. Skirts and blouses were her specialty. She'd hunch over her sewing machine and have a colorful outfit for a summer date in a day. I think I thought I didn't deserve it. And now the idea of accumulating more possessions was becoming even more burdensome to me. Why? I think I wanted to feel liberated from the worry that valuables carried.

"Simplify. Simplify," as Thoreau used to say. I was beginning to understand what he meant. Mother was constantly concerned with who would inherit her Wedgwood and crystal. She wanted assurances that her valuables would stay in the family. I only wanted the cookie jar. She thought I had no appreciation. She was hurt by my lack of interest.

I had even had discussions with my agent about giving up everything. I couldn't work for nothing, because I would undercut my fellow players; but I could, I thought, put myself on a meager budget and give everything else away.

I guess my notion of giving up material wealth had something to do with wanting to experience the feeling of complete surrender. But to *what* would I surrender?

The closest I could come to defining it would be the surrender to total liberation. Liberation from possessions, from the worry that went with them. Liberation from being encumbered, tied down. Liberation from needing to be insured, from needing to feel I needed.

I thought perhaps Mother Teresa had the right idea. She'd move into a donated Hilton Hotel suite with her nuns of service and proceed to have the place stripped of everything: drapes, carpets, furniture . . . everything.

Having accomplished that, she never compared or judged her material surroundings. She never felt deprived, because she had taken a vow to live with *nothing*. It must have been liberating for her in the most profound sense. I knew I wasn't nearly so evolved that I'd be happy living that way. But I was doing a lot of thinking about it.

In my discussions with my agent, I realized how complicated such an act would be. The decisions of who to give my hard-earned money *to* would be as burdensome as how to make a lot of it. My "movie star's closet" was crammed with clothes, both from pictures and from travels around the world. Decisions of what to wear became time-consuming and confusing, whereas to have, say, ten outfits—one for each day of the week, with maybe three or four that could slop over—would be a liberation.

Having lived through several Malibu fires, I remembered that most of what I wanted to save revolved around my notes, some treasured pictures and books, and my cashmere and silk sweaters. Nothing else was really important to me. I guess the sequined Bob Mackie-type gowns from my show would have been a practical salvage, but my mind didn't work along these lines. I found myself thinking more in terms of what I would need to survive, rather than what I would need to get up on a stage. Yet, why were so many clothes still in my closet? It's true that I wore them all at one time or another. Yet my idea of a good trip around the world would be to take one small suitcase that I could carry and live out of.

I had no real jewelry. Most of it had been stolen anyway. Ostentatious flashing of diamonds, rubies, emeralds, and the like was an invitation to mugging and, more to the point, a spectacle designed for conspicuous consumption. And for that matter, the old-fashioned movie queen image was dated anyway.

I had not been a collector of art or rare antiques. I had never wanted a yacht. I did not have expensive taste in anything really, except comfort. That was why I loved my cashmere and silk sweaters. Something that traveled light, wouldn't wrinkle, and wasn't heavy was my idea of luxury. Perhaps I *was* addicted to the idea that one travels fastest who travels alone. Yet when I took a trip, I always packed too much and never wore most of it.

Underneath all of it, perhaps I didn't really want to have more than my parents had had. Perhaps their experience during the Depression was still a part of me. They had talked of it often. I had registered every word of their fear and compromised dignity. Now, in my middle fifties, I was beginning to look at the effect on me in a more serious way than I ever had. On the deepest, most personal level, I wanted to work out who my parents had been to me. I knew that I couldn't get on with the future until I had learned and realized the past.

I had written so much about inner peace, balance, and harmony in cosmic terms, when all of it really came down to fallout from Mom and Dad on this earth. What a joke. You think you have a handle on God, the Universe, and the Great White Light until you go home for Thanksgiving. In an hour, you realize how far you've got to go and who is the real turkey.

Such was my state of mind as I finally pulled up to the front gate of the Burbank studio, and the old guard there looked into my face and said, "Gosh, it's so good to have you on the lot, Miss MacLaine." He went on to say that I had been one of his favorites since he was a youngster! I felt a flush of gratitude, smiled, blinked—and then wondered what that said about *my* age. As I continued on to Soundstage 17, the white walls of the buildings surrounded me, bringing back that familiar glare that always gave me a headache by lunchtime.

A parking attendant guided my car into a reserved parking space, asked if there was anything that he could help me with, and pointed out the makeup trailer. I proceeded to the makeup trailer, said hello to the makeup man, and sat down on the chair.

There was coffee brewing on the makeup counter, as an

A.D. (assistant director), bright and energetic in the personage of a delightful blond eighteen-year-old girl, cheerily asked me if I would like to have a burrito for breakfast. I declined, made my amenities to others in the trailer, and before the makeup man could apply a thin base of Max Factor Fair on my face, I lurched out of the chair, ran to my assigned motor home, forced open the door, stumbled forward to the bathroom, and threw up. "What was it?" I thought. Was it the fruit? The freeway? First-day nerves? Could I be afraid of the three-page monologue? Or could I, having relived the past on the way that morning, simply be getting rid of old stuff and making a rather physical transition into something new and unfamiliar?

The A.D. came after me. "What's wrong?" she said. "Nothing really," I replied, in between heaves. "I'm sure I'll be all right." The last thing in the world I wanted was for anybody to think I was incapable of being disciplined. The thought of not being able to perform what was expected of me made me feel even worse. I would, above all, get through this first day and not hold anybody up. In fact, holding anybody up on any day would be a fate worse than death for me. I would live up to my obligations regardless. I was my mother's daughter.

I knew when the A.D. said, "Okay," and left my trailer that it wouldn't take five minutes for news of my vomiting jag to go around the entire crew, worry the director, and potentially necessitate a change in the schedule. Just worrying them bothered me.

The first wave of nausea over, I sat down in my motor home and began to meditate. I visualized a perfectly calm stomach, using white light etched with blue. I began to feel better, as the visualization became real and penetratingly worked its healing magic. Taking deep breaths and trying to smile, I made my way back to the makeup trailer and sat in the chair again. The makeup man applied rouge to my cheeks and the nausea welled up to match.

I ran back to the motor home, threw up again. Now, for sure, they'll think I can't work today, I thought. I vomited again, sat down, meditated, felt better, returned to the makeup trailer, crawled into the chair, whereupon the makeup man applied eyeliner and eyelashes. Again the nausea welled up. Nothing like making sickness a farce, I thought. I bolted out of the chair a third time, ran back to the motor home, leading the kind driver in the parking lot to wonder whether I was perhaps seriously temperamental. I threw up again, finished, and feeling better, returned to the makeup trailer.

The pretty A.D. had watched all of this and said, "Don't you want us to reschedule today?" "No," I said. "I'm going to be fine. Now I'm sure of it. Let's say that I just threw up three times: one for mind, one for body, one for spirit."

Everyone in the makeup trailer laughed, the tension was broken, and lo and behold, I was fine.

To this day I'm not really sure what happened. When I look back on it now, I realized I was going through a transition of coming to terms with aging, work, time, parents, and myself; and I was inherently dramatic enough to express it on the first day of work, another trait my mother had handed down to me. Frustration might be profound, but dramatic release was a definite outlet of choice. Sometimes even I was impressed by its potential effect on others.

Chapter 2

~ Makeup Trailer

I SAT IN THE MAKEUP CHAIR trying to relax with my eyes closed, allowing the makeup artist to do whatever he wanted to do with my face. How many hours had I spent in makeup chairs all over the world? Zillions. But not as many as most actresses. I simply didn't have the patience, and I had never wanted them to make me over. I sort of liked my face the way it was.

I had always been suspicious of the formulas observed for making up people's faces to be photographed by the camera—the lip line that conformed to cookie cutter prescriptions, the eyelashes carefully glued to create a cheek shadow when lit from above, the arch of the eyebrow usually plucked so that it could be more controlled, the contour of the rouge that accentuated the high cheekbones, the mixtures of the eye shadows that accentuated eye color—all those techniques were observed and duplicated as though out of a magic silver screen makeup textbook. As much as I had been conditioned to be disciplined and fulfill what was expected of me, I didn't like the idea of looking like everyone else, even if they were beautiful. I didn't like consensus beauty.

I was imbued with the need to be my own individual self, which included my makeup (I couldn't sit still for it) and my dressing habits (I made the worst-dressed list nearly every year). My attitude seemed to carry with it a devil-may-care carelessness, but in truth I think I was refusing to be repressed, molded, or sculpted into the vision that other people had for me. *Because* something had been traditional was enough reason for me to rebel against it. I wasn't loud or obstreperous in my nonconformist attitude, I just walked away from it. I wouldn't be there. I'd disappear.

And now, as I sat in the makeup trailer gazing at myself, I realized I was allowing the makeup man to do anything to my face he wanted to. He'd know how to camouflage the telltale lines and the contours of aging. I had always been the youngest kid in the flick. Now I was the grandmother; I had become a survivor. I could use all the help I could get. I would accept such a need as gracefully as possible. At least I had learned to surrender to that.

I looked around the trailer. There was that look in the eyes of my coworkers which silently acknowledged that I was there before many of them were born. It had been almost forty years since I first came to Hollywood. I was now the one who had been around the longest.

And what did "longest" mean? Did it mean I knew more than they? No. I didn't really know any more now than I did then—in fact, probably less. The more I experienced, the more

I realized what I didn't know. And confidence? When you're young, you're oozing with it. Now I wondered where that had come from.

In fact, most of my Hollywood youth seemed like a dream, mirroring the very dream the town purported to be. Had I lived out a dream I had as a small child? Not really. I hadn't consciously remembered wanting to be "a Movie Star in Hollywood." Warren and I had gone to the movies every week of our lives and sometimes every day. We had given ourselves movie stars' names at periodic times. We played out scenes from our favorite films. But we never "had to" get to Hollywood. No. For me it had happened as an outgrowth of my training as a dancer in New York. I had been a chorus girl understudy who had gone on for the star in a musical comedy called *The Pajama Game*. A producer (Hal Wallis) saw me, signed me to a contract, and brought me to Hollywood.

And I had grown with it naturally, or at least that's how it felt. Yet the dream itself was just as elusive to me now as it had been every day of my life for nearly forty years. And now, sitting in yet another makeup chair, the dream images flashed away as each new layer of dream paint was applied to my face on this morning in 1989.

I remembered Metro, with its splashed white soundstages, seeming broader and higher and longer than the soundstages at other studios. Makeup and hair had *not* been taken care of in makeup trailers in the old days. There had been whole makeup *departments* then, housing the great artists of face and hair. Bill Tuttle or Frank Westmore or Wally Westmore and others applied makeup to the stars' faces in small cubicles. I used to watch the screen giants enter the makeup building hung over from the night before, shrouded in scarves, squinting at the morning behind dark glasses, fearing that their innermost horrors would be reflected upon their faces and recognized. I used to wonder if that would happen to me when I got older and more lived in.

I watched how the makeup artists respected the fears of the giants and applied their artful cover-ups with tenderness, gentle understanding, and real humor. "Keep movin'," Westmore would say. "Just keep movin', baby, and no one will notice what you really look like."

So we would sit alone with the movie Rembrandts who would sculpt and paint our faces into gods and goddesses for the big black giant (the audience) out there to worship. Sometimes the makeup artists would give us a gift of a certain base or certain rouge color or a lip tint to take home to attempt to wield our movie-magic vanity in real life.

The men, after having their makeup applied, would sit while the artists of hair gently and with real sensitivity secured a toupee over a bald spot that no one was willing to expose in those days. But the women, after makeup completion, would proceed to the hair department where Sydney Guilaroff presided over a counter fifty feet long, over which hung a mirror reflecting back some of the most famous and adored silver screen queens of the day.

I remembered the day I walked into Sydney's room to be met by a stunning lineup of spectacular women in various stages of hairdressing. Gazing back at themselves under artificial light that denied the early morning were Elizabeth Taylor, Grace Kelly, Audrey Hepburn, Kathryn Crosby (she was the only one who came fully dressed with alligator shoes and bag to match), Cyd Charisse, Debbie Reynolds, Jean Simmons, Ava Gardner, Lana Turner, and Marlene Dietrich. I quietly sat just adjacent to the hairdressing counter, awestruck. It was a movie fan's fantasy. There they were, these Goddesses, chatting and laughing, drinking coffee and laughing, paying close attention to studying their faces in scrupulous detail and laughing, finding lines and contours, and laughing. The act of laughing does magic things to the face, but they were also enjoying themselves, each one a topflight winner, confidently getting prepared for another day of what they were best at doing. They knew they would be camouflaged by a carefully set key light another two hours down the road in front of the camera. Failing the key light, a No. 2 "diffusion" could cover up years of "experience," as long as the male costar didn't look too "real" in his close-up. The women always knew they could be photographed through seven layers of veils.

On this relentlessly sunny morning so long ago, Sydney, clad in his elegant silk shirt, holding a long cigarette holder, flashing a sterling silver lighter, presided over his gaggle of goddesses in a way that somehow deterred competition, because he respected everyone equally. Sydney himself had been a close confidant and friend of Greta Garbo; and at intimate moments after the shooting day, when others had sped home to their families, he would often sit and tell me stories of the glory days when, erectly perched next to Garbo in a big black limousine, he would attend the mysterious Swede to make sure everything was right for a premiere. Once, he told me, he had taken her hand, pressed it to his face, and found that he had embarrassed her. Just once.

Sydney Guilaroff is a veritable fountain of fantastic memories relating to "the old days." He should write a book, because his memories are his life. His work is his legacy. The fantasies he created upon our heads were wonders to behold. Those were the days before face-lifts, so Sydney would glue what he called "sticky tabs" on the sides of our faces just above our ears. The tabs had been pierced with holes through which a small rubber band could be threaded and pulled by a hairpin into a pin curl nestled in the hairline, which would never show when the wig was placed over it. Natural face-lifts, to be sure, but guaranteed to give you a headache by mid-morning.

Dietrich had a trick whereby she used a thin gold chain pulled under her chin and up behind her ears. At each end of the chain were pins that could be secured to two pin curls also nestled behind the ears.

I remembered the day she took me on the set of *Around the World in 80 Days* and taught me how to light myself—"camera high, key light low," she would say. "If you have that, nothing much else can go wrong." She also said something about eating once every three days and drinking lots of water. Maybe that was how she kept the figure that made the rest of us drool.

Her behavior at costume fittings was legendary. She made no secret of it. She would stand for five hours at a time directing the placement of sequins and zircons upon her gown, while exhausted costume designers shuffled around her skirts on their knees. Several shifts of costumers were replaced as Dietrich, undeterred, had them move a zircon one more time. She also had a trick whereby, at the nipple point of her dress, she had a 10½-millimeter pearl sewn in to give her breasts a finished, confirmed "pointed" look. Marlene knew all the tricks. She even taught the practitioners of tricks some tricks. The quintessential pro.

Elizabeth Taylor always seemed to me to be living inside a kind of misty, dewy bubble. She had grown up in the movie business and had been a star for so long that she could, when necessary, hide herself in the midst of the souped-up protection it afforded its major stars. Her lush beauty and violet-blue eyes, enshrouded in those blue-black lashes, made her seem languid, but she was actually down-to-earth, not to say raucous, bawdy, and wholly, attractively irreverent.

Audrey Hepburn, on the other hand, was ethereal, lace

made of finely threaded steel. Self-control seemed to have been her salvation, yet her large, almond brown eyes seemed haunted by a memory that she alternately used and denied. I used to imagine it was her experience during the war.

Grace Kelly was thin, very thin, cool; not an ice goddess really, but more of a detached diva. Even though she was crowned royalty in Hollywood, I had the impression that being a Philadelphia blueblood was both more important to her and, at bottom, reflected her real personality. This was before she went off to become true royalty in Monaco. I had heard that all her costars fell in love with her. I imagined that the adventure would be one of cracking the reserve.

Debbie Reynolds was pert, perky, precious, and punctual. She was bubbling with enthusiasm and right on the button with every comedic assessment she made. I had no way of knowing then, as I gazed at her in the mirror, that our lives would converge later on and that my face one day would be made up to be the face of Doris Mann, a character based in part on Debbie's life.

Jean Simmons was a close friend of Elizabeth's, married then to a man whose real name was Jimmy Stewart. On the screen he was known as Stewart Granger. She had beautiful high cheekbones and a perfectly proportioned face, striking even without makeup. That day, forty years ago, she was wearing a bulky yellow knit sweater, which I was to inherit some ten years later during a particularly cold night at Elizabeth's house. I remembered that sweater now and suddenly wondered what had happened to it. Had I left it in a foreign city during one of my peregrinations around the world?

That first day in the hairdressing room, Ava Gardner didn't say much. But then, and even later, she didn't have to. She was beautiful beyond description, and nothing she could have uttered might have enhanced the magic of that perfection.

I remembered thinking, "Well, at least she has big hips . . . she's human."

I remembered the day, many years later, when Frank Sinatra told me of a fight he and Ava had had, because she spotted lipstick traces on his handkerchief. "Pride," he had said, "can destroy you." He went on a bit about their personal conflicts, but what stuck in my mind was his recognition of pride.

Frank, as a matter of fact, on that morning when he talked about Ava, had been in one of the makeup rooms, not really caring that the door was open and his bald spot was being painted with a color that delicately matched his own hair. It didn't matter to him that a faulty light angle usually made the painted head shine.

Later that same day, I had had one of many Italian "dago" lunches in his dressing room, with Dean and various and sundry others. Frank had a swagger and a command that intimidated people and rightfully earned him the title "Chairman of the Board." He could also, however, be extremely vulnerable and exceedingly generous in his appreciation of someone else's talent. I always thought he was responsible for my good performance in *Some Came Running*. "Let the kid get killed," he said to Vincente Minnelli (the director) and to the head of the studio. "If she dies, she'll get more sympathy. Then she'll get nominated." He was right. Frank's a good guy. At least he always was to me.

Dean was a favorite of mine. He was one of the original wits. He could look at an inane situation and, out of it, construct twenty minutes of comedy material that could go right on the stage. Whenever we worked together, I felt as though I'd develop a hernia from laughing, never knowing from one take to the next whether we would finally get through what had been actually written.

Dean Martin and Jerry Lewis had dressing rooms right up

the block from me. Jerry was always a high-tech fanatic, who loved the new technologies in sound, film, and tape recording. Dean would go out and hit golf balls. As soon as he got to work (6 A.M.), he'd go out and hit golf balls.

So one by one we Magi of magic would be turned out of makeup and hair, some having gone through a make-over process taking four hours, onto the streets of Metro.

The women stars, for a nine o'clock "ready" call, reported to the studio at six, one hour for makeup, one-half hour for wash and set, forty-five minutes under the dryer, another half an hour for comb-out and style. Then the wardrobe department got us. We were stuffed, trussed, and jammed into corsets, scientifically designed brassieres, underwear with lingerie straps that would never reveal themselves, even in a hurricane; and while we stood in our underwear, the body makeup people applied the finishing touches to what used to be real skin and what was now "reel" skin.

I particularly despised the body makeup. They put it on us with cold water sponges, and I remember one woman whom I seemed to have assigned to me with every picture I did at Metro. She had false teeth, which she clicked and clacked as she ground them while attempting to cover up my freckles. Since body makeup rubbed off on everything, I found myself in a permanent state of tension and concern about soiling the wardrobe. I didn't know which was worse, my freckles or the tension.

Everyone hovered all the time. Makeup hovered. Hair hovered. Wardrobe hovered, so that a relaxed naturalness was almost impossible, unless you had been schooled from the beginning. I think that's what Elizabeth's bubble was all about. She had designed her bubble to make it bearable. I think I found it bearable because of the discipline from my dancing. From early morning to the last shot, I remembered being in a state of "tolerance." I can tolerate this, because I'm a ballet dancer. If you can tolerate ballet, you can tolerate anything. Well, almost anything.

I remembered how Baryshnikov had come to me well into the shoot on *The Turning Point* complaining that it was so difficult for him, because the psychological and emotional pressure to act was much more draining than what was required of him to dance. "I'm exhausted at the end of every day," he said, "whereas I would have plenty of energy if I had done three ballets."

Yet walking onto a soundstage and into the center of the lit set was more comfortable and more comforting in the old days than it is now. In those days the crews lived for the films they were making. Everything about their lives revolved around the magic they were creating. They were trained, schooled, disciplined, and each one a master of his own job. Perhaps it was because it was less democratic then.

When I first came to Hollywood, we worked six days a week, sometimes didn't go home until nine, and then started in makeup again at six the next morning. Then there was the pecking order of control and power. The director was not really the helmsman. The studio head was. And the studio heads *breathed* films. They were not deal makers; they were filmmakers. A director's final cut was unheard of then. And very few writers were even allowed on the set. But there was more of a sense of family, or did it seem that way because it was before the deterioration set in?

Stars took time in between takes to joke and reminisce with the crews. Directors could get away with "waiting for the clouds to be right." And the star who was beautiful, but couldn't act, was catered to and helped from every conceivable angle. The publicity departments created the image that the studio head wished to convey to the audience, so that one's personal life was usually protected.

Each studio had its own personality; whereas Metro was big, sprawling, and powerful, like the lion that represented it, Paramount was more intimate and intricate. There used to be a fish pond in the center of the dressing rooms at Paramount, where I would go sometimes during my lunch hour to sit and think. Ursula Andress and John Derek had a dressing room next to mine. They were a couple that amused me, because each looked like the other. Later, as I followed John Derek's career with women, I realized that each woman he chose looked like the female version of himself.

Lizabeth Scott, a mistress of Hal Wallis, used to take her script apart word by word and put directions that seemed like a good idea in the margins. She would go over them with me, ask me what I thought. I was just learning myself. What did I know? My margins were empty. But since Hal Wallis had "discovered" me (he was also a man I was to sue later because he treated me like a white slave), I thought I should listen to Lizabeth.

Watching her pore over her script, her platinum blond hair falling into her glistening lip-glossed mouth, I was reminded of Veronica Lake, who had been a favorite of mine when I was a child. I remembered hearing that she had to change her drooping, one-eyed hairstyle during the war because she was setting a bad example for war factory workers, who might get their hair caught in a machine that was producing a B-17.

Shirley Booth and Anna Magnani, both idols of mine, were the "old people" on the lot. They always ended up working with Danny Mann, the director who had done my screen test out of New York before I came to Hollywood. Of course, they were under contract to Hal Wallis too, as were Dean and Jerry, as was Burt Lancaster, as was Kirk Douglas. Wallis had a nose for talent but no idea how to handle it personally. I remembered how his wife-to-be, Martha Hyer, had asked a friend of mine during her early days at Metro if he would mind fathering a child for her, because he had good bone structure, strong teeth, and a seemingly fine genetic strain.

The young man turned her down, although he had been quite flattered to have been asked. He later headed up a studio, and we often joked about where that child of his might be now had he consented.

In those days, Paul Newman was the man who looked like a road company Marlon Brando. And Burt Lancaster pulled away from Wallis, who still thought of him as a trapeze artist, and built his own company.

Danny Kaye would hold court with friends from all over the world, listen in reverence to the suggestions of his wife, Sylvia, and then proceed with some electric clandestine affair on the side.

Actors were basically actors in those days. The idea of becoming a director, writer, producer, while one was an actor, was unthinkable.

Edith Head was the head of wardrobe at Paramount. Many a day we women were rounded up for fittings and ushered into one of Edith's fully mirrored fitting rooms, where a young, sleek fashion designer, called Pat Bartow, would design many of the costumes that Edith would pick up the Academy Awards for. Edith Head was one of the most stable and intelligent women I worked with, yet she always knew her place in the pecking order of power. I found it remarkable that she never changed, always the black bangs and long straight hair pulled back in a chignon, with her horn-rimmed glasses, scuffed slippers on her feet, and a black dress. Fashion designers seemed addicted to black dresses. I suppose they spent so much time concerning themselves over what others should wear that they wanted no decision-making process about what they themselves wore. The lint on their black dresses was the badge of their hard work and creativity. Every time I had a fitting with Edith Head at Paramount, or Helen Rose at Metro, or Orry-Kelly at United Artists, I was reminded of the truth that they had seen every screen god and goddess in the world stark naked.

There used to be a massage artist, Jim Kelley, on the lot at Paramount. He was a big burly man who was booked solid all day in between shots and on his lunch hour by actors and actresses whose bodies, he claimed, he could change with massage. It was before the day of the "no pain, no gain" addiction. So after the tensions of a hard scene, one by one we would pile into Jim's office, allow him to pummel us until it really hurt, hoping that the makeup didn't smear on his sheets or that the hair wouldn't be disturbed to the point of dishevelment, and walk away feeling that he had done the work for us.

The commissaries at Paramount and Metro and Fox were the places we would retire to during the lunch hour to be reminded that others were also toiling in their own work. There would be Clark Gable salads, Bette Davis vegetable dishes, Carmen Miranda fruit plates, Dean Martin prosciutto, Frank Sinatra spaghetti and meatballs, or Grace Kelly ice sherbets to pick from on the menu.

Agents used to come to visit on the lots. (In fact, if you found your agent in his office during the day you knew he wasn't working for you.) Children sometimes came to visit. Visitors came to visit. Now agents don't have to come; they are running the studios. And time is far too precious to allow family gatherings.

In those days we even talked to the newspaper columnists on the lot. Louella Parsons would wander in, half-tanked, with her husband and would remember everything that was said during lunch. Hedda Hopper, crowned in a bonnet of Easter Parade glory, would hold forth on her political angers. Mike Connolly from *The Hollywood Reporter* and Army Archerd from *Variety* had memories like steel traps for the gossip that kept their rumor mills and livelihoods going. Everyone seemed to know everything about everyone. Information was traded and dispensed as a tool of power. "I won't print this if you do that" was a line often heard. If a love affair was blossoming on a set, the crew knew that mum was the word. The wives and husbands were always the last to know if their spouses were "playing around."

It seemed to me that it was expected that leading ladies would fall in love with their leading men, and vice versa. It was almost as though the magic of the story should prevail, with a tacit agreement that, unless it was really serious and people were willing to change their lives, the affair would be over at the end of the shoot.

There was a more insular emotional environment in those days. The lights were hotter, the candle power more penetrating, the experience of the shoot more intense. We were truly living lives within lives, internal experiences within the experience of objective reality. We were purveyors of fantasy, oftentimes caught up in it. Perhaps that was why audiences caught the fallout of stardust in our eyes.

The Hollywood dinner parties were grander, more opulent, conducted for the sake of indulgence and show. I attended many a dinner party where Sam Goldwyn, for example, would preside over the head of the table, every single course served by white-gloved attendants, the dishes before us as likely as not on fire. Women were bedecked in jewels, men strutting about in tuxedos. There would be enormous cheeses served on great platters, a cavalcade of desserts, French champagne brimming in English crystal, the whole elaborate ritual from a borrowed culture topped off by demitasse imbibed in two resplendent living rooms, one for the women, and one for the men. This must have been a Hollywood nod to a time when ladies left the dinner table to the gentlemen, cigars, and port. The conversation also repeated the conventions of another day, the ladies discussing clothes, international shopping, furs and furnishings; the men talking business and sport. The social niceties thus observed, the sexes mixed again to view the latest films, which were run in projection rooms outfitted with yet more food, drink, and mounds of carefully sculpted chocolates.

There was no dope. There was no cocaine. There was no marijuana. There was, instead, booze, the luxury of opulence, and the faith that the magic we were creating was real to the rest of the world.

Billy Wilder's cynical humor tickled us. William Wyler's abstract mystery fascinated us. John Huston's tales of Irish recklessness exposed our own lack of daring. And Elia Kazan's New York/East Coast intellectuality often made us feel that we in Hollywood were hopelessly behind in social consciousness.

The Mirisch brothers had a production company that drew all of the best talent to it at United Artists. The lot was small; there was no makeup department, no hair department. Each individual seemed to perform the function of an entire department elsewhere. This was probably the beginning of independent filmmaking as we know it today.

Fox had a back lot that was a small country unto itself. There was even a huge lake. I remember the night I was being transported as Princess Aouda in *Around the World in 80 Days* on a chair carried by four extras, one of whom threatened to drop me in the lake if I didn't ask Mike Todd, the producer, for overtime. Being one who had arisen from the ranks myself, I'd been prepared to do it until, as they gently let me down on the banks of the river, I spotted Marlene Dietrich up against a tree, dressed all in black leather, smoking a long cigarette, while Mike circled her, berating her with a harangue of some sort having to do with why she was late. I watched, fascinated, and thought I'd get to the extra's request a little later. Fortunately, they printed that take, and I wasn't threatened again. I never did bring up overtime to Mike.

I made several pictures on the Fox lot and enjoyed as a dressing room a bungalow that would be large enough to house a small family today.

I remembered the relationship I had with Candy the Chimp, whom I worked with on a film called *What a Way to Go*. Candy and I took a shine to each other. She would come to my dressing room every morning to watch me get made up, while she sipped a cup of coffee with cream and two lumps of sugar. She would then go over the wardrobe, which was not insignificant, hanging neatly on a rack for the day's shoot. Then she'd climb on my back, and together we'd ride my bicycle to the set. Candy was upset with me at the wrap party when she saw me kissing and hugging so many other people, and finally, in a fit of jealousy, she bit me in the hand and that was the last I saw of her.

Much later, the Khrushchev visit to America came to the Fox lot, presided over by Spyros Skouras and others. They had asked me to do the Can-Can for Khrushchev. Irene Sharaff's costumes weighed about sixty-five to seventy pounds. I thought I would go into cardiac arrest doing the entire number without cuts. At the end of it, Khrushchev's comment was, "The face of humanity is prettier than its backside." I countered, in juvenile bravado, by saying, "He was just upset that we wore panties."

I remembered so well that day, because I had gone to the Fox commissary where the Skouras–Khrushchev debate had occurred. Joan Crawford had sought me out in that commissary. She came to visit me on the set, had lunch with me—and then, back in my bungalow, while she was dressed in what she claimed were her fake diamonds and turquoise (the real ones being left in the safe), I couldn't help but focus on how predominant her freckles were. I wondered how much body makeup she was subjected to every morning, because I couldn't remember seeing her freckles in *Mildred Pierce*.

She talked of her life, her baby-doll straps, her ambitions in Hollywood, and invited me that night to have dinner with her. The dinner to me was vague, as I thought about it now, but I remembered sitting at a long Citizen Kane table—she on one end, me on the other. The impression created was one of distance, an ambiance of intimidation. Perhaps that's why I couldn't remember the subjects we discussed.

The Fox lot was where I was reunited with Dean Martin, with whom I had done five pictures, Bob Cummings, with whom I had worked in Japan on *My Geisha,* and Bob Mitchum, which continued the personal relationship that had kindled between us on *Two for the Seesaw*. Mitchum was a man of high intellect and low expectations—of the world, of himself, who knows why—one of the most intelligent men I had ever met, with a photographic memory and a capacity for booze that could have retired him with the title. He was forever making B pictures, giving as an excuse, "Better they should happen to me than someone else."

I remembered lying in a giant champagne glass with him for hours, covered with a golden silk sheet and surrounded by the crew, who were trying to make us look beautiful together, while at the same time showing irritation at our intimacy. Mitchum was a man who, with all his talents, would go to any length to deny them. It was as though he didn't want to be charged with the responsibility of living up to them. He referred to himself as "a poet with an ax."

In that bungalow on the Fox lot he would hold court, telling stories of his bygone days, holding us spellbound with his talent as a raconteur, stretching out the stories, never getting to the point, until sometimes as late as eleven o'clock at night. We would stagger out of the bungalow (other actors and some grips) and drive home, swimming in the word pictures he had spun around us and wondering why we stayed listening hour by hour with a 5 A.M. call ahead of us.

At the end of one of those storytelling binges, he presented me with some brownies he said he had baked. I ate them for dinner when I got home. An hour later, I thought I had achieved Nirvana. Clearly he had included his own "special" ingredients.

I remembered that Fox's expectation of *What a Way to Go* was that it would be the big hit of the year, while on another soundstage around the corner from where we were, shooting history was being made with a little musical we heard about called *The Sound of Music.*

Dream makers were not always correct in the evaluations of their dreams. And where were all these people now? Mitchum was still slugging it out in his granite cigar store Indian fashion, like a walking mountain of endurance.

Paul Newman had become a respected sociological assessor of our culture's values, a racing car enthusiast, as well as a fine director. Dean Martin outlasted Jerry. Robert Cummings continued with his vitamin company until, at the age of eighty-something, he still looked fifty. And Dick Zanuck, who was the head of Fox at the time, came to work one morning to find that his parking space had been removed by his father, Darryl, and Dick was banned from the lot. He went on to produce independently some of the best films in town and to marry a woman who provided the push and inspiration he required.

William Peter Blatty, who wrote the first picture that I

did on the Fox lot, called *John Goldfarb, Please Come Home,* went on to write *The Exorcist.* He patterned the protagonist, Chris MacNeil, after me—using my yellow Jaguar, the French couple who worked for me, J. Lee Thompson, the director who directed me in *Goldfarb* and *What a Way to Go* and who had a habit of shredding his scripts and eating them. One day he ate a rewrite, which had no carbon.

Blatty and I often had long discussions in my bungalow on the Fox lot about the nature of good and evil, whether spirits existed, and whether the polarity in the universe was harmonious.

We used to have séances with the kids in the neighborhood at my big house in Encino, which is where he told me the idea for *The Exorcist* was born. He presented me with the book on New Year's Day. I opened the door. He stood there unshaven and gaunt and said, "Read this. It's gonna be a hit." I took it to Sir Lew Grade, with whom I had a contract at the time. He read it and said, "This will never work." I went on to do another film about the same subject, called *The Possession of Joel Delaney,* which never made a ripple. Blatty went on to make *The Exorcist* with someone else and made history.

I remember Bill Friedkin, who directed *The Exorcist,* coming to my apartment in New York while he was shooting with Ellen Burstyn, watching me as I made blueberry pancakes for breakfast. He clocked how I moved, talked, sat, rushed around, even how I cursed with Southern "eloquency." I remember Blatty coming over during the shooting of *The Exorcist,* discussing the mishaps that were occurring—sets burned down, one of the grips getting killed, and something to do with an air conditioner with a mind of its own, turning itself on and off at will. Blatty said it was the spirits controlling the film. On reflection, I was glad I didn't make it but got into the positive side of the "force" instead!

* * *

Sitting there in the makeup chair, I found I had fast-framed about twenty years of my past in Hollywood and it occurred to me to wonder why. Was it just the role I was about to play? Or something deeper? And on the heels of that thought I realized I was making the transition into the adjustment of getting older. I could no longer pose as a character actress. I actually *was* one.

I guess the transition had really begun after a string of bad films, a television series that was a miserable and unintelligible flop, five years of being out of work, and an excursion into political activism that left me as disappointed with the Democratic Party as I was with the roles I was being offered.

Being true to my survivalist nature, I pulled myself up by my bootstraps and went back on the stage. Perhaps nothing had ever given me as much pleasure as the collective response of the audience to what I had been trained to do in the first place. It was pure joy for me. Hard work, physically taxing, sometimes terrifying, but it made me feel alive again.

Soon after that I began playing older parts, people's mothers, and women whose wisdom and experience showed on their faces. There's an adage in our business. If you have a hit once every five years, you can still survive and sustain your career. Fortunately, that happened to me. With *The Turning Point* and *Terms of Endearment,* it didn't really matter what I did in between, and I suppose my Oscar for *Terms of Endearment* signaled a capstone in my long, hard-working career that gave me the freedom to venture into areas that my friends warned me might jeopardize everything I had toiled so hard to achieve. Namely, metaphysics. The journey within.

So important had that investigation become to me, and so fulfilling its rewards, that now, living in the world as it had become, it was impossible for me to conceive how I could ever have lived without it. With the creeping deterioration that was infecting our world, I wondered how anyone could live happily anymore without some kind of deep internal spiritual belief.

As I thought about my past, I realized that most of my life had been a search for my own identity, as well as the identities of the characters I had been required to play. This may well be an occupational hazard of acting, or perhaps the root reason why so many people think they want to be actors despite the obvious and multiple uncertainties of the profession. Many are really in search of themselves. And suddenly, sitting in front of a mirror, I felt I had been a fraud. I had said I knew what I was doing. I had said I knew who I was. I had said I had a handle on life and was confident in the future. But now, as I looked back, that perception had not been real. I was not aware enough of who I was to even realize that I had been straining at the very seams of self-image, and using overachievement to deny it.

When you're a person to whom money means little, to whom power is burdening, and to whom fame is an invasion of privacy, success has to be defined by different criteria. I was always a person who needed internal assurance, internal fulfillment, and internal knowledge of a greater truth than external achievement offered me. I never denigrated external success, but now I was beginning to appreciate it from a different perspective. Oh, the number of things I had done on a whim without real understanding of my intent or the consequences!

Yet, when the makeup trailer began to fill with people who came to greet me, bring me flowers, and some just to have a look at how I was holding up after so many years, none could have known what a tapestry of images was passing through my mind as I sat there submitting to the application of yet another expertly designed Hollywood mask.

It hit me again that some of the people who walked in the trailer to wish me good luck had not even been born when I was already a star. I wondered how they had even heard of me. In fact, more than a few had been more turned on by my books than they had by my movies. There was an unbridled openness, appreciation, and curiosity about who I was now. With varying techniques and overtures people would sidle up to me these days, longing to talk about life and meaning and "our cosmic role in the universe." How could I articulately explain I didn't know? I was no closer to the answers now than I had ever been. Having lived a life of social and political activism, having traveled all over the world, having had deep and abiding relationships, some tearing, some joyful, some a mixture of both, having tasted success and failure in equal measure, I couldn't really explain how it all had happened or why I had done what I'd done. That was all. I wasn't really sure what any of it meant. However, I was now convinced of one thing. I couldn't do anything much about the world and the deterioration I saw occurring in so many places. But I could do something about myself. I had finally realized, with all my social activism and political involvements, that the act of changing the world to become a better place began with understanding and changing myself. And I realized, as I chatted with the people in the trailer, that I was involved in some emotional cleanup, a kind of wrap-up and balancing of who I was, what I had been, and what I was going to do with the rest of my life. To them I was a person who had solved many of life's mysteries; centered, secure, and peaceful. To me, the day that lay ahead was as precarious as it had ever been, except that perhaps I was now learning to accept it as an adventure I had chosen to have fun with and from which, hopefully, I might learn something.

My makeup completed and the natural "curly wig" adorning my head, I took a long, deep breath, thanked everyone, and left the trailer. The California sunlight blinded me as I walked back to my motor home; this time I wasn't going to be sick again. I would sit down for a few minutes and do what I had learned to do some years ago. I would concentrate and attempt to figure out what was bothering me, before I went to work.

Chapter 3

~ Intermission: Time Out

I HAD ALWAYS BEEN A positive person, rarely given to depression and fear. My anxieties had usually related to whether I would live up to what was expected of me. The happiest times for me were when I felt deserving of reward after good work. I allowed myself my just deserts; and because I was a hard worker, I knew the reward would be deeply fulfilling. As I thought about it now, rewards had more to do with time than anything else. Time to me had always been something that one needed *to use,* preferably to further creativity.

I rarely refrained from *using* time. I couldn't just let it be—do nothing—let time flow through me, rather than "contribute" as I flowed through it. I had regarded time as a scarce commodity, a rare and limited essence of life, and could not bear to waste a drop of it.

Nonuse of time produced profound guilt in me. Wasting time made me fragmented, impatient, and churlish to be around, feeling as though part of me should literally be somewhere else. I felt cut off from myself if I wasn't achieving something with the "time" at my disposal. It was really upsetting for me not to be fully extended, and probably this painful guilt was at the bottom of my need to overachieve.

Now in my mid-life, I was faced with what society would claim was a running out of time. The subtle desperation such a concept produced in me was not so much about the advancing acceleration of old age and eventual death but more about whether I had used the time I had been given to its fullest potential. Sometimes I could only sleep peacefully at night when I knew I had accomplished a great deal during that particular day.

Someone had once defined me as a "terminal Protestant" because of my work ethic values. I understood what they meant. Mine were values that tended to blur the overall picture. The tunnel-vision view of the need to achieve the maximum out of any immediate time span shut out past and future. Something about not seeing the forest for the trees.

I had served time all my life, and now that it no longer stretched out to infinity I was actually contemplating whether it was possible for time to serve *me*. I could perhaps be the master of time rather than the other way around.

As human beings we lived our lives as slaves to time. To all other creatures, life (hence, time) was infinite. We alone punched the clock from morning till night, reducing our lives to mathematical fragments. It seemed time itself was an invention of our consciousness. Yet few of us felt, at our accelerated pace, that we had time for anything to be really fulfilling.

Science had been teaching us that because we are self-aware, time was the concept by which we could define and gauge ourselves. Yet time didn't actually exist. It was only a concept. And now life had gotten to the point where we were governed by our own invented concept. Time: the clock (even by its own definition round and timeless). The clock itself was unmoving. Only the hands moved and they had no destination, set to measure the endless circadian rhythms of the sun and our planet.

A clock was truly the representation of its task—an expression of infinity. It embraced the past, the present, and the future in its hands all at once. If the past and the future existed simultaneously, then what role did our concept of time play? It served to limit us, it seemed to me. It served to make us anxious and worried.

At our places of employment, we were measured daily by how much time we put in, when the coffee break would occur, how long we had for lunch; and finally the addictive clock-watching enabled us to at last call it a day. Something was wrong with that.

Instead of focusing our attention on the task at hand and getting lost in it, we focused on how long it was taking. So our measurement of time stunted us, as we constantly tried to squeeze our feelings into whatever minutes or hours we perceived as ours. Why couldn't the workplace be a place of creativity where fulfillment on many levels was possible? If the task itself was sterile, or dull, why not take the time to make relationships at work more meaningful? Instead we were categorized by fragmented expectations, beating and cheating the clock whenever possible, deceiving ourselves and our creativity in the process.

And why did we decide that the age of sixty-five was the "time" to retire? Who said so? There were societies, unlike our economy-motivated "civilized" societies, where age equaled wisdom and knowledge and respect; therefore, retirement was not a concept anyone in those cultures had to cope with. Age did not loom as a threat, but rather as a time of peaceful participation in the lives of family and community, a time of valued contribution and continued self-respect.

In the West we worked according to the *hours* we put in, rather than the depth to which we experienced pride or joy in what we were doing, or the degree to which we achieved a positive exchange with the people we encountered at work. Why couldn't our values include simple respect for work well done, engendering *self*-respect no matter what the job? The product and creativity would improve one hundredfold. Our contributions, no matter what the age, could be measured by the tasks we accomplished, rather than the time they took. Time was not an accurate yardstick for contribution.

I had learned that when I was unaware of time and totally lost in work, or in contemplation, the quality and the quantity of what I was doing improved. With no time limits, I was happier, probably because I could allow myself to feel the "infinite" scope of everything. This certainly was not a factor of age. It was something anyone could do, at any age. *Age had no meaning when one ceased to measure time.*

When I gazed at the stars, for example, I found myself lost in time, because I knew the light of the stars I was seeing belonged to the past. I was enjoying the past in the present. If I could see past light, why couldn't I see future light? And if I could see future light, why was I a slave to time *now*.

Time, as we measured it, was a limited concept of the infinite—the infinite being too broad in scope for us to take in at one gulp. So we limited infinity to the parameters of our own puny capabilities of tolerance.

I had made time totally relevant to myself to the extent that it dominated every moment of my days.

I was flying faster than I needed to from continent to continent, so that I could become even more slavish to time when I arrived. My attitude toward time created a physical response that denied the body's natural rhythms. My body responded to the artificial parameters. If I felt there wasn't enough time for rest, I was tired—not enough time for love, I was lonely—not enough time for reflection, I became harassed. And my physical self reflected my time deprivation until there were periods when I almost felt that I had no time to exist. So my body also reacted better if I ceased to measure time.

I began to realize the equation was really very simple. Consciousness of time equaled stress, equaled emotional and bodily distress. And now a new form of time lapse was catching up with me, creating its own sense of urgency. The infinite vistas that stretched ahead when one was seventeen were no longer there. In my questions regarding old age, I was reflecting not only the desperation of having lost control of my own use of time but of its inexorable passage. I was still measuring myself by achievement against time, instead of achievement for its own sake.

So in all senses—emotional, spiritual, and now very much physical—I needed to radically change my attitude toward time.

Chapter 4

~ Motor Home

I SAT IN MY MOTOR HOME thinking about how much "time" it would take before they called me to work. How many motor homes had I waited in over the years? This one would be my retreat and sanctuary for privacy for the next three and a half months. I loved the idea that there was a kitchen, a bathroom (complete with sink, tub, and shower), and a bedroom where I could lie down between shots, plus a living room in the middle with stereo, chair, table, couch, and portable telephone. And all of it was on wheels and could move from place to place. I always felt a little bit happier when I knew that something I considered home could move.

As I sat down and looked around, I saw my wardrobe hung around the trailer on racks, as though I had been invaded by a department store dedicated to making me look like the character I was playing, instead of myself. The colors of the clothes hanging were parfait, light blues, peach, pink, pale yellows, and tinted whites.

I walked over to the kitchen and opened the refrigerator. Inside were bottles of Evian water and containers of nonfat yogurt. I guess the people in charge of my motor home thought I was a health food addict.

There was a television set on a ledge and a built-in stereo softly playing FM symphony music. I retrieved some water from the refrigerator, took a few sips, and sat down on the sofa.

I closed my eyes, crossed my legs, put my forefinger and thumb together, and began to let thoughts drift across my mind like clouds on a lazy summer sky. Such a lilting feeling, I drifted deeper into myself. Suddenly there was a knock at the front door. A pleasant, dark-haired, mannish-type woman dressed in blue jeans and boots opened the door and came in.

"How are you feeling now?" she asked.

I opened my eyes. "Oh, I'm all right," I answered. "I'm not sick anymore and I'll be fine."

"I'm Myrna, the first A.D.," she said. "Really nice to meet you. I've admired you."

I nodded and thanked her.

"Would you like us to call in one of the other actors and give you a few more hours to rest?"

"No," I answered quickly. "I couldn't bear the thought of not reporting when I'm supposed to, and I'm all right, really."

She looked at me a bit hesitantly and I said, "Honestly, I'll be fine."

"Okay," she said. "Just wanted to make sure."

"Well, tell me," I said, "are you ready for me?"

"No," she said casually, "not yet."

"Well, when will you be?"

"Soon. I'll let you know," she answered. "Talk to you later." She opened the screen door of the motor home and left.

"Hurry up and wait," I thought to myself. There it is again. That's the way it is. Scurry, scurry, scurry to be on time because they made it so pressing and so necessary, and almost never were they ready when they said they'd be.

I shut my eyes and began to meditate again. "Maybe I'll align my chakras," I thought to myself. So I placed my mind at the bottom of my spine and visualized that I was twirling and spinning a red ball that corresponded to the energy center of the first chakra. "Fear and survival," I thought. "That's what this chakra deals with. It's a good one for me to spin this morning."

Just as I began to spin red light, another knock came on the door. "Can I come in?" asked a cheery voice.

I opened my eyes. "Sure."

In walked the wardrobe girl. "Hi," she said. "I hear you weren't feeling well."

"No, I'm all right now," I answered.

"We'd like to try on this dress," she said, "and see how you like it. We never had time to get to this in the fitting room."

"No, I guess we didn't," I answered. "Okay. What does Mike want me to wear?"

"Well," said Sarah, "he's not real sure. He thinks he might want you to wear slacks, but it's a process shot and you'll be sitting down. So they won't really show. The top will, we have to decide on that."

"Okay," I said. "Let's put on the top."

I got up and went to the bedroom where I took off my street clothes and slipped into the top. Back in the living room

Sarah handed me a pair of slacks that she retrieved from a hanger. I wondered what size they were. I wondered if I was thinner now. I was standing in my underwear, one leg in the slacks, when there was another knock on the door and in walked the motor home driver.

"Hi," he said. "I'm here to see that you get what you want for your motor home. Is there anything I can stock the refrigerator with?"

I quickly grabbed a towel and put it in front of me, which didn't seem to deter him at all. "Oh," I said. "I'll let you know what I want later. I'm not as pure an eater or drinker as you probably think."

"Well," he said, and he had a long list in his hand which he began to read from.

"Uhm, what's your name?" I inquired.

"Tony."

"Okay, Tony. Can we go over this later, because I think I'd better do this fitting now?"

"Oh, okay. Sorry," he said. "I'll be outside if there's anything you need." Tony turned around and left.

I dropped the towel and put my other leg in the slacks, hiked them up, and was glad to see that I could close the size 10 without too much trouble.

I turned for a moment in front of the mirror. Sarah nodded. "Good. I think they look great," she said. "Can we try another pair, just in case you get out of the car and they show?"

"Okay," I said, unzipped the slacks and waited, standing in my underwear, for her to hand me another pair. Again, there was a knock on the door. In walked a delivery boy.

"I have flowers and a fruit basket here," he announced. "Where should I put them?"

Again I whipped the towel in front of me. "Over there," I said.

"These are from the studio," he said. "Looks like you could live on this fruit basket for the next month."

"Sure," I said. "Thanks."

He looked at me—not at my body, but at my face. "Sure did enjoy you in *The Apartment*," he said.

"Thanks," I said, "but I've done about thirty pictures since then."

"Oh," he said, "well, I saw that on television last week, and that's the one I remember."

"Okay. Thanks very much," I said. He left. I dropped the towel and put on the second pair of slacks. They fit too.

"Good," said Sarah. "Well, we can choose either one of these."

"I wonder," I said, "how long I'll be able to get into these, knowing what's out there on the catering table."

Images of my passing the catering table and taking a bite of something each time drifted across my mind as one of the joys of making a picture. There were doughnuts, muffins (six kinds usually), M&M's, peanuts, blue corn chips, avocado dip, chocolate candy, cheese and crackers, fruit, cookies, and whatever specialty the caterer had made the night before while dreaming of how he would please the crew the next morning. I always began a film five pounds lighter than when I finished, simply because of the agitation of waiting, which produced in me the craving to eat.

I tucked in my stomach as I took the second pair of slacks off. I was already beginning to feel agitated and impatient at having to wait for them to call me.

"Here, Shirley," said Sarah, as she handed me a terrycloth robe. "Maybe you'd want to sit in here and wait wearing this."

"Thanks," I said, taking it out of her hand a little too brusquely. "Wonder how long it'll be?" There it was again. I couldn't relax, because I was waiting for Time to dictate its wish.

"Who knows?" she said. "But we'll be able to get a rhythm on this film pretty soon. I've left the rings here, the watches, there's some costume jewelry. Why don't you nose around and see what you think. I'll leave you alone now and come back later." Sarah smiled and left my motor home.

I began to pace up and down the newly vacuumed carpet. "Oh, God," I thought, "the number of times I've paced in a motor home waiting for the A.D. to call me: the number of times I've rushed onto a soundstage only to be met by the crew and other technicians, while the "above-the-line creative talent" tended to mysterious things in the solitude of their own trailers. The creative people on a film included many echelons of expression—no echelon more important than the other, no one individual more important than the other really, except for the fact that the actors are the ones with whom the audience identifies. It is the actors up there who enable each person in the audience to lose the trials and tribulations of their own lives and hook into the drama of what has been created on the screen.

During the rehearsal period of this film, I had attempted to allow myself to accumulate all my past experience as an overachieving female star, stirred the mess around in the pot of my own conscious mind, and let it come out of me as a light soufflé—but with depth of feeling about what it is to play a movie star after having been one. Somehow it never mattered how much experience I had had. It was always, and ultimately, a new anxiety each time.

I remembered overhearing a director of mine at a rehearsal and photo shoot, during which the press had been allowed to come in. I had said something about wanting to stand aside and not be next to a much smaller and thinner actress, when

I overheard this director say, "She wrote the book, you know," referring to me.

I never felt that I had "written the book." I never felt that I had really, finally and definitively, nailed down my cumulative experience in a way that enabled me to relax and be confident in the command of my own craft. I wasn't overly anxious (nausea was not my usual way to start proceedings), yet I somehow never felt that I completely knew what I was doing. That would have to wait until I was so caught up and involved with a scene that I could forget everything that went before in my life, or how I would step aside and watch myself in judgment in the future. And even as I thought of these things, pacing now in the motor home of yet another adventure, I was aware that perhaps my purpose in this business was not to succeed in being successful, but rather to work through and overcome the personal obstacles that movie work tended to magnify.

I didn't like to be kept waiting. I didn't like to be afraid of being fat. I didn't like to be unprepared. I didn't like to feel self-conscious. I didn't like competition. I didn't like insensitivity. I didn't like destructive criticism. And I didn't like the priority that technology held on a movie set. All of the above were feelings that were necessary for me to overcome if I was going to be a happy, contented, "well-centered" person. "How funny," I thought to myself, "that I'm still working on those issues, seemingly the very same ones that plagued me forty years ago."

Did this mean that I hadn't really resolved them, or did it mean that I was just working on a higher octave of tolerating them? So many times lately I had realized that for me the movie business wasn't about the business, it was about using my "reel" life to understand my "real" life, and insofar as the business of making movies was based on creating the illusion to become real on the screen, so was my life based on the creation of what I would make of it day by day.

What was the difference really between acting in a scenario on the screen and acting in a scenario of my life? I was creating both. Each seemed as real to me as the other. Structurally, a good screenplay had three acts, and I was probably now edging out of the second act and into the third act of my own life. I was going to work in the reel experience with characters that I would learn from to enhance my real life. There would be comedy, insecurity, achievement, and gnawing anxiety in both. And, to top it all off, I was playing a movie star who had a daughter who wanted to succeed but was plagued with her own insecurities. Why had I drawn such a script to me, and what did I have to learn from it?

The people I had "created" to work with were the most talented our business had probably ever produced—a costar, who was acclaimed as the best actress of our time, and a director who could do anything. Both were equally accomplished and adept at comedy and drama, and both were exquisitely available to their own anxieties and demons.

How would my mechanisms of professionalism and command of craft stack up with theirs? I had been schooled, conditioned, molded, and sculpted by Hollywood/West Coast values. They had been formed by New York. Did that necessarily mean they would be cynical about our forthcoming experience, or was I the fundamentally cynical one with many more years of experience but of an inferior quality.

I thought I had found my character in rehearsal and was beginning to come to the conclusion that parts of her were not unlike myself. I was certainly not playing Debbie Reynolds, but our experiences had somehow been similar. I liked her and found her honest and direct, tough but tender. She had been a part of my past and somehow now, at this juncture, it seemed as though so much had led to this moment, which was not really about making the movie but getting on with the rest of my life.

"You're going to have to risk being yourself in this," Mike Nichols had said during rehearsals. "You're going to have to let yourself touch your own fear and your own conflicts," he had said. I knew what he meant. I would have to have the discipline to throw away my experience, my mechanical craft, and my tricks, and just feel—"feel" my life instead of thinking about it—"feel" the character instead of conceiving it—"feel" me instead of analyzing myself. The mystery of self had always been an adventure to me—*my* self, as well as others. I loved questions about people's *selves*—their underlying reasons for behavior and attitude. I never ceased to be interested in the subconscious, the unconscious, and now the superconscious.

This was where acting and spirituality merged. Each character I had played had been a help in knowing myself. Perhaps that had been my motivation for being an actress. I had, in effect, been seeking the experience of being alive with all of my selves. I wanted to feel feelings that transcended thought when I was playing a character. I wanted to know what couldn't be measured. I wanted to understand what couldn't be named. I wanted to be in the center of feeling where no time existed. I wanted to lose myself in just being the character.

"Just being" was perhaps the very nature of creativity. I needed to relax into "just being" before I could become a character. So, in order to become a creator of a character, I needed to identify with the essence of life.

I sat down on the sofa, hoped no one else would come in the motor home for a while, and closed my eyes again. I would surrender myself without judgment to whatever came up for me. Maybe that was creativity anyway. Maybe my character would emerge.

Out of that creative impulse, where one doesn't judge, perhaps I would feel the connection to the divinity of all creation. So that the experience of creativity, in its purest form, would be the experience of eternity. Perhaps I loved the creative process so much because, to paraphrase Joseph Campbell, "Creativity is the expression of the eternal presence of God." If I felt in accord with that universal being, perhaps I would lose my anxiety and my sense of judgment about myself and everyone else.

Perhaps I would liberate my feelings from the prison of judgment that they seemed to be sentenced to. The acting experience then could go deeper into my own mystery, where the real self transcended all thought.

I closed my eyes, and even in the attempt to let myself go I realized I was thinking too much. We actors were supposed to be children of wonder, each of us a kind of emotional canvas on which writers and directors and camera geniuses could create and manipulate diverse images.

This was, of course, a colossal contradiction; and yet, in the end, when it came to acting a great part in a really good script with fabulous co-workers, the operative name of the game was "surrender." They expected us to surrender our conscious identities so that creativity could prevail—surrender to inspiration; surrender to instinct; surrender to intuition; surrender to giving up one's own contradictions; surrender to the character, which should become second nature enough to allow oneself to be possessed.

Were we actors primarily expected to be channels for those we were playing? Or were we actually participating in the expression of characters that we had inevitably drawn to us, because they were and are aspects of ourselves yet to be experienced?

And the really fine directors—the impresarios of emotional

pace, the conductors of the rhythms of our talent, the orchestrators of our illusion—were they secretly longing to play all our parts? A really good director has to know and love all his characters, just as a really good actor has to know and love his character.

So when each actor loves his part and each director loves all the characters equally, there is really no room for competition, or at least not without sabotaging the creativity. Wanting to do one's best is different from feeling competitive, and surrendering to the character you love is surrendering to the best in yourself.

I leaned against the back of the sofa and let my thoughts drift, trying not to analyze or hook into any one of them. I breathed deeply a few times and let my shoulders go, my stomach go, my hips, and finally my legs and feet. I felt the feeling of "being" begin to prevail.

Slowly, slowly, I surrendered to it. I would also, I thought, create a reality where no one would now knock on my door, even to tell me they were ready for me.

Chapter 5

— Sachi

I HAD LONG SINCE LEARNED that without such reflection time, I could be in trouble. I needed to knit the fabric of my thoughts together, needed to see and feel the harmony. If I didn't I became irritable, short-tempered, and rude. I had come close to that today. I needed to give myself a present of time . . .

Meditation could be full of surprises anyway. I never knew what would come up. An internal adventure, you might say, that somehow was always relevant to what was bothering me. It was the language of the subconscious that triggered an understanding in the conscious mind. A kind of alchemy could take place in meditation whereby what seemed an illusion became a reality simply because it was experienced. Daydreams or nightdreams, it made no difference. If the feelings were experienced, the feelings are real. Maybe all illusion had its basis in reality. Could life simply be the coexistence of illusion and reality?

I breathed deeply and let myself go. I relaxed. A picture began to form and swim into my mind. It had water around it, full of light and pulsating energy. What was I seeing? Was it real or was I making it up? I tried not to question with my mind, hoping to observe with an eye in my heart. There it was—I saw a tiny, tiny baby being formed in my own body. It had an exquisitely angelic face, masses of blond angel-hair, and ethereal arms and legs that wrapped and floated around a plump body. It was my own daughter, Sachi. My daughter. She smiled at me, chuckling at my confusion. Why was I seeing her at this particular time? I laughed. It was too incongruous. Then Sachi spoke.

"Oh, Mom," she said with teasing wisdom. "This is the creative process. You can make it what you want, which you will, because you are going to film a comedy–drama. But there is nothing incongruous about seeing me now as you embark on a mother–daughter story. You are going to draw on your experiences with me. I will be here for you, and you will translate it onto the screen. That is part of our agreement."

I choked. This was our agreement?

"Oh, Mom," she said again. "You know we are friends from so many times and places. Here we are again, with so much to learn about ourselves and each other."

I felt as though I were seeing and hearing, within my own self, this tiny profound being who said I had agreed to give birth to her. There was no mistaking her wisdom, her knowledge, her compassion, and even her almost cosmic humor.

Then the image began to speed up. She grew within me with liquid grace, sometimes laughing as she felt the power of her physical body, alternately confused and irritated that so much of her well-being depended on me and my own movements and frame of mind. Her form blossomed into definition, her personality taking on traits that complemented the form she was living in. She was a distinct entity whose soul I could actually feel using her little body as a channel of expression. Who would she become? What could I do for her? What was this agreement we had with each other? What did she know about our relationships in other times and places? And would we accomplish what she said we had come in to do this time around?

Her eyes remained calm and sparkling as I asked these questions. She seemed to know everything—so much more than I did. She seemed to be centered in the truth, and aware that she was in possession of it. Truth? And what was that?

I saw her face become serious. "It doesn't matter," she said, as if a dialogue of this nature was not only natural but in need of being recognized. "You are me and I am you. We are all reflections of each other. You may think you are hearing me, but you are hearing *you,* because *you* are creating both me and the conversation. Relax with this and use this creative power in everything you do."

Suddenly she was no longer a baby within me. She was born, squawling and berating the air, her face stripped of its wisdom and serenity. She seemed lost and confused, helplessly dependent upon physical surroundings of which she had no knowledge.

Then someone placed her in my arms. She looked up at me. Recognition, a memory of two souls. She relaxed. The crying stopped. Her eyes melted through me, forging a connection in me with their soft heat. I felt her love power stir in my heart.

What were we meant to do together? Why had I never had any other children? Was our task together so consuming that I couldn't handle more than one? What could some mother with ten children have agreed to?

Now Sachi began to walk, and simultaneously, from some objective viewpoint, I remembered the day it happened. She stood up on the floor of black and white checkered linoleum, her arms raised in pixie triumph. I had a camera and captured her first step.

Then I was walking away from her playpen and she cried deeply, and with overwhelming loneliness. I wondered what she was so afraid of. Perhaps she sensed the future—the years I would be away from her when she lived in Japan with her father.

"It was all an agreement, Mom," she said to me. "We all knew what we were doing. You didn't put me on the plane alone for the first time, with my dog tag around my neck, without my agreeing to it. On a deep soul level, I know that. You know it too. So don't feel guilty. You did what you had to do. So did I. I will take responsibility for that. Now we need to work through what we have learned."

And what were those lessons? Perhaps I was drawing so many powerful mother–daughter scripts to me because they were teaching me. I was learning, both from the "script" daughters *and* from the mothers I was playing in the scripts. And at this juncture in my life no relationships were more important to me than those with my mother and my daughter.

In actual fact, what could be more profoundly disturbing and exquisitely joyful than a mother–daughter relationship? What could possibly be more fraught with the creative combustion of the universe than two females who were charged with the task of creating and reflecting each other? The thought of it gave creative combustion a new definition. The female energy itself called into question long forgotten attitudes relating to tolerance, nurturing, patience, intuitiveness, emotional support, and matters of the heart. The world was not resonating to these attitudes in any serious way. We were still caught up in male attitudes of dominance, the "logical" intellect, power posturing, and willful manipulation.

But now we were facing a new age of feminine nourishing in an attempt to survive on the planet. Not only were men having to find and accept the feminine in themselves, but mothers and daughters were having to find the necessary gentleness of acceptance too. The goddess energy, the guru masters called it. The right-brained approach, the doctors and scientists called it.

The other half of ourselves, I called it. I had been operating with my masculine energy most of my life. That was how I became an overachiever. I was well versed in the ways of willful perseverance, intellectual analysis, logical, linear thinking. What I hadn't allowed myself was the power of surrender, the ecstasy of allowing what will be to be. I had not heard the music of the universe with my heart. I was dancing with my mind and, as a result, I was discordant with the natural harmony of the symphony of life.

I could feel it all around me too. So many of my friends were having problems, real problems, in their relationships, marriages, and work, with money, and so on. It was almost as though the earth itself were spinning in a rhythm different from that of the human race. We were dissident, out of harmony, and didn't even know it, and it was happening so fast that the acceleration of confusion was alarming. Yet barriers were coming down all around the world. People wanted to join each other, touch those who had a different way of life, experiment with freedom, and express individual opinions.

The problem was nobody knew how to do these things and still keep order and harmony. Our young people knew there was something more to be experienced in their internal reality, but because they hadn't been taught to nurture and respect it as real, they went to drugs to provide a chemical elation. Greed seemed to prevail as a hedge against the coming annihilation of meaning. Crime and perverse violence continually threw us back into the dark ages of devil fear, and devil worship was alive and well and winning the hearts and minds of at least some twisted humans. We seemed to be plunging headfirst into the abyss of a new millennium with no sense of harmony, security, or peaceful evolvement and survival. What had we become and why had it happened?

Sachi's face appeared again. She was wearing a bonnet with a flower centered on the top. Her pug nose was sprinkled with freckles, and her smile was a thousand suns.

"It's okay." She laughed. "It's all happening just like it should, Mom. Like we all planned it. We just like to learn the hard way." She was chewing a huge wad of gum, which she fashioned into a bubble with her tongue. The bubble burst all over her face, leaving electric sparks of gumlike light exploding in the air. "See," she said, "even an exploding bubble can be beautiful."

Sachi, I thought, who are you? Are you my teacher, my mentor, a master of knowledge in your naïveté? Should I listen to you, or change you, or teach you away from your own wisdom? How can you know more than I? I'm supposed to be strong and help you learn. I should protect you from my own fears, my own anxieties. I should shield you from this out-of-control world for the rest of your life to make up for the times when I wasn't there.

Suddenly I was overcome with the realization that the first lesson I had taught her from the time she could reason was the lesson of negativity. "Don't do this." "Don't talk like that." "Don't touch this." "Don't, Don't, Don't."

In a burst of understanding, I realized that I, and probably many other mothers, instilled the concepts of negativity before their babies even had a chance to feel themselves, their individuality, and much less their creative will. Sachi's development was set in motion the first time I prevented her from making her own move. A negative format that was repeated and reinforced far too often within the convenient framework of being for the benefit of the child. No wonder our children responded in life more to the negative than to the positive. That was what they learned first.

What had I done to the individuality of my daughter, all in the name of loving protection? How had I suppressed her desires, her will, her creative imagination, by calling something silly or not having the time to pay homage and attention to her childlike dreams, which could blossom into a blazing adult reality someday?

No wonder so many teenagers finally rebelled by angrily denouncing their parental figures for not recognizing them as capable of doing anything right! They felt physical energies surging through their bodies, and we adults attempted elaborate explanations for controlling, denying, and suppressing them. We left no room for growth in freedom, in self-expression to its ultimate.

I must have suppressed my daughter's subconscious mind in ways I couldn't even fathom while she waited in frustration for release. She would now have to dig through the rubble of negativity I had heaped upon her and try to unleash her natural self. That self had been originally accessible to her. Now it was locked behind doors to which I had the keys, just as my original self was locked behind doors to which my mother had the keys.

"No, Mom," said Sachi, wearing a sarong and eating a juicy mango under a tree, "you don't understand. Give me some credit. I'm as responsible for what's going on as you are—

even though you created me. I wanted all of this. What I don't want is for *you* to hide yourself from *me*."

I sat up. "What do you mean?" I asked.

"You don't let me see *your* pain," she answered. "Your pain about me. Your pain about yourself. Why don't you trust me and let me see it?"

"Trust you?" I asked. "Why would that be trust?"

"Because you would be respecting me and trusting that I could help you maybe."

"But I'm your mother. I shouldn't burden you with all that."

"You're more than my mother. You're my friend. But I've been your mother. Remember?"

I remembered.

"You know how maternal I am about you," she continued.

"Yes, I know."

"Well, allow me that talent again. I know how to do it. Maybe better than you do."

I flushed with embarrassment.

"No, never mind that," she said. "We all get to be many characters, right?"

"Right."

"Well, just trust me that I'll be there for you. I will, you know. You've just been too busy worrying whether you have or haven't been there for me. You're too worried about what you've done wrong."

"I know."

"Why do you do that?"

I thought a moment as she slurped her orange mango. Her fingers glistened with its slimy juice. Why did I always feel I couldn't bother her with my problems?

"Because," I said, "that's the way it was with my mother.

She never let me see who she really was. So I thought that's what mothers were supposed to do."

"Or not do."

"Or not do."

"Well, what do you think mothers are supposed to do?" she asked. She threw the mango pit away, reached in a basket beside the tree, and retrieved another fruit. Delicately she bit off the end and squished and pummeled the mango juice into her mouth.

"Do?" I asked. I couldn't answer. "I don't know. I don't know what mothers are supposed to do. I never learned that, so I don't know."

"Nobody knows," said Sachi. "They just do what feels right."

"But," I heard myself protest, "maybe what feels right wouldn't be the right thing to do."

"Why not?"

"I don't know. Maybe it wouldn't be good for you."

"Let me be the judge of that. I told you, you don't trust or respect me."

"Oh."

"Yeah."

"I'm sorry."

"Okay. So give me a break."

"How?"

"Tell me the truth."

"The truth?"

"Yes. Tell me what you feel, everything—about me, about your mother. You never told me much about how your mother was with you."

I sighed deeply to myself. Where to start? I was struggling with it. I couldn't really get her clear. She wasn't clear to herself—how could she be clear to me? And what bothered me more than anything was that in her twilight years, the perceptions I had of my mother were fading. I tried to untangle some of the webs we had spun around each other. And as time progressed and our conversations became more honest, I found my mother talking more and more about *her* mother and *their* webs. Her deepest guilts centered on how she may have hurt or troubled her mother. It was almost more than she could bear. And her memories of those guilts centered around her teenage years, her college experience, and her feelings of responsibility relating to the death of her father. Somehow she felt that the burden of raising her brothers and sisters, as well as *herself,* was hers. Her need to share her mother's responsibilities was profound. I wondered why. What was the agreement between the two of them? Did we all dovetail somehow? And, as Sachi had said, were we really reflections of each other in order to learn about ourselves?

I remembered how depressed and unsettled I was becoming over my mother's attitude about life in her old age. She seemed so negative and judgmental. I knew that fear of dying became amplified as the years dwindled, and that personal anger would then be inevitable. But I was having difficulty being around her. During lunch with a friend of mine in Washington, D.C., I unburdened myself about Mother's "dark-sided feelings." My friend was a psychiatrist and, wanting to help, he said something that astonished me, coming from a man of traditional training.

"Have you considered," he said, "that your mother's attitudes these days might be a reflection of your fears and anxieties?"

I didn't know what he meant.

"Perhaps," he went on, "you *expect* her to be this way and, therefore, commission her with the task of emulating those emotions you expect to feel with age in your own life."

"You mean I am creating her to behave this way out of my own negativity?"

"Yep," he said, "and I think you'll find that if you release those feelings in yourself, they will disappear in her also."

I pictured Mother sitting across the Potomac River in her living room in Virginia. I could see her sitting alone, upright in her chair, upset with me that I wasn't with her. With hurt dignity, she would lay a guilt trip on me when I walked in, sighing with righteous indignation that I took so little time to come to Virginia. Anyway, how could I rob her of what time I did give her by having lunch with someone else? The picture in my mind was accurate in my opinion. So what had that to do with me?

I excused myself and went to the ladies' room. On the way back, I called Mother. The hurt silences were there in between sentences on the phone. "Oh dear. How can I change this," I thought.

"You've missed your lunch with me," said Mother. "I know," I answered. "But I'll be home soon." "All right, darling," she answered, with that loving understanding use of the endearment that was meant to provoke guilt on the deepest level possible. I returned to the table with my friend and, for another hour, discussed the objective reality that I could create another attitude in my mother by first changing it in myself.

I practiced seeing her happy and full of interest in whatever I had been doing, devoid of her own feelings of isolation, her sense that she had been left out. I saw her face crinkled with smiles, her eyes lit with positive curiosity that I might have a tale or two to share with her. With wry humor she offered me some leftover food, instead of presenting it as a silent reproach for the coldhearted sadness of abandonment. The vision I was creating at the lunch table warmed my heart and, in fact, propelled me to go back to Mother much earlier than I had planned. She had turned into someone I wanted to be with, in my mind.

I thanked my doctor friend, got in the car, and went back to Mother in Virginia.

When I walked in the door Mother was sitting upright in her rattan chair. She had finished her own lunch without me. But when she looked up at me as I walked over to her, she smiled. She was old and full of her own wise opinions, but her face was open and childlike. Her first gesture was to put her arms up and reach for me.

"Oh, darling," she said, "it's so wonderful to see you. Let me get you some lunch, and let's sit and talk. Tell me everything you've been doing, and I'll do the same. You look wonderful. You've changed."

I was so caught off guard I couldn't laugh or even respond with the same love she was showing me. I sat down and tested her a little more. We talked of movies, the world, how she was coming along, and the inevitable rambling that always accompanies old age. Finally, after about an hour I said, "Mother, what's happened? You seem so much happier than you've been in years."

"Yes," she said, "you're right. I was getting sick of my negative attitude. So I decided to give it up. I like myself a lot better this way."

"When did this happen?" I asked, unable to comprehend the swiftness of her change. Or had I been wrong on the telephone?

"Oh, I don't know," she said. "Recently."

We sat long into the night talking woman to woman with no rancor, no pressure points, no manipulative buttons to push. It was a joy. She seemed to have found a new and serene place within herself.

"There's nothing much I can do about anything at my age," she said later, "so I might just as well be happy and accept it."

"You see?" said Sachi. "Why don't you take a lesson from yourself and your mom . . . relax, be yourself. You are you because of her, and she is she because of her mom, and so on. We women need to understand each other."

I heard a knock on my motor home door. I opened my eyes.

"We're ready on the set," said a new A.D. I hadn't met yet.

"Oh, okay. Thanks," I said, trying to bring myself back to reality. Reality? What was real? I closed my eyes again. Sachi was gone.

Had I been dreaming? It felt more like a "real" illusion that I had created. To me, once an illusion was created in my mind it became a reality. I saw it; I experienced it.

We actors played with this notion all the time. We were masters at allowing the subconscious reality, in all its abstraction, to permeate our conscious logical minds until we churned the mix into quite another third objective reality we used in our work.

We were magicians of the alchemy of balance. We perpetuated emotional illusions until, by consensus, the reality became real to an audience of individuals who allowed themselves to be moved by whatever triggered their own dormant, unexpressed feelings. Illusion and reality became one and the same, depending upon one's perspective. They coexisted in order to create life. There was indeed more to life than conscious reality. In fact, perhaps most of what we loved the best about life was born in the subconscious illusion.

I loved leaving the door open to alternative realities. There was a logic to the confusion it created. Out of confusion came a broader-scoped clarity. But most of all, I loved the notion that this life I was living might possibly just be a dream that I was dreaming from another reality I was living somewhere else. Making a movie was a subtext to that dream.

I happily got into my size 10 slacks and walked out into the California sunlight, blinked, crossed the street, and headed for Soundstage 17.

I was about to play yet another mother in a film about the sticky complication of a mother–daughter relationship. The theme was big and personal. And in my need to understand its intricacies, I was clearly drawn by the subject, apparently using my work to help myself. If I could understand the characters in my films, perhaps I could understand the characters in my life—myself included.

My character in *Terms of Endearment* had been a mother who demanded that her daughter live life according to her expectations. Her constant, negative, nagging fears, along with projections of disaster, finally manifested in the daughter's death by cancer.

As I was making it, I was reminded often of my mother's fears for me. She had fears that weren't the slightest bit realistic. It was as though she needed to worry in order to have an identity. If she could talk about what might go wrong instead of focusing on the joy of things going right, she knew where she was. The positive perspective would call into play her reluctance to trust it.

"Oh, Shirl," she'd say. "That will be difficult, won't it? Be careful, darling. You never know what could go wrong." Aurora, in *Terms,* was much more incisively destructive than Mother. But they both worried a lot.

When my mother got sick with her own cancer, I wondered if the disease was hereditary, or was the psychology of negativity a much more potent killer? When I sat by the hospital bed waiting for my screen daughter to die, I never allowed myself to contemplate the same potential event in my own life. I didn't want to give it any energy. I was learning more and more that thoughts carried power capable of manifesting into reality.

Until the making of *Postcards* I had never acted my roles by believing they were true for me. It wasn't my style. I found it self-indulgent. I acted the character in whose life these events occurred, and used only part of myself to react. Sachi's potential death was not something I was willing to contemplate or exploit just for the sake of a movie. That could have been part of the problem that Debra Winger and I had working together. She really believed she was dying of cancer, and I was acting as though she were. I came from the discipline of the stage. If I really believed that what I was doing was real, eight times a week and twice on Wednesday and Saturday matinee days, I would be taken away in a white coat.

I had learned, through the discipline of dancing, I think, how to orchestrate and conserve and manipulate my emotional tapestry to serve the character without damaging myself.

I could see that Aurora Greenway was projecting her daughter's death through her negative ramblings, but Aurora couldn't.

So as Aurora admonished her daughter for not taking care of herself, and essentially, for living a life unpleasing to her mother, I was able to examine those same aspects in myself. Aurora taught me a lot. When I finally leave this world, I hope it's because *I'm* ready to, rather than succumbing to any negative conditioning visited on me by anyone else, and I hope the same will be true for Sachi.

As I was contemplating aging and death in my films, the constant realistic reminder, of course, was my own mother.

"I'm afraid to die," she said to me often. "But I think I'm more afraid to live."

"Do you regret much?" I'd ask.

"Oh, I don't know," she'd say. "I have you and Warren regardless of what else I didn't do."

"So you poured your creative energies into us, didn't you?" I'd say. "You made us what we are."

"Oh, yes. And I'm so proud. What more could a mother want?"

I laughed whenever she wore her big floppy sweatshirt during her walks. The front read "Don't bother me. Both my children have Oscars." My agent gave it to her.

She'd sit with her toes pointed in, hunched over a bowl of soup with an almost manic twinkle in her eye. Then she'd dispel the pixie in herself by crossing one long lean leg over the other and, with dignified bearing, become a character out of some long-forgotten royal family. My mother had bearing, all right. And she never let you forget that she had gone through a lot to bear it.

I wondered if Sachi had the same thoughts about me. Here we were, a triad of women springing from completely different backgrounds, yet born into each other's lives and each sparring both with life itself and with the intricate impacts we had on one another.

I came from a middle-class American Mason–Dixon line background, with a Canadian mother and a small-town Virginia father. My daughter had come out of an American mother and a father who was American but thought and lived like a Japanese. She had been educated in America initially with one parent (me); but then in her crucial formative years (six to twelve), she had gone to live in Japan with her father and been conditioned accordingly. The impact of the Eastern culture had been stronger than that of the Western, because it had been served up by her father when she was old enough to register it consciously.

How do two such women ever really understand each other?

My familial experience had been traditional. My mother and father lived together upholding American values and ethics recognized by the surrounding community. Sachi's familial experience had been a separated father and mother, and her social input had been Oriental. The twain would have difficulty in meeting.

Sometimes we seemed so close and yet we were actually worlds away from each other. Our problems together were not like the problems I had with my mother. I knew Mother well. She knew me well. The stickiness came out of long-schooled knowledge of each other. I often saw her in myself, which I alternately accepted and rejected. "My mother myself" was a theme familiar and often disturbing to me. I had seen my father through my mother's eyes, because she had always been the parent in attendance.

Sachi and I didn't really know each other that well—not the way a day-to-day existence would dictate. She had not seen her father through my eyes, nor the culture that surrounded her when she began to be capable of integrating it. I had been more of a friend and an absent mother, which had its good and bad points. We were not competitively involved with each other, as is usually the case; instead, we sometimes suffered from *lack* of knowledge about who the other was.

So our relationship was not one of undoing and resolving the knots we had tied ourselves into over the years. Ours, at the moment, was one of accepting that those ties existed as golden threads of loving communication that we each needed to learn how to understand.

Mother and I were almost staunch with each other in terms of our emotional territory. We were often competitive and insensitive to each other, because we were so familiar. We knew each other's buttons and pressure points. That produced a combustion that was intolerable at times.

Sachi and I were only just establishing our territory with each other, subtly discovering particular sensitivities and pressure points and never really feeling the temptation to exploit them to serve a power struggle; rather, were trying to *find* them so we'd each know who the other was. In fact, we were each afraid of the other in terms of trigger points because we didn't want to jeopardize the love we knew was so deep, yet so unexpressed.

I thought of my mother in terms of how to get along with her. We never discussed how much we meant to each other and how deep our love went. Whereas Sachi and I were always talking about what we felt and continually looked for ways to feel comfortable in expressing our feelings. We hadn't been together enough to know how, but we also hadn't been together enough to know how to sabotage connection.

I remembered the time she called me to announce she was going into surgery for endometriosis.

I was at my house in the Pacific Northwest, and, with her demanding schedule, she could only work the surgery into the following morning.

I was apoplectic. I was writing and had a deadline on my book, but I would be there regardless. She said it wasn't necessary. But then she gave me the gift of asking me to be there.

I sat in the front seat of my car the next morning, while Mike (who ran my house) drove me toward Sea-Tac Airport. There was a traffic jam. If I missed the plane, I'd miss Sachi's surgery. People in the Northwest talk slowly, they walk slowly, and maybe they even think slowly. They are, however, more thorough and they never forget to stop and smell the roses. What I couldn't tolerate was how Mike seemed to be smelling every rose along the way, even when there was an opening for him to pass a car and make time on the road.

"Patience," I thought. That's certainly one of my big issues in this lifetime. What would we pick up by passing anyway? A few seconds?

Well, a few seconds is what my catching the flight ultimately came down to. We pulled up in front of United Airlines at 6:55. I ran to the United desk to buy a ticket (I had made a reservation). The supervisor told me it was no use. I said I was getting on that plane no matter what.

I kicked into my acting overachieving success gear and, not knowing what to expect, I visualized myself on that plane. I raced through the security check. For the first time ever the uniformed authority flaunters made me dump out all the contents of my tote bag. They were troubled that I would hijack the plane with my cuticle scissors. Someone looked up at my face and recognized me. She ordered the others to let me go. I wondered how many faceless, unfamous individuals traveling with manicure sets would miss their planes that day.

I ran to the underground train that would speed me to Gate 17. I bounded out of it and raced up the escalator stairs, as people stepped aside, sensing a woman in an emergency. The door to Gate 17 was closed.

I looked out the window. The jetway was being pulled away. No one was in attendance. I made a decision. I pulled open the door and bounded down the jetway. The flight person in charge of pushing the jetway button gasped when he saw me. Apparently afraid I wouldn't be able to stop my momentum and would therefore run right off the end of it, he pushed a reverse button and the jetway stopped in mid-motion.

As if on cue, I saw the pilot in the cockpit turn around

and look at me. He was literally pulling the 747 away from the gate when I waved my arms at him. "Stop! Come back!" I shouted, knowing he couldn't hear me, but in order for him to get the full effect of my emotion *I* needed voice-sound effects. He looked startled.

By that time an airline official had been told there was a maniac on the jetway and for some reason the pilot was holding up his departure. The official was a woman who recognized me. "What are you doing, dear?" she asked. "You know we can't stop the departure now."

"But you must," I pleaded. "I have *got* to be in Los Angeles in two hours. I can't *not* be there. I *have* to get on that plane."

"Let me see your ticket then," said the official.

Thank God, I thought. It's possible. She won't mind if I don't have a ticket.

"I don't have a ticket," I said. "But I promise I'll buy one when I land."

She literally laughed. She waved the pilot on, who was watching with an intrigued expression on his face.

"Impossible," said the official. "We have another flight in two hours. Let me help you with *that*."

I turned toward the pilot and waved some more, this time with even more mustered intensity.

Then I turned around and ran back into the airport. By that time a senior official had been dispatched to deal with this crazy movie star. She had a kind face, but even if her face had been the Temple of Doom I knew I really needed to impress her. I can't say that what I did was an act—I really honestly felt it. However, it is not a choice I would have made in a scene. In fact, I would have strongly balked at a director who suggested I do what I did.

I got down on my knee and burst into tears. "My daughter is very ill," I sobbed out. I looked over at the pilot who was now witnessing the scene through the cockpit window. (I made sure I played it up against the window of the airport, which, by the way, was well lit by the morning sun.) The pilot seemed mesmerized. He wasn't going to move. So I had a little time.

"My daughter is going in for surgery in three hours in L.A. I *have* to be there! I *must* be with her! If I'm not she'll feel I've neglected her; and I already feel guilty about having done that in her life." The kind-faced official stared at me. This was not the kind of confession one expected in an airport departure lounge. "Please," I went on, "please."

I turned toward the plane. It was still stationary. "You see?" I said. "The pilot wants to take me. He hasn't left yet. He's probably already missed his place in the take-off line." I was reaching on that one. I knew it.

The official looked out at the pilot. He waved. She looked back at me. "Let me see your ticket," she said.

I thought of all the movies I had seen about people during the Second World War who didn't have the proper papers for freedom. Whole movie scripts had been written about how they talked their way onto trains and planes to cross borders. My little speech seemed singularly unimpressive and more than a little melodramatic.

"I promise I'll buy a ticket when I arrive," I said. "Don't let an airline ticket stand in the way of my being there for my daughter. *Please*!"

No one could resist that. Besides, I meant it. I thought of the controversy over the journalist's fabricated tears in Jim Brooks's *Broadcast News*. The tears had been real in the first take. But on coverage he needed an "Oscar bottle" (bottle of glycerine) to achieve the original effect.

I wasn't sure I could have done a retake on my airport bended-knee scene. As it turned out, it wasn't necessary.

The senior official (who I think might have some guilt dues of her own) melted. "All right," she said, as she waved to the pilot, who was an eager participant just waiting for direction. She pushed another hidden jetway button, and like "sesame" the door opened again. She led me down the jetway toward the plane and knocked on the side of the door. I wondered what it would feel like to make a sudden emergency escape from that door. When automatic and traditional procedures are interrupted, emergency pictures flood the mind.

Suddenly the stewardess inside the plane appeared. The plane was open. I was going to live the visualization I had concentrated on while being judged a dangerous scissors hijacker at the security point. It wouldn't make a bad third act ending, I thought.

"You are so wonderful," I said to the senior official lady, meaning every word but fully realizing how patronizing such a truth sounded under the circumstances. "What is your name?"

"Linda," she said. "And I've enjoyed so much of your work, especially *Terms of Endearment*. I identified with that."

So she did have a daughter, and there were unresolved issues in her life too.

"Make more movies like that," she said, "and you can get on any plane without a ticket!"

"Thank you, Linda. I'll never forget this." I wanted to mention that she should see *Postcards* for more of an update on mother–daughter relationships.

She pushed the jetway button, which was now beginning to sound with the frequency similar to a department store elevator alarm.

I walked into the first-class section and sat down, feeling privileged beyond belief and even more guilty because of it. No one looked up. They were reading the *Seattle Post-Intelligencer,* preparing for business in L.A. Since so many from L.A. were moving to Seattle, I wondered how many more times a scene like mine would be duplicated in the coming years.

I sat back in 1A, put my feet up on the bulkhead, and prepared to be there for Sachi. She would laugh at my drama, and she would also have been fine if I hadn't made the scene work for me. *I* was the one who needed to be there for her. *I* needed to repair the past by attending to her in the present.

When I arrived in L.A., I rented a car and drove to Sachi's place to pick her up. She is a suggestible person who, knowing she would have a general anesthetic a few hours hence, was already in a slightly spaced-out mood.

She was completely prepared to depend on me to make sure she had everything. Her little hospital bag, even though she was an outpatient who would come home that night, was stuffed with hair paraphernalia and pajamas and slippers. She seemed fragile and apprehensive, yet capable of strong resilience in the face of adversity.

Her boyfriend arrived, and my sense of being so exquisitely needed was slightly interrupted by his presence and the prearranged agreement that he would drive her to the hospital and I would stay with her until she could come home. I wondered what kind of mother-in-law I'd be when she eventually married.

I had obviously never been a typical nurturing always-attendant mother. I knew there were those who would say I had not been much of a mother at all. In fact, *I* would say it—wrongly maybe, but I'd say it.

I thought of how her father and I had agreed that an upbringing as a movie star's child in Hollywood was not designed for stability and a healthy way of life. I had seen too much wealth, power, dope, and money ruin too many of my friends' children. So we enrolled Sachi in an international school in Tokyo, Japan, where Steve lived and worked.

We were separated most of the time, but our marriage was comfortably open to us and admittedly unorthodox to others, but it didn't matter. What we felt Sachi needed was loving support from us—even though I couldn't always be with her—a good education, and an approach to life that would contribute to the world instead of Hollywood. I knew she would be loved and nurtured by Steve, and I knew the governess we had hired was loving and attentive.

As the years slipped by, and we nearly always spent her long school vacations together (one month at Christmas, one month at Easter, three-and-a-half months in the summer), she seemed to be developing into a sensitive and charming person—not too overloaded with self-assurance, to be sure, and shy sometimes, but incredibly sensitive to other people's feelings and anxieties, and always responding in a loving and compassionate way to anyone who was in trouble and needed help.

But now, as we lived our lives and our relationship in my middle-aged years, and she in her thirties, we were seriously involved with working out our mother–daughter issues and were more than committed to resolving whatever difficulties we had with each other.

It wasn't easy. We went to therapy together, where I learned how remiss I had really been during her childhood. I had lived with the illusion that her father had really been there for her, but that had not been the case and Sachi had never complained to me. She had borne her loneliness without me, without him, and ultimately without a family sounding board to bounce off against. In some ways that was an advantage for her; but I now felt that I had let her down, because I had not been aware of what was going on with her when I wasn't there.

Sachi had begun her own quasi-spiritual search, never as curious about such matters as I was, but still intrigued enough to want to resolve her own identity and what that meant to her spiritual growth as a human soul alive in the world. She seemed quite willing to accept her life, her childhood, and her problems as issues that were hers, chosen by herself, and designed to serve her enlightenment. She always has believed that we participated in the choice of being mother and daughter and that we have been around together for many lifetimes. If you asked her if she believed in reincarnation, she'd probably say no or she doesn't know. But if you asked her if *we* knew each other from some other time and space, she wouldn't hesitate to confirm it. She couldn't prove it, she'd say, but she felt it.

So Sachi, given her troubles and problems, has always taken responsibility for them, never assigning blame to anyone else. That doesn't negate our problems together or troubles she may be having with anyone else, but it does make it more possible to work them through.

One of our issues has been my guilt at not having been there for her as much as I feel I should. My mother had raised me in the traditional way. She cooked my meals, kept the house, helped me with my schoolwork, my dancing, and my boyfriends. She was, on the face of it, always there for me. Yet the first realization I had in my own therapy years ago was that I had an orphan's psychology (the psychiatrist's term, not mine). I knew it was true, but I didn't understand why it was so. How could I have an orphan's mind-set when my parents had always been there? I was to learn later that it had only to do with the quality of the time we spent together, not the quantity.

That made me feel much better where my time with Sachi was concerned, but it didn't assuage the guilt.

So when I sat beside her hospital bed as the nurse attempted to insert the IV into her arm and Sachi winced in pain, I grasped her other hand, squeezed it, kissed it, and wondered how many other moments of pain she had experienced in her life that I had never even known about. She was so brave as I saw the vein in her arm reject the needle. The nurse was gentle, but the forcing of the needle was more than I could bear.

Sachi looked over at me with a desperate plea in her eyes. How many of those pleas had I missed? How much had she borne without me in her stoic courage, accepting a childhood fate that had been essentially that of an orphan?

"Please," I said to the nurse. "Couldn't you give her a topical anesthetic to prevent pain before inserting the needle?"

The nurse looked at me and nodded with an apology. "Oh yes," she said, "but that can only happen on the third floor. Here on the second floor this is how we have to do it."

I could hardly contain myself. I looked over at Sachi. An imperceptible tear spilled from her eye. Then she nearly fainted. The nurse pulled the needle from her vein.

"I'll tell them," she said.

Sachi's ordeal was over until the third floor. She stopped hyperventilating and began to joke about her aversion to pain—a typical thing for her to do. Her stoic willingness to accept the pain had almost signaled a secret understanding that she felt she deserved it somehow, and in the final analysis, regardless of whether the pain was physical or psychological, she had somehow not done something right and was therefore being deservedly punished.

"I'm such a wimp," she said. When I heard her say that, I knew she would utter those same words regardless of what she was going through. Would I have been able to alleviate those feelings had I been there for her? Had I made her fearful by my absence or by my negative programming to protect her when I was with her? Had I stamped out her individual courage by insisting that she be too careful? My mother had done that to me, and it turned me into a rebel instead. How had I affected Sachi?

Soon the orderly came to wheel her bed into the elevator. Sachi wore her hair in a blond ponytail. Little loose wisps of hair played around her face. Her sea blue-green eyes blinked in slight confusion. What would happen to her when they took her from me? Could anything go wrong during this routine operation? What could I say to her to reassure her?

"I love you, Mom," she said as though reassuring me in that way that children who have touched real heart pain understand. She was more concerned with my fear than her own condition. How true it was that regardless of how remiss parents are with their children, the children are usually concerned with leaving the parents alone. They identify with abandonment. We children ultimately feel responsible for our parents—I of mine and Sachi of me. Why was that? Were all parents fundamentally identifying themselves with their own mortality through their children? And if parents let their children go, were they in effect relinquishing their guarantee of immortality? Did the children pick up on that? All those thoughts scampered through my mind as they led Sachi away on the stretcher bed. What would I do without her? Would I feel that I had programmed her demise should something happen to her? Again I thought of Aurora.

What would they find when they opened her up? Was it simple endometriosis? Or would it be more? Again my own flight of dramatic fantasy horrified me. I turned it off. I didn't know where it came from. Could it be true? Was acting out a fear a way of expunging it or would it really manifest into a reality?

"I love you, Sachi," I said, trying to invest thirty years of meaning into those words. "Just trust that it will all be all right, sweetheart. Trusting is half of everything."

Sachi looked up and over at me as she disappeared down the hallway. "I will, Mom. I know. I love you." Then the elevator doors closed behind her.

I waited for word that she had gone into the operating room. The doctor had promised to tell me. I checked with the nurse in charge of the waiting room.

"She's not out of surgery yet," she said. The nurse was slightly goofy from some kind of booze. (I found out later that she wasn't really a nurse, just a volunteer that read the communications from upstairs.)

Not satisfied with what was going on, I set out to find Sachi, wondering at the same time if I would embarrass her by barging Aurora-like into a pre-op room wanting to know what was happening to my little girl.

I found her. Like a homing pigeon I followed my feelings to a door without a window. I opened it and there she was alone, lying peacefully in her stretcher bed staring at cartoons on the wall that some hospital supervisor thought would be amusing right before surgery. She had been there for hours.

Again I reflected on all the moments of stoic loneliness she must have endured over the years. I leaned over and kissed her. She was so endearingly grateful that I had found her. She had been amused by my insistence at finding out what was going on. I had thought I would embarrass her.

Such misconceptions we have of ourselves and our children. I had always shielded her from my pain, my anxieties, my fears and desperations. In our therapy together, she had pointed out how distrustful of her that was of me.

"Why don't you let me know you?" she had asked. "By sharing that with me, you trust me, respect that I can handle it, allow *me* to be there for *you*."

I had never seen it that way. I hadn't wanted to burden

her with my woes. She had enough of her own. But as I was learning, *woes were not the issue—what we did with them was.*

It all came down to the mutual trust we had of one another to allow ourselves to be vulnerable. Such an allowing was the ultimate act of love. My mother had never allowed herself to share her pain with me. Sometimes she shared her burdens but never her pain. I had never done that with my daughter either. It was a tradition that Sachi was now allowing me to break.

The IV nurse arrived. Sachi began to hyperventilate again. I took her hand.

"Don't worry," said the nurse. "You're on the third floor now. Here you get a local anesthetic so the IV won't hurt."

Sachi smiled.

The nurse quickly applied the local, put the IV in as Sachi looked into my eyes, and when it was over Sachi never even knew it had happened. She broke into a sunny smile and her mood elevated ten notches.

"I just had a needle with no pain!" she gushed. "Everything's fine now, Mom. Don't worry." Soon after, another orderly wheeled her away to surgery, and I knew she really would be fine.

The operation was successful, and there was no further threat to look for.

I waited for her to come out of the anesthesia and, except for the fact that the nurses thought she was some other patient (insisting that she eat and drink a great deal while still asleep!), her gradual coming around was uneventful.

When she was discharged I drove her home, put her to bed, made some dinner, and relaxed into the time and understanding that it took to be a mother.

For the next three or four days we became mirrors for each

other. I took her to my place in Malibu. She drifted into sleep, dreamed, talked of her dreams when she woke, and slowly regained her strength.

She had been rehearsing a play for a theater production and was scheduled to open in her first preview five days after the surgery. But Sachi wasn't nervous or apprehensive; on the contrary, she seemed balanced and completely in the present. It was incredible for me to observe her. I would have been projecting far too far into the future—would I be well enough, how would I choreograph a move corresponding to the surgery?—and on and on. Not Sachi. She lived in the moment of her healing process. I was impressed. My daughter not only had guts but a wonderful pool of inner calm.

We watched television together, made meals together, dished about mutual friends, and talked about our lives as mother and daughter and now equal friends. She was going through some rocky shoals with the man in her life and dealing with the basic question of potentially being alone as a young woman in the world today.

At the end of the week she was well enough to go back into the world of show business, and I was to return to the Pacific Northwest. She didn't want me to come to the preview. She wanted me at the actual opening instead.

I was dressed and ready to leave for the airport. I walked into the living room. Her back was to me, and she seemed to be looking out the window. I could feel something was wrong.

"What is it, sweetheart?" I asked as I rounded her chair and looked into her face. Big tears slid down her cheeks. She was trying not to lose control.

"I'm so lonely," she said. "I've loved being here with you so much, and now I have to go back to my life of being strong and independent again. I love being a little girl. I don't like having to be a woman. Survival scares me. I know how to do it, but it's so lonely." She sobbed as she spoke. I put my arm around her and held her. Even as I hugged her, I was afraid that such a comforting gesture would contribute even more to uncontrollable sobbing. I wanted so much to take the hurt away, not to provoke even more.

God, did I know what loneliness felt like. How often I had felt that sense of lonely survival. Each time I waved a plane into the air carrying her father back to the Orient, it took days for me to adjust to his absence. Only later did I realize that bonding through dependence never works, whereas bonding through freedom always does.

Sachi was beginning to realize something that took me until I was in my mid-forties—feeling sovereign in oneself made it possible to have relationships with others that weren't dependent.

As our time together during her convalescence progressed, we had each found each other again; and longing for contact and loving communication, we slipped into the joy of interdependency so successfully that the outside world didn't exist for us. Our lives were each other. The future without the interdependency didn't exist. And now that Sachi was well and the real world beckoned, the wrench of separation was difficult for both of us.

It was a time period analogous to the way so many of us lived our marriages, our love affairs, our family lives. The joys were obvious; the drawbacks less easy to work through. How could we live completely in the joy of someone we loved without the inevitable pain of separation?

Sachi and I sat together talking about how to deal with any relationship we loved having and yet being able to regard it with some distance so as to give it breathing room and space.

She had been without traditional family experience in her childhood, so her need to hang on to anything that resembled that was deep. Yet she was reserved in giving herself to it because of her fear of its going away. My reservations in giving myself to it were based on the potential of feeling suffocated and having my freedom inhibited. We each had different and opposite fears that nevertheless proved groundless, because we allowed ourselves to feel the love for each other. As most wise sages have said, love conquers everything. I would, out of love, always allow her her freedom while being there for her. And she, out of love, would do the same thing for me.

Marriages were certainly based on the values we had been conditioned to be afraid of or trust during our childhoods.

A great psychiatrist had once said to me, "In our adult lives we work out our problems with our parents through our love affairs. We work out problems with our siblings with our friendships." It made sense to me.

As I sat talking with Sachi, her tears now subsided, I was aware that I was concerned with missing my airplane. Hadn't that always been symbolic in my life. I had not often taken the time to simply feel a situation, give it time to percolate. I was seeing that I needed to take more time to savor the spices that love and communication afforded.

As soon as I made the decision that my plane didn't matter, the doorbell rang. It was David, one of Sachi's best friends, who had come to pick her up. She sprang from the chair, anxious to see him and then to get on with her day.

"Don't miss your plane, Mom," she reassured me. "I have things to do and so do you. I'll be fine and so will you. Thanks for taking care of me. You're a great Mom."

With those words, I welled up because she had assuaged so many years of guilty concern.

Our midnight talks, the morning recap of dreams, the musings out to sea, all flooded through my mind again as we said good-bye to each other. Many times in our lives we had parted with an airplane waiting for me and a friend tending to

Sachi or vice versa. How was it possible to be a working mother and still feel responsibly attentive to one's family? Again I had to remind myself, it is the quality of time spent that matters, not the quantity.

Also something else occurred to me. Each of us has forgotten the child within: the carefree, joyful, nonjudgmental child. I was trying too hard to be a proper mother. Sachi was trying so hard to become a mature and proper adult.

Maybe we were both emphasizing society's concept of maturity with all its repressions too much. Perhaps we should each take the time to find the child that still existed unrecognized and unnurtured within each of us.

We were our own children really. We now needed to raise ourselves. We were each suffering from neglect and input that scared us, coming from parents that had in turn been neglected and frightened by their parents.

It was time to look to ourselves now—to find the child within us that had gone for too long without nourishment and allow it to play, to feel carefree, to indulge in games that were fun and to feel peace, security, and love.

Perhaps we needed to perceive the world a little bit more through the eyes of our child within. Because without the conditioning of society, that child is basically trusting, nonjudgmental of self and others, and indeed only interested in enjoying life.

Sachi and I kissed each other good-bye. A second childhood would be fun. But it couldn't come until we had each worked through what our mothers had programmed us to be—all out of love.

Chapter 6

— Postcards

I OPENED THE THICK soundproof door to Stage 17 and walked onto the set. It was dark and quiet. The crew milled around the camera with first-day jitters I could feel as I approached them.

Mike Nichols sat hunched in his director's chair munching trail mix. His eyes sparkled with a kind of manic anticipation as he chewed. "Good morning, my darling," he said, embracing me. "Are you certain you feel well enough to work? We can change things if you want."

I was embarrassed by his sincere concern for me. "No," I said quickly. "I'd rather die than keep you guys waiting or disrupt the schedule. I'm fine, really."

Mike patted my shoulder and dipped into the trail mix again. "Forgive me," he said. "I've just quit smoking." He looked like a sensitive, frustrated cherub who would secretly rather expire from food than cigarettes anyway.

A voice of tender "put on" called me from behind. "Hello, Mommy," it said. "I hope you're all right."

I turned around. It was Meryl Streep. Mommy? Oh, God, how am I going to pull this off? She walked over and embraced me. Should I hug this monument of genius as a protective–defective mother character or as a fellow actor who held her in awe? I opted for a friendly show-biz clinch, remembering that all in good time we would create a mother–daughter reality for those fans out there who would hopefully willingly succumb to our illusionary movie magic.

The Judds, I said to myself, just keep in mind the Judds. The mother is well preserved, and the daughter acts like the mother. Otherwise, how was *I* going to make anybody believe it if I didn't?

"What happened to your tummy, Mummy?" asked Meryl.

Immediately I realized she was prepared and already in character for our scene. Did this mean she was never going to be Meryl?

"Oh, I guess I ate some bad organic fruit," I said. "Maybe the alar is more healthy?" I tried to make a joke. "Or maybe it's the three-page monologue I've got to spout on this first day."

Meryl laughed, tossing her blond hair over her shoulders. "I know," she said. "It's creepy having to do this before we even know where we are. They're having trouble with the process screen anyway."

I looked at the setup. Meryl and I were supposed to play the scene sitting in the front seat of a car, which was erected in front of a screen with miles of process freeway traffic behind us. Someone hadn't shot enough freeway footage, so either I had to act fast or we would wait until they spliced together more traffic footage.

"Hello, dear," said a comically singsong voice from the shadows. It was Carrie Fisher. She had written the script of *Postcards From the Edge* and had decided I would be best to play the part patterned after her mother. Not that I was supposed to play Debbie any more than Meryl was going to play Carrie. "We'll transcend the actual people," said Mike. "You play a mother who happens to be a movie star who can sing and dance, and Meryl plays the daughter who has just gotten out of drug rehab and attempts to straighten out her life with her work and her mother."

That all made sense to me, since Debbie was an old friend of mine whom I liked and respected for having survived the Hollywood wars. I had called Debbie as soon as they approached me to play the mother. I wanted to be sure she hadn't wanted to do it herself and, if not, what she felt about me.

"Oh no, dear," she said. "I can't play myself. Besides it isn't really me. I didn't even do a good reading. You'll be great. You're funny, and the mother has to be funny. You'll be fabulous. Have a good time with my daughter's wonderful script. Carrie is a brilliant writer, and she knows what is right." She and Carrie were obviously working out their own mother–daughter problems. Carrie's script was the result. I wondered if Sachi would ever write about me. I wondered what my mother *really* thought about what I had already written about her. Mothers and daughters were certainly in fashion. It was about time.

I thanked Debbie. We talked on, and later that week I saw her with Jay Leno on *The Tonight Show* discussing her life, the book she had written about it, and how proud she was of Carrie.

Debbie had been very helpful to me when I first went into live performing. She controlled all of her shows and knew about sound, lights, musicians, and potentially dishonest business managers.

"Watch every penny," she warned, "and, if possible, get a relative to run things. You can always trust your family."

She gave me hints about costuming, trucking equipment, and how to deal with theater managers. She had worked her way up and learned her lessons every step of the way.

What was most interesting to me in playing the wonderful part that Carrie had created was the karmic balance of it. Twenty years before, I had been contracted to play *The Unsinkable Molly Brown* for MGM. There were some complications, because I was also under contract to Hal Wallis at Paramount. In the middle of the difficulties, Debbie called me. In what I thought was a real act of personal honesty and courage, she asked me if I would let the part go. I remember her words: "You'll have lots of parts, dear, but this might be the last good one I'll ever get. Let the old mother here have it."

She charmed me. I loved her for it. I let it go, and she made history with it and is still bringing happiness to people all over the country on the stage with her own production.

It seemed karmically balanced that I would now play a character based on her life.

Meryl and I took our places in the front seat of the car. I quickly ran through the dialogue in my head. I knew Mike was a stickler for having precise rhythm with the words. He had a way of being so diplomatically kind with his insistent and correct discipline. He was an artist who had been hard on himself for years and, feeling happier lately, he had seemed to come to terms with his artistry and his desire to believe he was a man of great decency. I liked him a lot. I think he was feeling the same way about himself.

The cameras rolled (there were three of them), the process screen behind us cranked up, and Mike quietly yelled "Action."

There I was, playing a long scene with a woman I considered to be one of the great actresses in the world. I was required to play everything looking straight ahead, because I was driving the car. I couldn't look into Meryl's face. I couldn't really see what she was doing. I had all of the lines. She simply reacted. I knew she was eating M&M's as I spouted my dialogue. I heard her well-orchestrated chuckles and grunts in response to what I was saying, which seemed appropriate to her character and the scene. I knew she was wearing sunglasses to shield herself from the harsh world outside of the rehab clinic, and I could feel her seem to tolerate the colorful "mother's" dialogue as I plowed through the three-page scene, all of which, I thought, was written to enhance the character I was playing. I was wrong.

When I went to the "dailies" the next day, Meryl had, in my opinion, acted me off the screen. She seemed able to find comic nuances that I never dreamed were there, perfectly legitimate to her character and to the scene, without disturbing the balance. The woman was brilliant; and for the first time in my life, I felt that I was possibly outclassed.

This would be a new experience for me. She made me feel competitive, which I was uncomfortable with. I liked being friends with my fellow actors. I had always acted *with* people before. This felt like an exercise in simply staying in the race. Then I realized she wasn't even acting really; she was *living* the part of the daughter, who was suffering from comparison with the mother.

So as the days and our work progressed, we developed a relationship based on mutual respect and admiration. Because she was *living* her part, I can't say that I got to know her. For me it was an experience of hands-on observation of the seminal process of actually becoming a character; something I never wanted to do myself.

My working relationships with Anne Bancroft, Audrey

Hepburn, Debra Winger, Shirley Booth, Dame Peggy Ashcroft, Sally Field, Olympia Dukakis, Dolly Parton, Daryl Hannah, Julia Roberts, Teri Garr, and many other fine actresses carried with them a certain personal intimacy, something of ourselves, apart from what we were playing.

With Meryl, I never had the pleasure of actually knowing her. But she happened to come along at a time in my life when I could recognize such a phenomenon as that of not being able to meet and know a part of myself. I couldn't seem to "get in there" far enough to know her as my daughter as well as she seemed to be able to know me as her mother. Central to my role, of course, was precisely the kind of self-centered unawareness of others that would naturally shut out any intimate understanding of another person. So perhaps I was more on the mark than I seemed to myself, but it was Meryl's vision and definable secrets in our screen relationship that belonged exclusively to her and that allowed her to forgive, and accept, and admire, and ultimately, to love that mother. She was able to mine the gold of our on-screen relationship as a one-person expedition, reaping the profits to her satisfaction and needing no one else to accomplish it. She was a magnificent one-woman band, playing and orchestrating her emotional instrument, oblivious to the fact that some of the rest of us felt as though we were acting alone. Perhaps that is the destiny of a real genius. Or put another way, perhaps that is the true meaning of channeling. When one channels divine talent, one is connected only to the source of it, and the physical presence of those who are also in attendance is irrelevant. A channeler puts aside the conscious mind and surrenders to another identity. That's the phenomenon I saw in Meryl.

Meryl could do what she does whether anyone else existed or not. Her thrill in acting seemed to come from abdicating her own identity completely and becoming someone else. It was an identity decision I had never been able to make, nor did I want to. But, as I worked with her, the mystery of why and how she did it filled my days with confused wonder. Was the basis of her ability founded on complete knowledge of surrendering herself or complete detachment from who she was? Or was she a consummate technician who had researched her character thoroughly?

Since I had become such an ardent student of consciousness and inner reality, she served as an archetypical example for me. To me, acting itself had become a metaphor for life. We could each choose how we would approach our own truth, much in the same way we approached our roles. We were both blessed and cursed with the canvas of freedom we had at our disposal. We could make our illusion any reality we chose. And the million choices open to us with each character were open to us in our own lives as well. We could play with each other or we could play alone. We could believe our inner fantasies and make them work for us in the "real" world, or we could believe only in the objective world and, as a result, feel the inner isolation of emptiness. Of course, one was not mutually exclusive of the other. The trick was how to balance the two.

As each day passed on *Postcards,* I felt like writing some postcards of my own. We each grappled with the incongruous marriage of cinema art and technology. Mike's directorial vision was sometimes not met cinematically, whereupon he had to deal with his tendency toward impatient perfectionism with his crew and cameraman. On the other hand, he was exquisitely aware that the letdowns and defects were not so much about his finished product but more about how he personally was handling the process.

Each actor who came to work—Dennis Quaid, Richard

Dreyfuss, Gene Hackman, Gary Morton, Mary Wickes, to name a few, and myself—seemed to be dealing with the accelerated manner in which we were attempting to keep pace, not only with our desire to do good work, but with an even more serious question of living and functioning in this *world* with some degree of joy and optimism.

Because the freeways were choked every morning, sometimes causing delays of up to two and three hours, we often fell behind. The studio that financed our picture was bought by the Japanese, causing concern as to who would ultimately have final creative control.

The dark-spirited success of *Batman* worried everyone as to the basic mania-going tendencies of the public. *Sex, Lies and Videotape* caused a flurry of insecurity in the minds of comedy scientists like Carrie and Mike. How could someone as inexperienced as Soderbergh (the writer–director) have produced something so flawless?

Tommy Tune came to California to stage a song for me, a gesture of great generosity considering his own out-of-town problems with *Grand Hotel* waiting for his return in Boston. Tommy was calm, focused, and almost centeredly balanced in his attitude that whatever would be would be. He would go the last mile with his talent and commitment, and the rest was up to providence. Tommy knew that smelling the flowers on the way to the contest was everything.

Mike even changed his approach to the number the very day before we shot it, which required restaging and an entirely different playing style. Instead of panicking, we slid into the last minute changes with a spontaneous certitude that it was going to be much better and the adventure would be in adjusting to change in an incandescent way, rather than hanging on to the security of the past, which didn't work as well. Again, the thrill of working with such artists was discovering

Kathlyn Corinne MacLean, graduate of Acadia University, Nova Scotia, Canada.

Ira O. Beaty, Esq., graduate of and teacher at Johns Hopkins University.

Daddy holding me the day he named me after Shirley Temple. Maybe I heard it and tried to live up to her.

— My Dad's mother and father dealing with their son's offspring.

— Daddy brought me a new toy. I think I had a tantrum later.

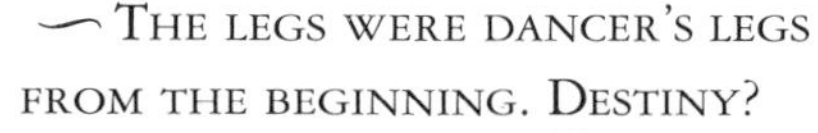

— The legs were dancer's legs from the beginning. Destiny?

—Welton and Ada Beaty on the veranda in Front Royal, Virginia.

—My reaction to sharing my parents with a new arrival.

—I learned "adorable" really early. The red curls and big bow didn't hurt.

— This is how Warren and I felt about having our pictures taken. It hasn't changed much.

— Somehow cars were always present to remind us of the date and other more down-to-earth matters. Me—five; Warren—two; teeth— zero.

MY SORORITY PICTURE...SUB-DEB CLUB...CHIC-ER THAN GREEK!

MOTHER COULD HAVE BEEN A MODEL.

DAPPER DADDY WITH MATCHING HAT, JACKET, AND TROUSERS.

— WARREN AND ME THINKING ABOUT OUR FUTURE.

— WARREN AS FOOTBALL PIANO PLAYER, ME AS WOULD-BE FOOTBALL QUEEN PERFORMER.

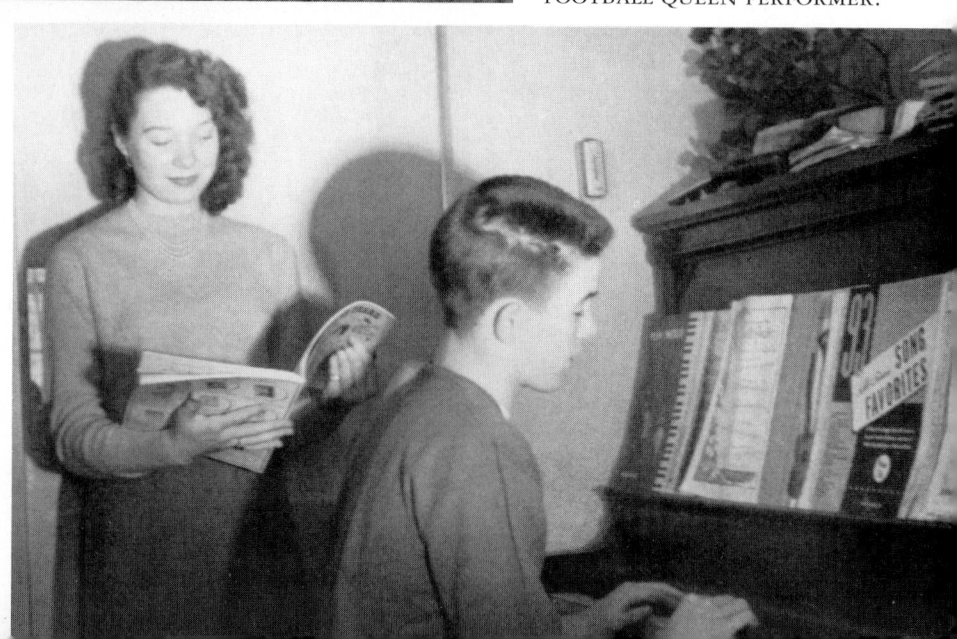

— I played the Fairy Godmother, which some would say portended the future. I was too tall to dance Cinderella. None of the slippers fit.

— Maya Plisetskaya I wasn't.

— I was a "post card" dance-hall girl in the subway-circuit production of *Oklahoma*. I was sixteen going on thirty... I played this part most of my life. (Fred Fehl)

Even I don't recognize myself. It was my Rita Hayworth vamp period.

Beaded eyelashes and lips that would give collagen a bad name.

—What a family.

—Talk about having your nose to the grindstone. *Some Came Running*, 1958.

—Dean teaching me to smoke, drink, crack jokes, and act natural in Vegas. The guys with the pinky rings were ringside.

—My beloved Mort.

We started *The Apartment* with thirty-five pages of script. Wilder and Diamond wrote the rest as we went along. I wondered where they got the idea for my suicide attempt!

Jack always wondered if the dog was part of the deal—hooker-wise. *Irma La Douce,* 1963. (Photofest)

—MITCHUM AND ME IN "REAL" LIFE AND "REEL" LIFE. (PHOTOFEST)

Glenn Ford "roped" me into *The Sheepman.* The producer said I wasn't pretty enough. Who cared?

Michael Caine's first American picture. My second Oriental makeup. My eyes remained slanted forever after. (Photofest)

Guess who on the *Can-Can* set. Whatever happened to glamour?

(© Bob Willoughby)

Vittorio de Sica, whom I adored as a father-director. He loved putting on my dresses and showing me what to do.

Danny Kaye, whom I adored as a friend. He'd take me across the country to dinner. He was the pilot who flew the plane and the cook when we arrived.

—I used to visit Liza, age nine, after a day's work on *Some Came Running.* She'd dress up and perform for me.

—My waist cincher was pinching. Shirley Booth was Dolly Levi in *The Matchmaker.* (Sterling Smith)

—Audrey taught me how to dress. I taught her how to cuss. We remain dear friends. I love her.

— GENE KELLY RECREATING OLD HOLLYWOOD MUSICAL SEQUENCE AS HE CHOREOGRAPHED *WHAT A WAY TO GO!*

— YVES MONTAND AND ME IN JAPAN ON *MY GEISHA.* HE HAD JUST COME AWAY FROM HIS RELATIONSHIP WITH MARILYN MONROE.

their personal recognition that the process was just as important as the result.

I remember the time Mike rehearsed a tracking shot for a full day. It involved a long shot of a helicopter, landing the helicopter, actors stepping out of it, walking to sets, playing a scene, close-ups inside the sets, exiting the set, more walking, and finally opening into a crowd scene with many people who each had business and lines and activity that was choreographed.

On the board it was scheduled for a three-day shoot. But after rehearsing it for one day, Mike got it in a few hours. While front office memos were being passed in overwrought concern about the time and money going down the drain one day, the next day we were three days ahead of schedule.

As a matter of fact, even with retakes (two or three days' worth) and a day off for Memorial Day, the picture wrapped nearly two weeks ahead of schedule. That had *never* been my experience in all my years in Hollywood. The reason was because Mike had a vision in his mind, and he stuck to it; the actors were well-rehearsed, prepared, cooperative, and loving with each other; the studio stayed out of our way; the catering table was fabulous (health food, junk food, doughnuts, chili, soup, sandwiches, chocolate bark with nuts, birthday cakes when necessary); good, well-furnished motor homes; nice teamsters; a good script; a makeup trailer peopled with experts who went out of their way to attend to us; and reasonable morning calls that respected the creative working rhythms of people who were mostly from New York. But I think the real reason it all went well, swiftly and expertly, was because Mike was happy with his new wife Diane, and he wanted to get back to her.

Those were all positive aspects of the shoot. But each person was going through his or her own negative struggles, too. As the days passed I began to face, more specifically, that

I was truly confronted with getting older. I could feel my body respond with less triumph to exercise. I needed to get up earlier to stretch and digest my food before exercising. I couldn't pivot as quickly with a comic spontaneity without wrenching my back. Working with choreographed props and business had been a delightful lark in my youth. Now I needed time to work it out. My brain couldn't retain the lines in a long monologue the way it used to. Most of my professional life I had been able to whip through line memorization with a cursory glance at a scene and know it. Now I literally needed to do what everyone else had always done—study my lines the night before.

Even some of the new shooting techniques were disturbing to me. I was aware of the developing lines in my face and the stomach and hip bulges in my figure. With one camera, I could maneuver to soothe my vanity; with three I knew two of them were getting angles I couldn't do anything about. But that wasn't the real problem. Appearances have never bothered me. Lack of being in control has.

For instance, people have asked me how I could "let" myself look so ghastly in *Postcards* in the scene where my daughter finds me in the hospital after a drunken automobile accident. I didn't "let." I *knew* it was necessary for me to look absolutely terrible, almost pathetically vulnerable, so that my daughter could break through and respond to that vulnerability—and help restore the brassy bravado of an aging actress. It was a breakthrough scene in our relationship. And never mind that I had to be made artificially bald! As long as I *know* what's happening I'm happy with it. But there was no doubt in my mind now that parts like this were coming to me, or I to them, because my status in life had changed.

Madame Sousatzka, for example, was a tyrannically possessive music teacher who endeavored to mold a young man's very existence for the sake of his art. She then needed to summon the courage to let him go so that he could fly, even if with uncertain wings. Perhaps that was why my mother had found the film so painfully moving. Perhaps she identified with that fledgling talent *and* with the teacher.

My part in *Steel Magnolias* was an exercise in humorous cynicism. I played an old bat whose verbal, biting negativity and permanent state of outrage allowed me to dip into my own capacity for crankiness and entertain a whole town by being the local curmudgeon. Expecting the worst in others was an adventure for me.

In *Waiting for the Light* I played a bizarre ex-circus-performer who tricked people into believing in miracles.

As I graduated into character parts, one thing bothered me as I trod the path of epic character women. There was never a love interest or sensual sensitivity any longer to the parts I was playing. Hadn't been for years. Did that mean that women in their fifties no longer were perceived as sexual beings? Surely not. Perhaps the parts I was being offered really reflected what was missing in my own life?

It had been four or five years since I was involved in any kind of "meaningful sexual relationship." Was I therefore drawing characters to me who were devoid of those same joys in life?

As for myself, I didn't really feel I was missing anything. I felt happy and fulfilled and creative and contributive and vital and hopeful. Why then, when I stopped to examine a character I was commissioned to play, did I feel an identification with her in my own life? Were my "reel" characters acting as catalysts for the examination of my "real" life? None of my recent characters had men in their lives. None of my women were even interested in men. They didn't evidence loneliness, anger, longing, frustration, or even sexual fantasy as a result of a missing partner. Neither did I.

I seemed to love going to parties and events alone. Except for the pressure of the press, I never minded showing up unescorted anywhere. It felt liberating and fun for me to be able to come and go with my own rhythm. I could leave early if I was bored (which was almost never), or I could stay until breakfast was served (quite often). I had a good time operating on my own, working the rooms full of fabulous people, trading stories and jokes, and dishing about others and their lives, and I noticed that I seemed to be expected to come and go alone; and whenever I took someone with me (a friend from out of town, a vocal coach, etc.), I noticed a spark of prurient interest light up the eyes of the curious who seemed to have their equilibrium disturbed by the thought that I might actually have settled on a new someone with whom to involve myself.

Perhaps it was my reputation as a spiritual, metaphysical lecturer. Somehow the opposite sex didn't fit into that image. Intense interest in matters of the spirit apparently negated sex.

And maybe that was true. I hadn't really realized that the state of being in my life was essentially sexless until one day I began to count the number of times I had actually made love in the last few years. Let it suffice to say—not many. And I hadn't even missed it. It had somehow given me up. Where had it gone? Was that it for the rest of my life? There were any number of opportunities, I guess, but the funny thing was—I didn't notice.

I found that I couldn't relate any longer to people who found themselves involved with sexual jealousy, an obsession with someone they couldn't have, a heart-wrenching love affair, a deep need for "a relationship"—even those in the spiritual movement who, above all, wanted to meet their soul mate. I just couldn't relate to that anymore. It seemed pointless to long for another to ratify one's own identity. What was wrong with the one I already had?

So even at parties and gatherings I noticed (when I thought about it) that men no longer interacted with me with sex as a high priority. It was there certainly, but only slightly. Perhaps I frightened them off. Was that because men still related to us primarily as sexual objects, and I now demanded a different perspective.

To be fair, I was not the only Hollywood star experiencing the "lifting of sexual pressure." Quite a few women whom I would describe as "willful achievers" were going through the same phenomenon. We often discussed it. Granted we were each on our own spiritual path, which gave rise to the conclusion that we had found, or were looking for, solutions to our deeper identities that we intuitively sensed had not that much to do with men. And each of these women was as happy as I in the liberation from sexual obsession. It was an addiction, or a dependency, we were glad to be rid of; and, in most cases, they too had woken up one day to find that they hadn't even thought about it in some time.

The culture around us, however, was geared to a different *modus operandi*. Everything around us, on television, in films, in the stories, in the ads, and even in the humor of the day, was constructed to either discuss, joke about, or deeply analyze how to be attractive and consummately expert with our sexual impulses. No one spoke to those of us who were now marching to a different drum. It was as though they didn't want to know. I was beginning to realize that we had previously been sexual victims of a product selling, profit and loss culture and system whose very basis was dependent on sex addiction.

If some of us had found that sexual nonaddiction was more peaceful and satisfying, we were decidedly out of the mainstream because it didn't sell sexual products; and, as a matter of fact, our way of physically presenting ourselves represented our "feelings" as a much more important priority. We were uncomfortable in tight pantyhose, short skirts, uplifting bras, and the "feminine" accoutrements that were designed to achieve the male perception of what a sensual woman should be. You might say we even looked unisex when we were most comfortable. And why shouldn't we be comfortable? Wasn't that one of the goals in life—the comfort of being in the skin of one's own being, rather than gussying up for someone else?

At first I thought that my comfort in wearing long cotton leg warmers under my clothes was a dancer's concern for easy muscles, but I'm not so sure. I just liked the warmth of leg-warming cotton under loose-fitting clothes, and it wouldn't have mattered to me that in the dance of undressing with a new lover, he found that he had to peel off long underwear rather than a bikini. It just didn't matter to me that his sensual expectations might possibly be dashed. If those were his requirements, I didn't want him anyway.

Was I spouting values of liberation here, or was I just getting old and didn't much care?

These questions came up for me as I worked through the character traits of the parts I had been attracting. The women were either eloquently cynical in their assessment of life or in a complete state of denial as to their sexual identities. My question was, "Were they a reflection of myself, and, if so, what did I have to learn from that?"

I seemed in so many ways the feminine opposite of my brother, Warren. He was a man who was exceedingly "left-brained" in his approach to life, needing to control his mechanisms of perfection, intellectually analytical, and above all needing to be in charge of his destiny. He was also a man of sexuality, whose appetite at the moveable feast was legendary. How could we be so different? Were we the clichéd example of male and female crossbred within the same family?

And what was this business of masculine and feminine anyway? I had always thought I had a pretty good balance between my masculine and feminine traits until a teacher I admired greatly pointed out that I had always been attracted to macho men, because that was the aspect of my own personality that I didn't yet own. That made deep sense to me. Was I now owning that aspect of myself? I never was attracted to spiritual, sensitive men. I liked the guys who knew what they wanted and with brains and humor went after it. And now? Neither. I wondered if I was denying something or whether I had, as most of my friends believed, outgrown and transcended the "need."

We made jokes about evolving enough to finally get above the second chakra (the second energy center of the body being the sexual center). I certainly didn't rule out falling madly and passionately in love in the future. But when I examined such a thought, I didn't really want, ever again, the "mad" passionate swirl of a relationship in the way I had always had it before. Perhaps that was the rub, the conflict, the missing link.

I asked Mike Nichols why he got married again. I'll never forget his answer. He said, "I was perfectly happy being on my own, ordering up pizza whenever I wanted it—but when a love came along which I knew in my heart was a gift from God, I took it."

I had had so many "gifts from God" though. How would I know when it really came from the Source?

And what would I do if that familiar "love swirl" hit me again, keeping me awake at night at the sheer wonder of its intensity? And what was that intensity based on? Hadn't it been based on some need in myself to experience myself differently—some all-abounding desire to meld my "isness" into the being of another in order to feel whole? Was I, were we all, looking for the other half of ourselves that resonated in our cellular memory from another time and place, reminding us of the completeness we felt long, long ago when we were one with the universe and therefore with ourselves?

Perhaps the sexual revolution (of which I was a part) had,

in the final analysis, played itself out because we had abused the search for that completeness by looking on the outside instead of the inside? Were the sexual diseases so prevalent in our culture residue examples of the abuse we heaped upon ourselves and each other in the frantic, desperate desire to find what used to be the other half of ourselves, which never did and never would exist anywhere except within each one of us?

Perhaps I had simply come to the understanding that every sexual relationship I had ever had was really nothing more than the enjoyment of myself while I was involved with it; and now, because of age and a certain amount of wisdom, I had come to the realization that sex was nothing more than a language and dialogue through which we could experience another human soul, which was a reflection of the missing and unrecognized parts of ourselves anyway.

Perhaps I should take heed from the characters I was playing and recognize, without pressure, that in one's fifties and sixties, a manless existence could really be the state of the art of living, because the women themselves were more fabulous than ever and the men were the ones missing something.

While working I felt more than ever that the social and emotional environment of creative people on the film was analogous to the utopian dream of society. No one holds back much, feelings are freely expressed, yet there is a respect for the order necessary to function. There is a leader on the set (the director), yet even he answers to a leader in the front office.

The marriage of creative individualism with industry (money) works fairly well for the most part. There are explosions of individual temperament and protest (born out of insecurity usually), but always there is the hidden acknowledgment that such artistic combustion is vital to the health of the whole.

Creative people in show business know they are dependent

upon the people with the money. But the converse is true also. The often unexpressed admiration and awe with which the money people regard creative eccentrics is amusing. Yes, we are obstreperous children to them, yet the family of opposites can't function without such a mix. The "bosses" are often reviled and ridiculed by us creative children, yet they serve as parental figures who hold the power and the permission without which we are not allowed to play and make magic.

Arguments, anger, fear, and sometimes even literally physical combat serve as outlets for resolution, sometimes making it unclear who is more childish, we children or the parent bosses.

When Columbia was bought by the Japanese "bosses," Nichols's creative reaction was to put his film in a can under his arm in protection until he could determine what kind of business parents they would be. At the same time, those who now controlled the family were completely dependent on the emotional and spiritual health and welfare of the genius children. Such motion picture relationships gave new meaning to symbiotic interplay.

One day, as Meryl and I were rehearsing for the musical number we were to shoot the following day, she involuntarily described the costume she would be wearing as her school uniform, adding that she had done her homework and hoped that her teachers and mother would approve of her work. Mike often talked of what he would be "allowed" to do regarding shooting and inventive expense. Carrie was constantly protective of the feelings and sensitivities of her mother and father, and I, in my adjustment to aging, tried to live up to my father's adage that I was a long-distance runner, not a fast-starting sprinter.

We were each playing our roles in the game of illusion, needing each other and the "parents" who "allowed" us to play. There were compliments from the front office about our work in the dailies. There were baskets of gaily arranged fruit and worldly delicacies that spoke, in gracefully sophisticated acknowledgment, to our appreciation of being appreciated.

The crew was, of course, more "grown up." They were pragmatists and played with technology. Sometimes, as we creative children sat singing songs with mischievously invented lyrics, they blinked in embarrassment at the free-flowing childishness of our spontaneity. They might even have been much younger than us in years, but their emotions were more controlled, regulated, and restrained. They were the "straight" people. The creative "above the line" talents were acknowledged to be the children who kept the familial project going, perhaps even activating the child in every person who would ultimately buy the tickets.

When Mike arrived for the night shoot, which included two musical numbers, and was disturbed by the color of paint of the walls, a slight undercurrent of "so what" rippled through the crew, but at the same time everyone knew that he "sees" things others don't. Somehow there was the understanding that color matters to performance, it matters to ambiance, it matters to deep visceral reactions in the minds and eyes of an audience.

We sat for three or four hours while the walls were repainted and dried. And because the new color produced a subliminal shift in feeling—surrounding the actors with enhanced focus—the musical scenes went better and were accomplished in two takes.

What was it that Mike's eyes saw? How did he know? And more than anything, how did he muster the courage to command the change at such extravagant cost in time? Only a creative child whose sole survival was realizing his own visions would do such a thing. Mike's dreams were infectious so that we all saw through his eyes.

Would a studio head in his right mind come charging

onto the set to tell us we had to go with "that" color because it was already paid for and we shouldn't keep three hundred extras standing around waiting? It wouldn't be the first time, of course, but I've found that the more eccentric the creative child, the more the "straight" people leave them alone. They are unable to identify with the freedom of eccentricity, and thus find it difficult to handle. They are literally intimidated by the insanity of eccentric vision.

Observing the intricacies of creativity over the years—both in myself and others—led me to examine, probably with too much scrutiny, the nature of the transformative process. What was it that enabled a person to realize and manifest his or her vision?

A simple light stroke applied to the canvas of creative imagination could change the entire perception until, to the objective observer, it became a new reality. How does the artist know? From what does he receive his knowledge? Overnight a transformation can occur, which gives the impression, because of its perfection, that it was there all along.

And wasn't that true in our lives? With a rearrangement of focus the entire drama of an event alters. Perhaps the reason show business and movies and theater are so fascinating to every culture known to man is because the creative expression is analogous to our lives in that we do indeed create the drama, the comedy, the laughter, the tears, by casting the characters therein according to what we need and want to experience. We can tolerate the responsibility when it comes to a fantasy production—but how about the "reality" of life itself?

Were *we* responsible for creating whatever we were going through? Were *we* drawing personalities to us that make us miserable, joyful, and confused? Were *we* the producers, actors, directors, and casters of our own lives? Were *we* then the enactors of our own transformation or the lack of it? The whole world seemed to be going through a transformation, because the individuals in it were taking responsibility for who they were and wanted to be.

An actor, writer, director, or artist understands the phenomenon of transforming the choices one makes into the reality of enactment. The choices are infinite and the decisions sometimes painful. Indecision can abort the flow of harmony. Fear can cause chaos. Insecurity can breed a breakdown of communication, and insensitivity can make war. But the combustion of all the suffering that goes into the variegated spectrum of creativity is what makes show business endlessly alluring. Was that not analogous to life itself? The world was a stage and all the people actors upon it learning who they were while playing their parts. The reviews or even the finished product were not as important as the process. The pleasure lay in the enlightenment along the path; the pain lay in the resistance to learning.

But regardless of how much moviemaking affords those of us in it the opportunity to know ourselves better, there always comes a moment when we suddenly are faced with what we are doing in our lives as actresses and actors and where we'd be without our work.

One morning I woke up early and flipped on a movie channel. The credits were winding down for *Billy Rose's Jumbo*—a big, old, MGM Hollywood musical about the circus, directed by Chuck Walters and produced by Joe Pasternak.

I had worked with both of them at Metro so long ago that it seemed another lifetime. As I watched the opening scenes unfold with the hundreds of extras and animals and high-moving crane shots, I was overcome with a nostalgia that segued into a depression so deep I had to turn off the television set.

What had happened to Hollywood? Where had my past gone? Why was everything so different now?

There was Doris Day gaily singing the thrills of bringing the family to the Big Top, riding high on a magnificent carriage drawn by prancing white circus ponies, her blond hair piled on top of her head, her smile flashing teeth brighter and more gleaming than polished ivory nuggets imbedded in an Indian statue.

And where was she now? Heading up an animal shelter somewhere near Santa Barbara? There wasn't even water in Santa Barbara now. There was fire and fear.

I remembered walking into Alfred Hitchcock's office in the old days just as a dramatic thriller starring Doris and Jimmy Stewart was being storyboarded. The assistant director was swaying and humming along with one of her hit records as it revolved on the turntable. He was caught up in an almost arrogant pleasure that he would be scheduling the time and talent of this marvelous performer. She didn't know him from Adam, unaware of her influence on his life and sensibilities. He would dine out for months on stories about "him and Doris" struggling to complete this "goddamned flick on time."

The screen credits had flashed the name of her husband, Martin Melcher, as an associate producer on the picture. That was a laugh. She had relied on him to be her manager, learning only after his death that millions of dollars had been lost.

My heart turned over as the moment brought back the rushing memories of what it had been like to be part of a business that was flourishing, and which, like the magic it created, would flourish forever. Or so most of the people living the dream seemed to believe, prancing and posturing with their power and talent like overindulged children gone amok in a candy store. And if the wizards who created and maintained the candy store did so because of what was in the cash register, they were no less caught up in the fantasy.

In the old days, the moguls of movies were so much more honest and humorous about what rogues they were. They were dedicated with a deep and childlike addiction to the game of making magic. They lived, breathed, manipulated, and made love to their own glittering, greedy creation.

The "deal" was important to be sure, but overriding it was how much was up there on the screen for the "people" to enjoy. Everything they did was in the name of their love for the mystery of the magic. Today it was for the love of profit and the sale of software to service hardware technology. Heart was out. Technology was in.

Perhaps that was what caused my depression. The spirit of our business was different now. Perhaps it was even gone. Certainly those people, like Pasternak and De Mille and Jack Cummings and Roger Edens, belong now to a past that almost provoked ridicule and cynical derision. Why was that? They had been such embraceable moviemakers. They had been patriarchs of power and passion whose attitude expressed pure delight in the knowledge that talent could potentially be immortalized on the screen, bringing joy and happiness to the small towns of America.

Of course they drooled over the profit they would make on someone else's talent; but *they* invested in the talent. They were part of the nurturing process, the developing and molding of what would eventually be a sculpted legend, like Lana Turner or Rita Hayworth and, yes, Debbie Reynolds.

They provided coaches, trainers, teachers, designers, writers, and even PR people who carefully, and most of the time sensitively, fashioned the desired image of projected imagination until a screen identity had been achieved. Each individual in the army of backstage people had a stake in the success of a star and a film. They were not detached. They were totally involved with the destiny of each project, sometimes foregoing time off and, more often than not, sacrificing time with their families.

In no other business had I seen dedication to getting the job done with such naive selflessness.

There was time in those days for show business stories in between setups, time for movie queen primping, time for temperament, time for on- and off-screen love affairs between the gods and goddesses of the celluloid. The front office knew everything and also when to let well enough alone.

Nowadays there was little talent for involvement. Everything nowadays was about money and about time being analogous to money. The basic character underneath the business had changed. I missed what we used to be. I was lonely for the familylike camaraderie that used to surround us as we bared our hearts and souls on the screen.

The movie business seemed to give people up, rather than the other way around. Why, then, hadn't it given me up?

Why were my brother, Warren Beatty, and I still around, battered and bruised but none the worse for wear? In fact, it seemed to me that the wisdom gained had enhanced our work. But why was our drive so deep and intense? It appeared nothing would dam up our chosen outlet of expression. We would somehow use our tragedies and loneliness as grist for the mill. No personal relationship or event in our lives, regardless of the impact, seemed to alter our need to continue to create, to be on top, or at least somehow to still insist on being in the melee.

I loved being alone and spending long self-reflective periods of time writing. But I always knew I was going back to bat again—to work as an emulator of human emotion decked out in an appropriate costume with hair and face to match. I *knew* I would always have the opportunity to become someone else on demand for the rest of my life. I never doubted it. The question was, Why did I *need* it?

I believe the need to be on top of the profession was a way of continuing to act out my parents' unfulfilled dreams, particularly my mother's. She had always wanted what I now had. She had told me so, and her old age presence was a constant reminder to Warren and me that her dreams continued to come to fruition through us. She wanted to stay around to witness our testament to her ambitions. Our accomplishments were motivated by her burning desire to see us succeed. She hadn't done it for herself. She had dedicated her life to us. I don't know if she actually sacrificed a budding creative career for us, but the implication was clearly there for me. For Warren? I don't know. I only know that her desire for us to "accomplish" permeated our very beings. It was in every film we made.

The depression that overwhelmed me when I "accidentally" turned on *Jumbo* probably spoke to the truth that I couldn't continue being in the business to fulfill my mother's dreams. I would go on now to fulfill my own dreams. It seemed preposterous that I had become Shirley MacLaine because my mother wanted it, but I think there is more truth to that than I had been heretofore willing to admit. I was doing it for her, and at the same time I felt slightly guilty that I had done what she couldn't. I felt a sense of competition from her, a velvet resentment almost.

Weren't most mothers a twinge jealous of their daughters? Would I twinge with a loving jealousy if Sachi became a star? It seemed that I felt the opposite. In fact, it would be a continuum if Sachi followed in my footsteps, and yet . . . and yet. That primitive fear that one's territory might be usurped was always possible. And so I plowed ahead year after year, decade after decade, to serve my mother's dream, which had now become mine, to thank her, live up to her expectations, and sustain my "stardom" regardless of what it took or the price I paid. I loved it, to be sure, but it was clear to any other thinking, curious individual that our professional longevity—Warren's and mine—was beginning to raise the proverbial eyebrow around town. What was the reason for our long-distance marathon? Others came and went. We were determined to stay in the race till the people went home. Our mother had subliminally, in her powerfully passive way, decreed it. We would become stars, and we would shed our light as long as she lived and breathed. And after that, what?

What would we do then? If there were no audience, what would we do? Would we have to turn around and literally consider having a long-term committed relationship? Never mind that this was the professed objective for most of the rest of the world. Show business relationships were notoriously difficult to sustain. Actors, actresses, entertainers of one kind or another—all felt the pressure of the now-and-then relationships, all, or at least most, were too mercurial, moody, inconsistent, self-centered, and vain to sustain long-term personal connections. We were perhaps more in need of approval from relatively impersonal masses of people. And it seemed that we'd go to any lengths to sustain that approval. If a particular relationship compromised that priority, it was doomed.

We sometimes didn't even realize the profound need we had to put ourselves first, above the relationship, in order to insure our position at center stage. It was a matter of survival for us. We felt we didn't exist if the focus of attention was elsewhere, while innate shyness expressed itself in anxiety about not living up to being in the spotlight.

Most of us were loving, social, outgoing, in a word, extroverted. After all, expression, rather than introversion, was the core of our work. Yet we were also territorial beings. We continually sought to find love and companionship, then as soon as we found it, our survival and territorial instincts would take over and we'd begin to argue and engage in the power struggle that we thought jeopardized our position.

If we didn't engage in the power struggle by trying to dominate, we evaluated the circumstance and elected to repress our real selves and "succumb."

I was quite capable of either game, and I had played both roles. I had been the woman I thought the man wanted me to be, down to the way I dried myself after a shower, or contained myself in a moment of hurt. I protected *my* territory by never really exposing it, by refraining from jeopardizing it. Or I'd subtly make my wishes and desires known until, depending on the wiles it took, I'd ultimately have my way.

Rarely, in a close emotional relationship, was I my real self, completely and totally accepting who I was and the person I was with. Such protective posturing was tailor-made to annihilate the prospect of lasting love.

We'd begin with harmonious feelings and the spirit of loving diplomatic compromise. God knows we in show business knew how to use charm and emotional orchestration to get what we wanted. Then, having achieved the desired relationship, we reached some kind of plateau that allowed evaluation of the weaknesses of the other. Paying a high price to survive in our business, we needed to shore up the knowledge of where the weaknesses and strengths lay in anyone else we were associated with. The nature of the struggle for top spot, for good parts, for strong alliances and powerful supporters dictated a mistrust in the positive aspects of close relationships. Manipulation became the name of the game.

Rather than truly share, more than anything else, we attempted to change the individual we were attracted to. We really wanted shadow versions of ourselves, because we would then be familiar with the responses without being threatened. The contrasting differences that had been attractive in the first place slowly eroded away.

In show business, the stronger, more definitive personalities usually prevailed in any one-on-one relationship. The gentler partner was required to conform with the needs of the stronger, carried all the emotional baggage, believed in the self-image the more powerful person held of himself, or herself, and supported that vision. That was when the real trouble started.

When another person became a shadow of someone else, there was no balance to the relationship. Gone were the stimulating differences, the fuel for the fires of passion. The differences that were so attractive in the beginning inspired discussion, colorful passions, and feelings. After well-schooled velvet manipulation had removed any disagreements, there was only a replica of self left.

How many times had I, and so many of my friends, been through this process? It seemed to be human show business nature: actress meets man, actress attempts to change man to reflect self, actress is then unhappy at disintegration of differences. It was all around me. Everywhere I looked people were doing this to themselves and each other.

I had finally given up the male-female contest, at least for a few years, and was happy with the liberation from passionate conflict. But I could see, for myself, and for so many others, that it would be more fulfilling to simply respect the individuality of another we loved than to perceive it as a threat, as something to be altered. Agree to disagree. Agree to respect the disagreement.

After all, wasn't real love the ability to respect another for what and whom he is without judgment? In my heart, I knew the differences were interesting, a path to objectivity that offered the scope of broader perspective, an enlarged or enlightened view. We should be secure enough to see differences not as barriers, but more as stimulating catalysts for growth. Why couldn't we just relax and accept?

Being alone for a while had made it more clear to me that the probable reason for the ennui in my life was the lack of those close combustible differences in another—someone who could challenge my intolerance, test my evolution in nonjudgment, and provide me with the opportunity to see just how far I'd be able to go in my capacity to accept another person for what he was without destructive criticism. I needed to allow, no, welcome, constructive differences.

I knew I'd lose by trying to change someone. I also knew it was going to be difficult to grow by being alone for much longer. I knew there were games to play and joys to share, but there was still a part of me that wondered if I could really live up to the evolved expectations I knew I should fulfill in myself, particularly at my age with my experience and so-called wisdom.

When I was younger, I didn't know any better. Now I was aware. I had been through some deeply profound relationships, endured many a power struggle, loved and given in, hated and demanded. I had been around the track more than a few times and finally given up the contest for a while. And, I had to admit, I was still enjoying the liberation from the competition and the power games of the Relationship Olympics!

Perhaps soon I would try the adventure of putting a relationship first, rather than myself. I had a sneaky feeling that if I was willing to do that, it would precipitate change and growth in everyone involved simply because of the commitment to accept and not judge. If I accepted another human being totally, he would probably reciprocate. Maybe I should try putting a relationship first, because by doing so I would ultimately "allow" the real me to emerge. That, however, had not been what I saw when I observed most of the marriages around me. Each partner seemed to have settled, somehow, into a life of compromised alliance. In the case of my own parents (where my view of marriage originated) the alliance was so compromised that frustration reigned.

The marriage of my parents was a manifest example of two people who loved each other but were not free to develop individually. Each sacrificed his and her creativity for the marriage. Mother was an extremely talented painter and actress. She longed to develop those talents but opted for marriage and children instead. Dad was a talented musician (violin) and a philosophic thinker (philosophy and psychology) but opted to fulfill his duties as teacher and school principal and as a husband and father. The school business carried what he called "peanut politics," which prevented him from enjoying it. But it was the only living he knew how to make.

Hence neither was really happy. Dad felt obligations as a father and husband above his own needs. And Mother made herself subservient to her marriage, her husband, and her children. Yet even within her subserviency, she managed to rule the family with matriarchal emotional power. Hers was the tyranny of the passive, the power of the deprived and repressed. Through her frustrated, suppressed creativity, Warren and I experienced enough fallout to last us a lifetime. What we did with that fallout was up to each of us individually. For me, I think I subliminally vowed that I would never allow myself to be colonized by customs, traditions, society, husbands, children, or marriage; and the same might certainly be said of Warren.

The haunted longing in Mother's face whenever I'd leave home for a new job—the choked tears that she might not see me again for ages—left me with a gnawing understanding that she didn't have a life. She never had. Not one of her own. She had given her life to me, to Warren, and to her husband.

She reveled in our successes and was always there for us, listening to our problems, our conflicts, our fears, and our triumphs. But underneath there seemed to be a resonant sigh of loneliness for herself. She seemed to be more in touch with what she *couldn't* do in her life than what she *could* do. On the other hand, she always said that her primary desire was to have a family and raise children. Yes, that was what she said. What she *felt,* I suspected, was another story.

One of Mother's unconscious conflicts was her fundamental sexism. It was a source of deep tension between us. She honestly believed men were more capable than women. She had bought the propaganda of the age of her traditional upbringing and carried it with her every step of the way. Perhaps it was sexism designed to justify her acquiescent position in the home. ("This is the work women are *supposed* to do.") Rather than summoning the courage to become more than a homemaker, Mother settled for the traditional definition of a woman's role in life (marriage, husband, and children).

So I always felt a subtle, but grating, resentment from her that I had broken out of the mold of female repression and dared to pole-vault over it. This was probably reinforced by the subliminal threat that a daughter always represents to a mother. She was dealing with my success, and yet, in an inverse way, so was I. I was somehow always holding myself back just a touch so that I wouldn't preposterously outsucceed mother. I became more reflective about my talent and potential instead of daring and outrageous. There are those who would say I was the personification of outrageous daring; but knowing my full potential for such things, I hadn't lived up to half of it.

Perhaps mothers and daughters have different reactions to success than fathers and sons do. The female evaluation of accomplishment is fraught with centuries of untried, unexplored yearnings. There were no real guideposts until recently. Women weren't expected to do much, and certainly it was recommended that they not rock the boat. But then a really talented mother comes along (my mother) who produces a really talented daughter (me) and, through her own frustration, acts as a catalyst for her daughter's expression—a negative role model you might say.

At least it was clear to me what I *didn't* want. Mother then was faced with what was clearly the unrealized potential of her own life. Of course, her children were the monuments to her life, but we belonged to our own lives now. What did that leave her?

Chastising me for my success was not something Mother would ever do. Not only was she happy for me, but I know she correctly saw herself as greatly responsible. No, her feelings about success had more to do with her own view of herself as a woman than they did with me. To her, Warren's success was inevitable and expected; men were supposed to make big accomplishments. But me? I think that was complicated for her, as it is for every mother and every daughter because they see themselves differently. The whole, complicated push-and-pull was encapsulated in a scene that happened when Mother was in the hospital after a bladder operation.

I flew to Johns Hopkins Hospital in Baltimore to be with her. Warren was coming later. Others came to "see Mother" too, but most of her visitors had heard that Warren and I would be there.

Mother told me about it. She was proud. One man in particular had longed to meet Warren. With a perfectly open and calm attitude, Mother sat in bed and said, "I told the man

Warren wasn't coming until next week, that he'd just have to be satisfied with meeting second best—you."

I felt the breath go out of me. I couldn't speak. I knew she believed what she was saying. When she realized what she had said, her hand flew to her mouth as if to smother the words. But it was too late. She had involuntarily articulated what had always been true to her.

"Oh, Shirl," she said, mortified at herself. "That was a terrible thing to say, wasn't it?"

My reaction then was probably the most hypocritical of all. "It's not horrible if you mean it, Mother," I said. "At least you're speaking the truth as you see it. Besides, I've always known it. I've understood how you felt."

Then I did something I never should have done. I would not allow her to see how much she had hurt my feelings. I wanted her to want and expect the same wonders from me that she did from Warren. But I couldn't let her see that. I wanted to scream at her, "Why do you expect less from me because I'm a girl? Why have you never expected anything from yourself because you're a woman?"

But I didn't. I sat upright in my chair beside her bed. I could feel my mouth quiver into a smile. Tears forced their way through my eyes anyway. I looked down, rummaged in my purse, and put on glasses until my feelings were smothered.

Our lives as women had merged in that moment. The truth was that Mother never did and probably never would believe that any woman could or should measure up to a man. Men were authoritative by nature and should be obeyed and respected as such. To have done otherwise with her own father, her brother, and her husband would have been heresy in the first degree.

For me to identify myself as a functioning, whole person without a man to prop me up was to her a false, unrealized identity. As she had said to me many times, "What do you really know about life and love and compromise? You live alone."

Now, heading into my later fifties, I could hear her words again, but with different ears than she had intended, and for entirely different reasons.

Perhaps I should consider a permanent marriage now. Not because I need anyone, but because it could hold the dynamics for a more interesting future. Within each relationship I had enjoyed, there seemed always to be two sides—positive and negative. If I could now perceive those opposites as creating a productive whole, I could perhaps come to the understanding that two people functioning together was a happier arrangement than one free soul alone. The question was, Was I ready for it? Or were there other things I needed to do on my own first?

Again my mother had been the stimulus for another octave of growth for me.

Part Two

~ FATHER STAGE

Chapter 7

~ Back to the Stage

ACTING IN MOVIES IS AN art that requires patience, tolerance, reverence for detail, and emotional faith. It is, in essence, what I would call the female expression. To preserve your sanity you need to be laid-back and accepting of wasted time, misperceived instructions, and authority figures who run the studios without understanding the films.

Performing on stage, on the other hand, is quite different. It requires a more assertive, aggressive thrust, an awareness that is left-brained, swiftly analytical, and above all a feeling of comfort in asserting power and control over an audience. It is, in essence, the male expression.

Movies are a more intimate adventure. Stage is outgoing. You stand in front of an audience and demand that they not only pay attention but succumb to all your tricks and timing. You must have everything your way, otherwise you lose control and it won't work. The light focuses only on you. The audience is dark; you are light. An entire symphony orchestra of some forty musicians must be subservient to your rhythm, your phrasing, your transitions, your emotional beat, your heart's will. You are, in fact, in immediate control of the manipulation of the audience's feelings. And it must be so in order for you to be good at it. You need to be very secure that you are comfortable with such power and, in fact, enjoy wielding it at your pleasure.

When you are in command, the audience feels safe. When you lose command, they become insecure. There is no democracy when you are the solo performer on the stage. It is a professional, artful dictatorship. The teamwork offstage is solely serving the one who is out there. And if the personal rhythm of those who serve your time in the spotlight is not in sync with yours, they must go. A backstage family exists, but the stage performer is not the child (as in movies). She or he is the father operating with all the masculine reflexes, talent, and instincts that are necessary to patriarchal requirements.

After *Postcards* was finished, I decided to go back to the stage. It had been six years. I missed the live performance side of myself. It was part of my personal resolution program I think, inspired of course by being in my fifties, to balance the female and male aspects of myself. I missed the love of live audiences for sure. But I also missed being in charge. Playing to a cinema machine for a few minutes at a time left me with a fragmented, disjointed frustration as to what I had really accomplished. I needed to know immediately. The *moment* was becoming more and more important to me.

It was usually a year before a film was edited, scored, and

released. I needed to know *now.* Film was a medium belonging to almost everybody but the performer. A terrific scene, a powerful performance, could be chopped in half, a large part of it left curled on the cutting room floor. By the same token, a bad scene—slow, out of sync—could be rescued. An entire story could be rewritten in the editing room, to say nothing of how a film's perception could be altered through advertising and marketing.

Doing my live show, no one but me was in charge. I was responsible for everything. It succeeded or failed on my merits, my taste, and my ideas. The mistakes were also mine. I needed to be in charge of my own destiny. And as my subsequent experience was to prove, I needed to be in charge of my own destiny more profoundly than I ever had before. This meant grappling with experiences on a much deeper level. It meant looking at my motivations in a much more emotionally courageous way. And, as it turned out, I came to grips with parts of my life and background that had nothing to do with show business but everything to do with, mainly, my father.

I'm not sure I would have made the decision to return to my performing roots had I known what physical, emotional, and spiritual pain it would put me through. However, the salvation of all of us, I guess, is that we mainly go forth in our lives unaware that such a step could be a life-altering, learning experience relating to those who conditioned us. That is what happened to me. Because of my return to dancing, I was able to give up the ties that bound me—ties I wasn't even aware of—ties that I unknotted and broke free from once and for all. The free-fall was frightening at times, but that's the nature of liberation.

Obviously, all people who put themselves through the rigors and rewards of the theater are answering a deep-seated call, probably a deep-seated plea, for loving, collective, instant approval—the electricity of being a human battery charged by the appreciation of the audience. You can't continue to get up there night after night, with the stomach clutched and the mouth dry, without the reward being direly necessary; and the reward must supersede the fear so as to be worth it. And for me, now, not only that. My body and physical condition had deteriorated. I knew it. I needed to lose weight and retrain muscles I hadn't used or even been aware of in six years. But still, I told myself, retraining the body at my age was not as much about the physical as it was about the consciousness. I had already begun to suspect that the "no pain no gain" theory was an incorrect way to work. Was it possible to get up every morning with hope and a chosen attitude that I was not going to experience pain? I wanted to see if that was true.

A dance trainer came to my apartment in Malibu every day for eight weeks with her gypsy bag dangling from her shoulder and her straight blond hair hanging behind her pierced ears. Mary Hite was rail-thin, taut, and strong—stronger than any dancer I had ever worked with, and very, very nice.

There was a subtle self-sustaining anger in her—an anger that kept her going from an accident she had sustained years earlier. She had been hit by a car, which shattered most of her body. The doctors said she would never walk again. She chose to overcome their diagnosis by studying every tendon and muscle in the body and, armed with that knowledge, going to work on herself. She accomplished a physical miracle through sheer discipline and hard work.

I wondered if she had come to terms with what happened to her. How did she feel about the driver of the car that hit her? She was still "workin' on it" she said, but it was clear that her anger had played a part in her recovery by somehow motivating her willpower. I thought a lot about Mary. If I were incapacitated like that, how would I deal with it? I was attempting to eliminate angry negative emotions in my life. Would that mean a difficulty in overcoming adversity? Did one need anger in order to survive?

Mary and I lay on the floor and did pelvic tilts and knee presses to the rhythm of the Malibu waves, quietly and easily. There was no loud insistent music, no shouting of encouragements, and absolutely no pain. My muscles felt "worked" but not worn.

We did relevés (foot rises to half toe) and stomach presses, leg lifts and arm stretches. The arm stretches were designed to "feel the breath" in the shoulders. The more interior "air" there was, the less pressure on the muscles. None of what we did felt overexertive, and never once did I break a sweat.

We worked for three or three-and-a-half hours each day, and inside of two weeks I saw that my body had changed and my strength was renewed in a different way. I had always thought that I needed to feel exhausted after a workout. To dedicate myself to the *pain* of discipline and working hard had been my credo. This time it was different. I was working correctly, instead of painfully.

The secret lay in easy alignment. If my pelvis was pulled out of my lower back, the alignment of my posture was correct; therefore, the strength was there. If I "breathed into my shoulders," I felt lighter and therefore took the stress off my thighs in a deep knee bend. If the center of my back had "air" in the center of the sternum, my lower back had no pressure. I was amazed. I thought of all the years I had worked with "muscularity" and force instead of breath and air and alignment; how I had strained and compelled my body to bend to my will. I could have saved myself forty years of pain. But pain had been addictive to me. It is to every dancer. Pain is not easy to give up. When you are trained to believe in pain, you feel your stamina and even your talent can't function without it. You learn to measure accomplishment by pain. The more the better. I wondered if relinquishing pain would serve me as well in performance.

As soon as Mary felt I was ready, we moved into a rehearsal hall. I put on my high heels. She winced at the insanity of my working in such shoes but knew I had to do it. I had worked in three-inch heels previously, because they give a beautiful ankle and leg line. The moment I put them on my feet I could feel the muscle memory return. Dancers know the phenomenon of the muscles remembering the steps irrespective of the mind. But this time there was a catch. My muscles remembered the old way of working. They needed to adjust to training in a new way.

Pain shot through my ankles and my Achilles tendon. My calves were remembering my old techniques. They weren't responding now. I panicked. I couldn't even run across the rehearsal hall floor with any grace. Then my back gave out. It was as though my muscle memory was so strong it dragged me back into the past.

Mary was undaunted. She had been through so much worse. "It just takes time," she assured me, "and you should really consider lowering your heels."

The next day we went to my shoemaker, who slaved by hand over each pair of shoes he sculpted. He said that if I lowered the heels, the original last of the shoe wouldn't fit. He had to make totally new shoes.

When a dancer lowers the height of her shoes, even if it's a centimeter, it's as though she is working with entirely new choreography, because the placement of the body shifts with each centimeter. That means that the muscles have to relearn the steps. It was not an insignificant decision, but we did it. We lowered the heels. That meant I had to wear the same height heels all day long in my daily life in order to accustom my body to the new placement. So I wore heels in the car, heels to the market, heels to dinner, heels in the house.

I also needed to tape my feet with adhesive tape in order to prevent blisters from forming, because the pressure points were now in different places.

Regardless of where I went, I carried adhesive tape, scissors, and Band-Aids in my purse. A blister could mean a few days without working.

Diet was as important as the correct exercise. At least eight glasses of water a day were necessary. Water keeps the system toxin-free and also lubricates the muscles and tendons.

Meat was necessary, because I needed the enzymes. But I found that lamb was too full of uric acid for me. Steak was fine. Dairy products clogged my arteries and, of course, fat was verboten. Sugar was a psychological reward, but too much of it (more than one dessert) made me too hungry for more. Fruit, vegetables, fish, pasta, chicken, rice, and steak became my diet. Protein (eggs, chicken, fish) for breakfast helped me lose the weight, because protein burns fat all day long. Food combining was essential. Protein with vegetables, never fruit. Pasta with vegetables, never meat. Fruit before the meal, never after. And never eat dinner later than eight at night. Water, water, water. Even more than the mandatory eight glasses a day. My car rolled with plastic Evian water bottles. If it was chilled, it was easier to consume. So much liquid washing through the system required extra vitamin intake and I took at least ten thousand milligrams of vitamin C every day, plus a vitamin pack of antioxidant vitamins three times a day.

I bought a mattress made in Japan, which was embedded with little magnets that helped align the electromagnetic frequency of the body to the vibrations of the earth. The Japanese had begun using these magnetic mattresses in their hospitals when they found that patients who slept on them healed much faster.

With every training-filled day, I got stronger. The weight came off, but what was more important, my body was firm and taut and more flexible.

I tried to remember my physical state and my attitude six years ago. It seemed a lifetime ago. Had I gone through such a training program then? I couldn't even remember. I could remember my original decision to return to the stage *fifteen* years before. That was the big one.

I had been thirty-five pounds overweight and hadn't done a plié in thirty years. Oh God, the memory of that regimen of pain brought tears to my eyes when I thought about it now.

I had returned from a trip to China looking and feeling like the Goodyear blimp, couldn't get a decent job in movies; I had done myself in where television was concerned with an obnoxious weekly series nobody saw (including me) called *Shirley's World.* I had campaigned for George McGovern for a year, only to find that the Democrats were as big a mess as I was. Someone suggested putting together an act for Las Vegas (which most struggling movie stars were doing then in the absence of regular work). I pulled myself up by my dancer's tights and started all over again. It worked, thank goodness, but the memories of what it took still rattled my sleep sometimes, and the sounds of the chains of pain haunted me now too.

Now as I climbed the Calabasas Mountains with my buddies at the Ashram, it was comforting to know they were still around and still encouraging. Yet, even they were saying that pain was no longer necessary to gain. Attitudes were changing.

For a few weeks, I got up every morning at six to climb mountains for five hours, then did an aerobics class, then a weight-lifting class, then jogged for six miles. After that, Mary and I worked for three hours, after which I climbed mountains for another four hours. It added up to something like fourteen hours of workout a day and it was crazy. I wasn't going to use any of that on the stage, and in my newfound wisdom about exertion I quit. Going the last mile was the old me. *Quality* in the mile I was treading was more important now. Angelo Dundee, the boxing trainer, had once warned me, "Don't leave your fight in the gym!" I came out of the gym and worked easier. It was the best decision of my physical life.

Along with my body training came the retraining of my singing voice. I knew I wasn't much of a singer, but I could belt and carry a tune. Yet I also knew that there was a better way to approach the art of making sounds than I had been aware of.

About the same time that I needed a new approach, a friend called me with a suggestion. There was a voice builder in town who worked with a self-discovered technique of not producing musical sounds from the "mask of the nose and face" but rather by forcing the muscularity of the throat open to produce the sound from the very center of the body. Although most of his students were singers, he had had extraordinary success with people who had suffered from an incurable voice disorder called spastic dysphonia (strangulated speech). It seemed to me that such a technique would work for me too.

We met. I had my first lesson. Gary Catona was a thin, middle-thirties, baseball cap wearer who loved Italian opera. He had been a singer, and from improper training he had lost his voice himself. He was unable to produce a sound. Out of sheer distress, he developed a technique of forcing the strong, resilient throat muscles open to make a passageway for the sound to come forth. By cataloguing his vocal recovery he laid down the foundation of his voice building system.

Heretofore he had been taught that the vocal cords were

fragile and needed to be pampered. Gary thought otherwise. He literally, through deep open throat techniques, forced the strength of the vocal cords to become more resilient, and found that when he tried to produce sound, the notes, now aligned with a new voice placement, not only returned his voice but enabled him to sing for hours without hoarseness.

He worked with Larry Carlton, a singer and jazz guitarist whose vocal cords had been reduced to a whisper by a gunshot to the throat. Gary felt that as long as there was even a piece of a healthy vocal cord intact, he could "over build" what was left into a normal voice. It worked—Larry is talking normally and singing again. And others who thought they were condemned to spastic dysphonia for life are talking in rich, baritone sounds as a result of Gary's techniques. Gary is neither a doctor nor a voice therapist. He says he works outside of traditional approaches as a voice builder.

My experience with opening my throat was more traumatic than anything I had been through in a dance rehearsal.

First of all, I had been so strongly trained the wrong way that Gary said my throat was as constricted and tight as any he had ever heard. So we decided to redirect the strength of these constricted throat muscles to force open my throat and free the sound of my voice.

Whenever I commit to something, I do it completely. Sometimes embarrassingly so. During the first few lessons I gagged, threw up, spit, hacked, coughed, and sputtered. I thought I was ready for nose and throat therapy somewhere in a clinic in Arizona. I carried a large bowl and a box of Kleenex with me to every lesson. Regardless of the trauma to my throat, I found that I was never hoarse when I finished. In fact, my voice was getting stronger and more resonant. That was enough for me, because two shows a night for four weeks are guarantees of hoarseness.

Slowly my throat opened, and I found that my natural singing voice was not a mezzo-soprano but contralto. I had a natural three-octave range, but I was much more comfortable in the lower register. That meant I had to have the keys to all of my orchestrations transposed.

Gary pointed out something I had suspected all along. I had been forcing myself to sing too high in performance, because I had been told it was a "brighter" sound. When a person finds his or her own natural voice and adjusts the keys accordingly and sings with an open throat, instead of nasally through the "mask" of the face, the voice is quite strong and capable of remarkable resiliency.

From the moment I began working with Gary, I felt I not only knew him but was remembering his technique from some long-ago time and place. First of all, I could feel my throat chakra open up as a result of working his way. Gary didn't know much about the chakra system, yet he was working with consciousness techniques as he taught.

When I explained that the throat chakra was the energy center of communication and expression, it made sense to him because of the experience of many of his students. He said they experienced an increased dream state revolving around areas that needed resolution in communication and expression in their lives. He said so many of them noticed a decided acceleration in the confrontation of long-denied issues with their parents and lovers and husbands and wives. They were also beginning to communicate more deeply with themselves and finding it easier to express certain aspects of their lives that had long been repressed. Along with changes in consciousness, his students rarely caught colds or sore throats because of the increased blood flow to the throat area during the vocalizing.

As we talked about all of this, it seemed to us that when the throat chakra is opened, it naturally opens up the emotional center of communication that the throat chakra represents. The very notion of sound coming from the center of one's being would also activate the heart chakra, which would come out in a more loving form of communication. And communication is two-way—with others, and with oneself. So all kinds of possibilities were being opened up.

As I heard my own voice sounds and the sounds from Gary and a few of his other students, I felt I was remembering a time of having heard those human sounds out of a long-forgotten past, almost as though it could have been a less constricted time period of communication. Perhaps before we had constricted our emotions and the open, free expression of them, we had been able to communicate with each other without being blocked in that particular energy center. It made sense to me and to Gary too when I mentioned it to him. He didn't think such notions were ridiculous fantasy at all—on the contrary. In fact, when I began to share some of the past life flashes I had during a voice-opening session, he said many of his students had reported the same experiences; and without any education in metaphysics, they had not known what was happening to them.

I realized that with Mary and Gary, I had been given two new teachers who were showing me pragmatic new ways to work from within. Nearly all the training I had experienced in my life had come from the outside in. Now in my advancing years, I found I had drawn in people who had been on their own paths in their own chosen fields, where out of deep adversity their only recourse had been inner strength, inner techniques, and inner realization.

Mary told me that my books had gotten her through her painful hospital years because of their metaphysical–spiritual perspective on life, and Gary hardly knew anything about me as a performer. He knew me mostly from my books too. When

I told him I believed his techniques came from some knowledge he had had eons ago, he said it sounded familiar.

So the teachers (Mary and Gary) appeared when the student (me) was ready. In fact, we each found we were teaching each other. It remained to be seen whether I could translate the new techniques to performance.

As time passed, I noticed that I was leaving myself less and less time to meditate, to do my own chakra alignment, and to simply take an hour to be by myself and reflect. There were not enough hours in the day, or so it seemed. That was a mistake. But I didn't see it. There were lots of things I didn't see as I prepared myself. But in life, as everything is a learning process, I would soon have to come to terms with the truth that I had not decided to go back on the stage simply in order to do a show. There was much more to it than that. But my understanding was to come later. One of my simplistic mistakes was to believe that I could promise myself that I would no longer do anything in my life if it couldn't be fun. That was truly putting the cart before the horse. I had earned that right, to be sure, but I was soon to learn that "having fun" was not as easy as it sounded. It would take a while for me to see it, but the signs had been there all along.

While I was adjusting to my new body and new voice, the creative meetings required to put together a new show were in full swing. I had gathered my old team around me. We knew each other, liked each other, and communicated with a kind of creative shorthand.

Buz Kohan would write lyrics, Larry Grossman the music, and Alan Johnson would stage and choreograph. Our schedules were tight, each person involved with other projects. We hadn't worked together for six years, and we needed to catch up on each others' lives.

Creative sessions between people in show business are not

understandable to anyone else observing. That's why anyone who's not in show business is called a "civilian." Emotions are raw, feelings are openly expressed, personal secrets are used as examples of identifiable truth, knowing that they will never be exploited. Jokes and gritty cynicism are the tension relievers, and creative suggestions between people who know each other are rarely couched in pre-presentational apologies. If you're confident in the team, you can hear "it stinks" without personal hurt.

Of course, the star has the final say, particularly one like me with a "mind of her own." And the sensitivities to my own discomfort at a suggestion were endearing. Each of the four of us functioned with equal security and expertise, never feeling that anyone else was overstepping bounds.

Much of the creative "processing" took place on the telephone, which sometimes left me with a sense of urgency relating to the time we had (three weeks). Three weeks was not enough. But it was all we had.

Out of the brainstorming sessions came the concept of the show, which dictated the opening number. So far so good.

Second numbers in any show are notoriously difficult to conceive. You come out, greet the people with an opening, and then what? If your second number works, you're usually home free for at least another twenty minutes. Alan came up with a great one that would utilize the dancers with me.

The next problem was how to end the first act. I wanted to work with an intermission this time out, so I'd have time to warm up my body in the dressing room, ready for the big dance number. When a dancer only acts and talks and sings—no big, body movement—for forty minutes prior to dancing, the body gets cold. The theater owners would love an intermission anyway. They could sell booze and candy to their customers.

A first act closing needs drama and an inspiration for the audience to return.

I decided to do "Rose's Turn" from *Gypsy,* a dramatic acting–singing piece. I, like every other performer these days, wondered what Frank Rich of *The New York Times* would think should I decide to play New York. I knew he adored Tyne Daly in the part, and so did I for that matter. However, I opted for doing something I loved every night, rather than succumb to what Rich might hate only once.

I'd open the second act with my mainstay tour-de-force dance number, which was a tribute to some of the choreographers I'd worked with (hoping I could get through the updated version), and the rest of the show would be some humorous takeoffs on my "New Age" beliefs and reprises of some of the things I had done in films (my hooker medley) and "I'm Still Here," the Sondheim song I'd sung in *Postcards.*

I made lots of jokes, and I talked with the audience in between numbers, which I loved doing. So with a big musical introduction of my company, allowing everyone to do an individual riff of their own, we'd have more than enough show.

The development of the concept seemed to be progressing nicely.

We hired a band. I decided to go self-contained, which meant traveling with eight musicians (two keyboards, bass, guitar, saxophone, drums, percussion, and piano conductor), instead of hiring an orchestra in every city augmented by a permanent rhythm section.

I loved my previous conductor, Jack French, but he hadn't worked enough with synthesizers. So we hired a conductor out of Vegas who had. He was recommended as being cool in time of crisis and very accomplished musically.

We chose a rehearsal hall with windows, good restaurants nearby, and a central location for everybody. It had a good wood floor (any other kind of floor, such as cement or linoleum, is lethal for a dancer because of lack of flexibility and spring). Television studio floors are crippling to dancers, because they are laid with cement (to insure smooth-flowing cameras). Dancers develop shinsplints and shattered backs from the rigidity of the floor.

There was a smaller studio upstairs for vocal rehearsals that would also serve as the band room where the musicians could rehearse and program their synthesizers with sounds, while Alan and I and the dancers toiled below.

We began with a new dance number. I have never understood how choreographers can take the pressure of having to move dancing human beings around in an entertaining way and produce two hours worth of show in a few weeks. What kind of dreams do they fall asleep to? And do they sleep at all? I have worked with many of them. They all suffer from temperament, anxiety, illusions of grandeur, sensitivity of such depth that they are often cruel, and—more important than anything—a desire to be loved and appreciated.

Choreographers come out of years of toil and suffering, first in relentless dance classes and then under the tutelage of another choreographer who has also gone through a conditioning of pain. It's a kind of exquisite love affair with sadomasochism. To force the body into the form and line they see in their own mind's eye is their never-ending task. The body has limits. A vision doesn't. So a choreographer can put a troupe of dancers through excruciating repetitions until he either comes to terms with the limitations or loses the love and respect of his dancers. Dancers will keep going, however, because they too have come from a schooled lifetime of hard labor. They are conditioned to obeying authority and, indeed, somehow identify themselves with suffering. A dancer will never feel anything has been accomplished if it has been easy. The choreographer knows that and behaves accordingly.

Alan Johnson, however, is different. I continued to ask for his help in putting together shows, because he—along with being talented and creative—is the nice one. I could never understand why he was different. He was a taskmaster but a gentlemanly one. If his feelings were hurt, he never struck back with cruel hostility. He somehow had himself centered and under control, and his talent flourished.

He held his dancers' auditions, but he and I both knew which four dancers he was going to use. He had worked with all four before. I had worked with two. There wasn't much work for dancers in California now, since the demise of variety-show television. MTV ruled and it was mostly rap-dancing—staccato, sharp, athletic moves that were more reminiscent of an entertaining and colorful aerobics class than the art of traditional dance.

So when Alan put out the word along the gypsy grapevine, he had his pick of the best dancers around.

Damita Jo Freeman was a black dancer with whom I had worked ten years ago. Her intelligence was blazing and her talent matched it. She had been assisting Joe Layton in choreographing shows for Diana Ross and Lionel Richie, as well as Whitney Houston and Cher. She was a choreographer herself, and when she called asking if she could get back to "real" dancing, Alan and I took her immediately.

Blane Savage had been a principal dancer in *Dancin'* for Bob Fosse and starred in the movie *A Chorus Line.* He was blond, fabulously handsome, funny, and had definite star quality.

Keith McDaniel was a principal dancer with the Alvin Ailey company in New York. He was dynamic, strong, and possessed a muscled body that inspired awe on the stage.

Jamilah Lucas had starred in *Sophisticated Ladies* and *Solid Gold* on television for years. She was drop-dead gorgeous, as well as strong and lithe.

Each dancer was a soloist and perfectly capable of holding the stage alone. I was honored that they would back me up. I wondered, in fact, if I could keep up with them.

So rehearsals began. Alan didn't like to have me around when he was creating new ideas. "Don't come to preproduction," he would say. "I want you to see it when I'm finished; then tell me what you think." Fair enough.

I had always loved to see the magic created out of thin air. It was a miracle mystery to me, but that was before I became "intimidating." I still operated with a gypsy mentality, feeling like one of the group, so it was sometimes difficult for me to accept the truth that when I walked into the rehearsal hall, there was a subtle change of charged energy. "What does she think?" "Is she watching me?" "Is it what she expected?" . . . and so on. "The Lady is here" was the hidden implication. "Let's do it full out now."

There is always a separation between the "star" and everyone else, regardless of how intimate the working relationship might be. The star is the one on the line, of course, so that is given unspoken priority. The star pays the salaries, the airlines, the hotels, the costumers—all the bills. The star, therefore, is in charge of everyone's contractual destiny. Even the creative behind-the-scenes talent has a hidden, subtle need to please the star so that instant approval is forthcoming.

That doesn't mean they won't tell you the truth. Quite the contrary, especially when they really care. But the separation is always there. The idiosyncrasies and temperamental shenanigans of other "stars" are a never-ending source of rich gossip; and even while participating in the gossip yourself, you know that the minute you leave *you* are the source of the next day's dish.

The star and her fears; the star and her strengths; the star and her talents; the star and her husband, boyfriend, or outside personal influences are the priority conversations. And that is how it should be. The others are there to serve the star, and everybody knows it.

Of course, in my case they were even more intense subjects of conjecture and gossip, because *I* wrote books on how to be more peaceful, centered, and free of the negative attributes that played such a part in the colorful gossip always swirling around the environment of a star. The real pressure would be on me. "How would she handle it?" "Would she live up to her tough, perfectionistic reputation?" "Would she stretch everyone else like she stretched herself, or had she learned through her own writing and investigation to relax with the demons of fear and possible public humiliation?"

Show business is all about wanting to be loved, wanting to avoid rejection. "Healthy" people rarely have such a need to be constantly reinforced with overt appreciation. "Healthy" people can settle for a more satisfactory, less stressful way of expressing their contribution in life. "Healthy" people don't need to dabble in the expertise of "magic" in order to feel fulfilled. "Healthy" people don't need to be somebody in order to be happy.

So the star reflects all those unspoken fears and anxieties lying dormant in "healthy" people.

Creative minds that work as a team to make a star look good are every bit as complicated as the star they serve. Maybe more so.

A lyricist's task is to feel the star's values and truthful emotions so impeccably that his words, coming from the star, sound real. Audiences always pick up falsity. And stars never feel they can express themselves on stage with words, so we rely on writers to do it for us. After that we change them! A symbiotic relationship, to say the least. For a lyricist and writer to put on the cloak of another is a kind of abdication of his own identity, yet at the same time an expansion of it. A really good writer *becomes* the star when he's working at his peak.

Then the musical interpretation of the star's body and voice is translated by a composer whose talent lies in the combinations of notes and chords and styles of music that seem the natural musical language of the star. They are well versed in the star's range of voice, emotional expression through music, and whether or not the audience will believe a song coming out of the star's mouth.

Each member of my creative team had worked with many stars, so they carried with them a backlog of respect and experience that is always necessary for trust when insecurity raises its inevitable head. I am always amazed at the sensitivity inherent in each creative person whose job it is to serve what is best for the star.

During the rehearsal period, anxieties become magnified—all sorts of anxieties. Personality traits that are the most troublesome become obviously those that one needs to work on and resolve. Rehearsals are sometimes better than therapy. The body, the mind, and ultimately one's spiritual balance come into play while learning something new, and at the same time attempting to perform it.

Some people learn fast but don't retain what they've learned. Others plod along but learn more deeply and thoroughly. Musicians have the advantage of speaking a common musical language, which is set before them to read. Dancers have no way of recording movement in a really articulate way, except of course by videotape (which we used later).

So the choreographer experiments on the bodies of the dancers until he sees what he wants. That process can be exhausting at the same time that it challenges one to stretch and build physical stamina. During the repetitions of combination after combination, the muscles record, as if by memory, what they are required to do. We know that feeling of "muscle memory"; and if a dancer learns to trust it, it is only necessary to get out of one's own way and allow the various parts of the body to remember and have their way. It's almost as though the cells themselves have brains and feelings, the capacity to be autonomous.

I knew that from experience over the years, yet somehow the process of learning for me was different now than it used to be. I now approached steps and body movement from an acting point of view. It was no longer a mechanically scientific exercise of learning by rote and repetition. Now I needed to know why each movement existed. I literally needed motivation! I was forever asking a choreographer "Why?" And "why" doesn't exist in the world of dance. But if someone found a way to answer me and it made sense, I never forgot a step. I could recite the Gettysburg Address and dance at the same time if I *knew why* I was doing a step. But there are some dance combinations that no one could give a motivation to. "Why?" is irrelevant to some things. Such a moment occurred during our rehearsal period when Alan gave me a new dance combination with complicated rhythms and uneven phrasing. It was unattached to any motivational thinking process, and it looked fabulous on the other dancers, who had learned it in a few minutes. Now it was my turn. I was the star. I was expected to give the combination a panache no one else could or I wouldn't be a star.

The company stood watching me. Alan demonstrated the combination for me. I tried it. Since I couldn't find a motivation, my mind went blank, my legs and arms worked in contradiction to one another, and I couldn't even hear the rhythm and beat, much less dance to it.

My mind scrabbled. Then it got ahead of itself, a self-destructive tendency I thought I was rid of. But the threat of potential humiliation in front of a live audience can be paralyzing. Instead of focusing on the combination, with its rhythms and phrasing, I zeroed in on the opening date and how little time I had to feel comfortable with what I was learning. I panicked. Frozen with fear, I stood in the center of the room feeling that everyone on the planet was staring at me, waiting for me to get it. Blank. And then a flood of humiliation, embarrassment. I felt like a total idiot: tears filled my eyes, and I doubled over and began to cry.

Immediately Alan called a coffee break and came over to talk to and comfort me. At that moment, I felt like a presumptuous fool to imagine I could still get up on a stage and entertain people. I couldn't even learn the stuff, much less make it pleasurable for people to look at. The paralytic craziness that strikes when the insecurity crunch comes is impossible to describe. A less experienced choreographer would talk about how wonderful it's all going to be, denying completely the reality of a mini-breakdown. Performers never want to hear that. We want specifics about how to climb our way out of the abyss. We know when we are in a survival modality, and candied reassurances are deeply annoying and even an insult. We want a plan, a mode of operation, a strategy, in order to see our way clear to the light again.

Alan's strategy with me was to give me different choreography. "You're the star," he said, "remember? You don't have to be a gypsy here." That wasn't good enough for me. "Why can't I learn as fast as I used to?" I wailed. "What's wrong with me?" And then, "Oh God, maybe I'm just too *old* for all of this." "No," said Alan, "you've been acting for six years. Your approach is that of an actress."

I thought about that—it made sense for a moment, and

then other doubts flooded in. I launched into a fear rundown on whether the costumes, the sets, the lighting designs, the tryouts, the previews would all come together in time. "Could we put the opening back a week?" I asked. "Why am I doing this! Aren't there easier ways to make a living?"

Alan didn't laugh. Nor did he point out that making a living was hardly relevant. He was much too sensitive for that, and besides, he had been through many mini-breakdowns with other performers. I derived much comfort from hearing about the problems of others. At least it meant I wasn't the only crazy one; the only insecure, blithering idiot. It meant that people I considered far more talented than myself had their own demons, and must have their own approaches for banishing them. Some, I knew, used tricks like booze and pills that I wasn't interested in, mostly because I'd lose control and I wanted to be firmly in control of my choice to be insecure! Anyway, a dancer's trained body and the drug–drink scene definitely do not mix.

Alan put a hand on my arm. "Remember the other times," he reminded me. "You've been through this before; everyone goes through it and everyone finds a way out. You will too. For now don't worry about these steps; and if we're not ready, we'll deal with postponing." His tone was reassuring and sensible. He saw me relax. "Now," he said, "I'm going to rattle the change in Puss's can."

Puss was Alan's Jack Russell terrier dog, a child to him. Alan took him everywhere, including rehearsal. Puss was stationed on a leash by the piano and next to his little traveling case. Puss loved to sing. When the rehearsal pianist launched into "I Hear Music When I Look at You," Puss hit a high C and held it for the duration of his aria. When he misbehaved, Alan rattled a can full of loose change at him and threatened to make a live painting of him up against the wall. Puss also took on his master's tensions, which Alan himself was so adept at disguising.

Puss had lived through the tensions of *Legs Diamond* with Peter Allen on Broadway, a revival of *Can-Can* with Chita Rivera, the act of Peter Allen and Bernadette Peters, numerous productions of *West Side Story,* the many Academy Awards shows, and now me.

I lifted my Evian water bottle and tried to finish off what would be my first of the day, knowing I'd need to drown myself in at least one more liter of water in order for my muscles and joints to work properly. The other dancers had discreetly moved outside into the sunshine and the musicians, thank heavens, were working in a room upstairs. I patted Puss on the head and paced around the rehearsal hall.

Alan was right. I had been through the PANIC several times in the past—in fact, each time we did a new show. I wasn't good at having patience with myself. I was relentless with my self-demands and wanted tomorrow's accomplishments to be achieved today.

I remembered the panic I had felt the night I opened at the Palladium in London. It was so paralyzing that I fell asleep in my dressing room, fully made up in costume, and woke to hear the overture playing. I had unconsciously designed a complete checkout, right up to the moment they announced my name.

Even with rapturous reviews, I wondered why people paid good money to come and see me. How could their experience with me possibly be worth it? Foreign countries and cultures flooded my mind as I paced around the rehearsal hall—the one-night stands for a month in Germany and the habit audiences had of stomping their feet in approval. In Berlin I had left the huge stage, taken off my makeup, and was taking a shower when the theater owner retrieved me for one last bow. I went on the stage dressed in my towel and nothing else. The waves of appreciation and approval washed over me. I didn't really understand why.

The instant interplay between a collective mass of human beings and a performer is a hymn to a kind of tribal rhythm. When it's going well, a transformation occurs that lifts the spirits to the gods, and passions are acted out with a collective creativity, reminding us that the call of the crowd can be as loving as it is cruel. The cruelty of a crowd can be informative too. I remembered the night I opened at the Palace in New York City. During some banter, I called New York the Karen Quinlan of cities (on a respirator, neither dead nor alive). The crowd booed. I experienced flop sweat and couldn't live it down for a long time.

Then there was the time in Vienna, Austria. I had a 106-degree fever, the flu, and four shows in two days. The crowd was so nourishing that after the first show, my temperature was nearly normal. Sure I worked hard, sweated out much of the virus, but I could feel the healing energy of the crowd.

In Sydney, Australia, I contracted ptomaine poisoning from a bad oyster and threw up in between numbers into a bucket in the wings. When you're out there with the lights coming at you like so many express trains and the music supports every movement you painfully attempt to make, your fellow dancers spurring you on because they themselves know that the only solution is to *do* it, you do just that. You DO IT, and soon you are soaring and dipping and flowing with the electric currents of the audience's response, oblivious to what you believed would not be possible to overcome in any other way but by an act of will. When you find that surrendering to the joy of giving an audience pleasure can be a healing, you are transformed. The trick is to *remember* the transformation and trust that it will always happen again, no matter what goes wrong.

I couldn't remember that magic as I paced the rehearsal hall now. Maybe I didn't want to. Maybe I needed obstacles to overcome, because I had been trained as thoroughly to believe that nothing was worth happiness and pleasure unless I struggled painfully for it. Perhaps I needed to play out the struggle more deeply than I ever had, in order to realize it wasn't necessary. On the other hand, I had promised myself that I wouldn't do a show again unless I could learn to have fun with it. Thus I constructed a built-in conflict. I needed both and they were mutually incompatible.

As I went through the passions and emotions of show business, I saw again how analogous to life it is. How many situations, families, relationships, and love affairs contained the seeds of the same conflicts—how to deserve happiness and creativity without mistrusting it?

I wasn't the only one going through personal struggles. As the date of our first run-through approached, fiery emotions kindled by insecurities gripped everyone. It was unlike making a movie, because the potential for instant judgment and chilling humiliation in front of an audience doesn't exist there. You can always do it again or fix it in the editing room.

Each dancer had his or her objections to the costume he or she was clothed in. That touched the feelings of the costumer. Regardless of how much experience teaches one not to take things personally, rejection is a new and wrenching shock every time.

The set designer didn't feel there was enough time to construct the bandstand properly. The orchestrations didn't arrive in time for the band to familiarize themselves with the music, which reflected on the composer. Some of the written material was late being delivered, which left us uncertain as to how long the show would run.

The shoemaker was backed up on his orders, which meant we couldn't work in our proper shoes.

The synthesizers were so loud in the rehearsal hall, we couldn't hear ourselves sing.

The costumes wouldn't be ready until we actually opened in front of a paying audience in San Antonio, Texas, which was our first play date.

Through all of these obstacles, the creativity continued. Living on the edge of heightened fear of humiliation with no time as a comfort zone can cause serious paralysis, or it can provoke the opposite effect. This is the enforced phenomenon that exposes the underbelly of anyone who wants to make it in live theater. It is what Mervyn LeRoy used to define as "more than talent." By that he didn't mean blood, sweat, and tears only. It is actually an indefinable quality a performer musters in that moment of crisis that knits together the capacity to push beyond personal fear, insecurity, and self-judgment, to blend with the projected original vision—grasping beyond one's reach, continuing to trust the dream, expanding into the imagination itself until you and the vision are one.

It doesn't matter if your crisis is sewing on two thousand sequins by six o'clock or finding the comedy in a tragic moment of a scene to fulfill the audience's expectation of you as a star—the stretch is the same. Your goal is in jeopardy unless you can pull together all aspects of the production and your own unused potential for manifesting the dream.

If a composer has written a song that is musically unrealized by a musician's talent, he must find a way to tactfully coax and sculpt that musician to a little more expression. If the intricate movement in a dance number can't be seen by an audience because of faulty lighting, the magic of the color spectrum needs to be plumbed and selected, so that everything can be seen. If a conductor's tempo is too fast to allow the audience to *feel,* he needs to sensitize his feelings to blend more in harmony with the collective response. And if the star, out of insecurity, rushes the material, the reasons why the people came in the first place are compromised.

In other words, live theater is bristling with such vibrancy that it requires all the people in it, regardless of their function, to test and balance their talent for combustibility in relationship to harmony. How far will the personal combustion go before it rattles the harmony of the whole? And which individuals are capable of recognizing the moment at which they must pull back and function as an integral yet sensitive part of the team?

Of course the "star" plays the major role, but is not necessarily more important than anyone else because the very principles of live theater are based on interdependency. It doesn't matter how wonderfully you play a scene if the audience can't see you. It doesn't matter how powerfully you sing a song if they can't hear you. And it doesn't matter how well *you* dance if the other dancers are not there as supporting entities against which you can be compared.

During the rehearsal and creative process (usually four weeks), it is inevitable, and even possibly desirable, that personalities will clash. This is the time when cliques are formed and lines of protection drawn. Creative artists like having their own people as support systems. Learning to work with new human rhythms is at first an obstacle to the imaginative flow, and it is necessary to take the time to become familiar with individual patterns. Then the dynamics of working together can take over. People who know each other create in shorthand and are comfortable with criticism, because they know friendship will override the personalization of arguments. When it goes well, it is an intensely satisfying process.

But sometimes the cliques of the "support systems" collide. That can be devastating to a project, unless the collision produces sparks that ignite a whole new process. It is a question of degree, I think. As long as just one individual involved in the collision of creative differences remains open-minded to the opposite camp, such wars are productive. It only takes one person. And as we were learning, each of us was that person.

The group around me was also very aware that achieving the ultimate goal of one's vision was not everything. Indeed, the *process* was becoming more and more educational. We often talked about this approach to our work. Theater was changing because of our personal attitudes. So was filmmaking. Yes, the director had the last word in films; and the star had the last word in shows like mine. Someone had to be in that position. But, whereas previously neither theater nor films were considered a democracy, these days a more open-minded creativity prevails.

It had something to do with how people in our business were growing personally. More people were spending as much time working on themselves as they were on a creative project. We were beginning to see that our talent was only as productive as our personal insight. If we were blind to ourselves and to others as individual human beings, how could we have any understanding with respect to the audience? We were learning that we could only see in others what we were capable of seeing in ourselves. Otherwise we were out of touch, locked into ideas and points of view that would divorce us from our own creation, and from the audience for whom we were creating it.

In any creative session, the outcome depends upon how willing the participants are to share themselves. Out of such sharing an atmosphere of trust develops, and as a result new and innovative entertainment evolves. The audience comes to feel. They come to be transported to another place. They come to be transformed. That being the case, we—the dancers, the musicians, the director—needed to fall in love with the process of transforming ourselves. Our rehearsal weeks provided us with that opportunity.

After emotional struggles at the start, I got to more practical matters. I developed metatarsal pain in my left foot. It was sharp and stabbing. I couldn't dance. I called my friend, Anne Marie Bennstrom, who is a doctor and chiropractor. "Well, my dear," she said, "you know that the feet represent the last spiritual connection to the earth, because we walk upon it. If you think you have integrated your understanding and harmony in every way but still have something bothering you, you will feel it in the feet. There must be something bothering you, yes?"

Bothering me? She must be kidding. How about my whole life? I was becoming anxious about the late delivery of some of my lyrical material. I felt I wouldn't have time to learn it and develop it properly. Anger was building in me at Buz, our lyricist. The frustration was under everything I did.

I thought about what to do. If Anne Marie was right about my foot, I'd have to solve it with my head and heart. I sat with myself for a while—a meditation you might call it—Western style. Slowly it dawned on me that, even though he was slow, he was good *and* he might be having problems himself.

I called Buz. Instead of berating him about being late, I felt better about complimenting him on what he had already delivered and said I couldn't wait to get new stuff. He sparked right away. "You really liked it?" "Yes," I said, even though I had already told him weeks before. "God, that's wonderful," said Buz. "Sometimes I feel I'm back in school delivering my term paper to a teacher who won't give me a passing grade." How many times had I heard that from every really good creative person I knew. It seemed as though anyone who was any good was constantly attempting to please parents, teachers, or various other authority figures from childhood. The past was constantly with us, alternately haunting and inspiring us.

"Well," I went on, "it's terrific and as soon as I can have your new stuff, I'd love that too." I waited a moment. "And Buz . . . I love you."

I heard a deep sigh over the phone. "Oh, that's so wonderful to hear," he said. "Thank you."

The material came the next day. It was no surprise to me that my foot pain disappeared simultaneously.

With that lesson, I began to release some of my tension. It's so easy to be told that tension never helped anybody. I *knew* that. We all knew that. But to live without it, knowing that it is our *choice* to disengage from it, was probably the basic issue of the next few weeks. My show would be a good environment in which to experiment with not only that process but the results . . . which would be my next lesson.

One day, during a break, we each shared our recurring nightmares. Much to my surprise, everyone had one. The dancers all had a recurring dream that they found themselves on stage and forgot the choreography. Alan's night-time anxiety was that the opening date kept changing. The set designer worried his way through a union strike every night. One of the musicians dreamed constantly that the airlines kept losing his instrument (bass guitar). Mike Flowers (our company manager) always dreamed the traveling trucks were lost and couldn't make dates.

My dream was one I had had since childhood. It varied slightly, but the premise was always the same. I found myself arriving at a theater for some reason, only to be told that it was my opening night. I didn't even know I had an engagement. I was completely uninformed. And rather than call my agent to ask what was going on, I would rush to the wardrobe department, put on some spangled outfit, call the dancers and the musicians to the stage, and proceed to try to learn a two-hour show in the half hour I had before the curtain rose. I could hear the people out front, and I was obsessed with living up to my apparent obligation to put on a show.

The anxiety built as I crammed steps, lyrics, and patter into my mind. Never once did it occur to me that it wasn't fair—that I didn't need to deliver a show. I *had* to deliver one. My survival depended upon it.

Then the curtain rose. The audience applauded at seeing me, but the terror was so excruciating I'd wake up.

Over and over I had that dream. It was a terrifying feeling of profound, paralytic anxiety over the promise I made to myself as a child to live up to what was expected of me. Who was expecting so much of me? Every time a difficult moment occurred in the rehearsal hall, the dream came crashing back to me. I was uninformed, unrehearsed, untalented, unenlightened, unprepared; and yet it never occurred to me that I didn't have to do it.

I associated my mother with that recurring dream not only because of her expectations of me, but because she wanted her children to live up to the unfulfilled expectations she had of her husband.

There was a hidden agenda in our family. Warren and I were driven not only to fulfill our parents' unrealized dreams but, in the process, to prove Mother correct in her aspirations for us in *spite* of our father's fears and his harshly critical attitude toward our efforts. She was in competition to prove her husband's criticisms wrong. She would make certain her children succeeded in this world, not only for herself, but because she saw her husband as a disappointing failure. He, of course, had the same vision of himself, which was why he was so harsh on us.

We *had* to do it. We *had* to be there. We couldn't disappoint her, or the audience, or ourselves, and we had to refute our father. In other words, there was no way Warren and I wouldn't become stars. It was bred into us by parents who were in competition with each other. One was driven to believe in success. The other was afraid of it.

My Dad had been a teacher most of his life. He was a good teacher too. He had also been the principal of several schools I attended. He loved teaching but had wanted to be a great musician and had been offered a scholarship to study violin with a splendid teacher in Europe. He decided against it. His reason, as he told me later, was that he felt he would make an investment in his musical future with a great teacher in Europe, only to find he'd return to New York and end up playing in the pit of a Broadway theater eight times a week, twice on Wednesday and Saturday—not his idea of high artistry.

Somehow I knew there was more to his negativity than that. He used it as an excuse so that he wouldn't be hurt by daring to achieve. His mother had been extremely cruel to him, having literally chased him with butcher knives and locked him in a closet once for two days. His own courage had been thwarted at an early age. He learned to be afraid even to try.

"Monkey," he used to say to me, "one thing my mother taught me well and that was how to fear. I'm an expert in feeling fear."

She berated him at every juncture, squashing his dreams and aspirations before they ever had an opportunity to develop. So his expectations of success were nonexistent. Daring to dare was a guarantee of rejection, pain, humiliation, and abuse. In fact, he'd often tell me that achieving success usually meant stepping on someone else (his mother?). He had come to equate success with corruption and would have no part of attempting it.

I believe all of these factors underlay his judgment of, and sometimes his cruelty to, his children. In the name of protecting us from the ravages inherent in daring to be somebody, he resorted to contempt and dire warnings of failure. I often wondered what brutality *his* mother had experienced. It must have been deep and abiding for her to teach her son the attributes of fear above all else.

I was left then with the dilemma of overcoming my father's criticisms and viewing him as a rehearsal for the tough world out there, or succumbing to the proposition that indeed I didn't have any talent and shouldn't even try. Either choice was a guarantee that stepping onto a stage would cause me profound anxiety. So *why* do it? Was it for audience approval? No, it was really a plea for my father's love.

At times in my childhood he had been cruel and emotionally humiliating in his judgments and comments on my developing career, but I think I intuitively understood that he was really commenting on and harshly judging *himself* for not having had more courage to develop his own talents. And how could he have developed the courage when he had had parents who were doubly critical of him?

When I sang for the first time at a school assembly in high school, the audience loved my comic rendition of "I Cain't Say No" from *Oklahoma!* But he berated me for believing I could sing at all and suggested that I certainly should not desecrate the words and music of Rodgers and Hammerstein ever again. I didn't—for years.

DANCE WHILE YOU CAN

When I lost the lead in the Washington School of the Ballet production of *Cinderella* and was relegated to dance the Fairy Godmother instead, I was destroyed. Instead of comforting me, Daddy stood over me on the stairs, *accusing* me, as though it were my fault, of having grown too tall, and sadistically pointing out that I wasn't a very good dancer anyway. I tried to bolt from him to the sanctuary of my bedroom, but he wouldn't let me pass. He wanted to drive home his point that I should give up and not try to be more than I was capable of. The more I cried, the more he attacked me.

I got sick and vomited on the stairs. It didn't deter him at all. I remember Mother looking on helplessly. Finally I slumped to my knees. The expression on Daddy's face was one of pained triumph.

He hadn't enjoyed what he'd done. He seemed compulsively driven to treat me that way. As, no doubt, his mother had treated him.

Soon after that I ran a relay race during an important high school track and field meet. When the baton was passed to me, I dropped it. As a result, our team lost the race. My father had been watching from the bleachers. I never got over the dreadful crawling feeling that I had proven him right by stupidly dropping that damned baton.

More painful than my father's lack of confidence in himself were the memories of my humiliation when I thought he felt I hadn't performed well. I suffered not only from feeling his assessment of my talent was low, but also from the recognition that my failure gave my mother nothing to hope for. I *had* to make something of myself, not only to prove him wrong but to give *her* a victory over him. She had set up the ground rules for the family. *We* were to succeed no matter what to assuage her frustrations. But more to the point, because she was our emotional support system, we fed into her competition with Dad by becoming successful. Our family unit then was a win–win setup for overachievement. We had to in order to get love.

Dad was prejudiced against success for fear of failing, and Mother was prejudiced against him for not realizing his talent. Warren and I would "accomplish" for both of them.

I remembered the times I questioned her about the conflict of having a family and a career. She was circumspect about it. "You can do both," she would say. "You'll have someone to watch the children anyway." Her values were permeated with the need to succeed, rather than the fulfillment of family love. There had been no doubt in her mind that we would become people "who would be recognized in the great capitals of the world." It was her foregone conclusion that we could mix having a family and career easily. On what she based her conclusion, I never knew. But because she was our mother, she must be right. But she wasn't.

We were still children somewhere in ourselves, and the audiences were now a collective symbol of parents for us. *Their* approval was what we needed so desperately—to be loved by them because that love wasn't present enough in our own lives.

These dynamics were often very subtle, but as all children are interested in emotional survival, we played the game of the family interplay in the best way we knew how. We learned the ropes of manipulating our potential talents early on since receiving love seemed to depend on it. But we were never really prepared or even educated to know what loving trust just for the sake of it was like.

Perhaps all show business beings come from backgrounds where love was rewarded in terms of competitive spirit. So many I know were similar in their reactions. We seemed to see ourselves as perpetual children, needing to achieve good report cards from the school of life as we lurched through our creative experiences wearing the uniform of the day, never late, always dependable, with smiling faces, churning stomachs, and literally living for the sought-after love and approval of whomever we challenged to sit in judgment on us. Audiences were, relatively speaking, a pushover in comparison with eagerly sought critical approval.

Perhaps some newspaper and television critics suffered from the same trouble as the performers, were harsh because they had not found the proper channels through which to please their own parents and authority figures, and the frustration tended to make them eloquently and wittily hostile, intent on showing off their own writing talents rather than making an honest evaluation of what they had seen.

I never knew anyone in show business who was free of the anxiety sickness—no one I knew was a professional actor or actress out of pure pleasure, void of the need to please. The arrogant, impossibly temperamental ones were more frightened than anyone. They used the offensive approach to mask their insecurities. Or even more sadly, some resorted to alcohol or drugs to dull the inner gnawing. And traditionally, psychologists and psychiatrists could always do land-office business in Tinseltown.

Some creative artists were openly honest about their fears. Barbra Streisand told me she not only wouldn't but *couldn't* perform live anymore because she was certain she'd forget the lyrics. Sinatra said his fear was that he'd open his mouth and nothing would come out. Liza Minnelli was always nervous that the creative people behind her were more nervous than she. Pavarotti and Domingo tested their voices all day long to reassure themselves that they would be able to even utter a sound at night. Baryshnikov wasn't sure his ankles would support him. Julie Andrews was afraid she didn't know how to talk to the audience.

For me, I didn't trust that the collective magic would be there. I didn't do any one thing particularly well on the stage, but I knew my energy and ability to make intimate magic worked somehow. So for me, I needed to trust the lights, sound, and music more than most. I couldn't perform without all of it working in harmony. If one of my people was out because of illness, I fretted that *I* couldn't do it without him or her. If the sound was off, it affected my ears, because I was self-conscious of my voice. If a blackout was late at the end of a number, I was sure the effect was distorted to an extreme. If a costume ripped, I was positive the whole dress would fall off—and at times it did.

During a dance number once, the top of my costume came loose exposing everything from my waist up. The spontaneity of such a moment is what audiences love. They adore having been there when something *unplanned* occurred. So when I rescued the moment by glancing down and saying, "Well, at least you know they're real," they cheered. The fact that the wardrobe mistress came out on stage and sewed me in for the rest of the show only added to the delight of the audience that *we* are not that different from them. Oh yes, it always works somehow, but to anticipate the problems before they occur is the hell of it.

And so during rehearsals we try to account for the future before it happens. To trust that somehow it will work out is not an easy exercise, given that our negative imagination is always worse than the reality.

Only once did reality exceed what one might possibly have imagined, actually to become life-threatening for me. I was playing in Oslo, Norway. Norway is one of three countries in the world that doesn't have an electrically grounded power system. That means that during an electrical storm, serious damage occurs from live wires.

On the night I opened, it poured rain. Lightning was flashing so dramatically, I felt there was a new Frankenstein being born. The manager of the theater came to tell me that if I used my live microphone, he could assure me that nothing would happen to the microphone equipment despite the increased electricity running through the wires. However, he couldn't insure me against the loss of my life!

There were over a thousand people sitting out there who had paid $75 per ticket. The theater in which we were performing was a government-financed project. A real scandal would have resulted had I not gone through with my show. So true to my recurring dream, I did what was expected of me. I performed the entire show without a microphone. My voice was shot for a few days, but again I had lived up to my obligation, and the government of Norway remained scandal-free.

So with my new show, I decided I would make the conscious choice to be less anxious. I would take some of my own advice; and, regardless of the programming conditioned in my childhood, I would empower myself to change. Around the third week of rehearsal, I was more balanced with my anxiety. If I didn't get a step right away, I quietly put it aside, working on it in a corner by myself. If I hadn't developed the drama in a song, I trusted that it would be there later. I knew I wasn't a singer anyway. I was an actress who sang. It would take time.

I had three scenes from movies I'd made as part of the show. If the props weren't ready, I relaxed, assuring myself that I could bring such mechanical problems together later. So in general, I made a pact with myself that I wouldn't allow urgency or any potential disaster to get the better of me. I was soon to put my pact to the test.

I had been feeling a dull toothache for a few weeks. Nothing to lose sleep over, but still I had learned to always attend to medical questions before departing on a tour.

I went to my dentist, who treated me to a series of tests, which seemed to revolve around the potential of root canal surgery. He recommended a root canal specialist, who told me about a man he treated who could meditate himself into such a comfortable state of being that he needed no anesthetic at all, even for gum surgery.

He had imagined himself on a beach, lounging in brilliant sunshine, the waves lapping gently at his feet. He could hear seagulls, feel the cool water on his toes, and taste the salt on his lips. He said the man was completely involved with the set and setting he had conceived in his imagination and never allowed the pain of the moment of gum surgery to divert him.

At one point, however, the man had interrupted the procedure while he retrieved a dry blanket from his car! The doctor waited while the patient imagined unfolding the clean blanket and once again assumed a languid position under the sky and beside the surf. At the signal, the dentist continued. He told me there was much less blood than usual and the recovery period quicker.

I, in my limited state of evolvement, chose laughing gas.

Since I never take any medication, my entire system felt clobbered when it was over. In fact, I couldn't really dance again for two days. I was dizzy, light-headed, and couldn't keep my balance. I didn't like being out of control. I was glad we had found the right tooth and it was over. That didn't last long.

Two days later, during my checkup, the doctor said the tooth next to it had a dying nerve too—a second root canal would have to be done. By now I really didn't have time.

I called a teacher friend, a teacher of metaphysics relating to the body. I was curious what dying roots in teeth meant in terms of consciousness. He said that dying nerves represent old values that are dying. "Root canals are often necessary when people give up their old ways of operating," he said. Then he asked if I was going through significant changes in my ways of looking at and feeling about my life and work. I hardly knew how to answer. I was in upheaval, not to put too fine a point on it.

He went on to say that venturing into areas with a new point of view was often accompanied by problems with teeth involving gums and nerves. Venturing out required new nerves, therefore, the old needed to die and step aside.

When I went for the second root canal, I told myself it was all happening for a reason—it was part of my growth. It was necessary to allow the old to pass away so as to make room for the new. It was part of a harmony I trusted but couldn't quite understand.

I didn't realize it then, but such a point of view was going to have to become second nature to me in order to get through the next seven months.

The night of our first run-through (without costumes and lights) approached. The bandstand was built. The musicians had programmed the music for synthesizers. The dancers were well-trained, and our rundown was complete. We hired the Pepperdine University theater to invite a few hundred people so we could get a reaction to what we had.

The invited guests trickled in; and after greeting them personally, I engaged in chatty conversation with a few friends, evidencing complete relaxation about getting up there on stage in a few minutes.

I bandaged my feet (blisters and such), attached my body mike with its battery pack, did some pliés, and we began.

Another reality occurs when a performer knows he or she has to rise to the occasion of entertaining people who are finally out there. All the years of experienced timing, the ability to ad-lib, how to pace your breath, how to give them a good time, come into play. It happened with me that night. Performance energy is a dimension different than rehearsal energy. It is higher, of course, but it is also more intense and leaves you unaware of anything but the audience. I have performed not knowing I was injured until the show was over.

Reaching down into myself and pulling up all the years of live enjoyment, I put on a good show. The audience loved it. The dancing was full out. I remembered everything. The comedy and drama were fine and, of course, everyone understood the magic would be more enhanced and complete when we had lights and costumes.

When it was over, I took a bow. My father flashed through my mind. Would he have liked it? I hadn't dropped the baton at the relay race. And I knew that what we had would work for the most part.

A few days later the entire company traveled to San Antonio, Texas. We chose that city for the first tryout, because the theater was available for us to set up our lights and sound and bandstand and have a few previews before we opened. The tour had begun. The real audience was waiting.

I took Mary Hite with me so I wouldn't shirk my bodywork. Her way of gentle but strength-building workouts had redesigned the alignment of my back and inner hips. I was using orthotics in my shoes, so I walked differently and my lower back, so far, was pain-free.

Gary Catona came too. He had redesigned my voice, because my restricted throat was now opened up. I was stepping out as a brand-new 1990 model of myself! As I was to learn soon, it required a great deal of adjustment.

Chapter 8

~ The Tour

SAN ANTONIO IS A QUAINT, cozy city, which has been attractively refurbished under the aegis of Mayor Henry Cisneros. Its relaxed environment was soothing for me. I walked the river (more like a canal); and with our composer, Larry Grossman, and some of the musicians, we ate huevos rancheros and drank Long Island iced tea in the sun like regular civilians.

Each person was dealing with his or her own problems relating to the opening of our show. With a kind of delicate tension under the conversations, people gossiped and chatted with each other, with me, and with the creative team that was responsible for putting it all together. A show on tour is like a traveling family. The members eye each other, have their likes and dislikes, their favorites, and an almost visceral understanding of the pecking order.

There's an old adage in show business. In any given company it's good to have somebody to hate. It releases pent-up tension. Usually the focus of anger is either the "star" or the director or some other person in a position of authority. The star often has a drinking or drug or temperamental insecurity problem, making him or her a natural candidate for unexpressed hidden frustrations. Stars either work the company too hard or not enough, are either too in need of attendance or totally aloof. Whatever. If the company's gossip can revolve around the star, the problem is solved. If not, they go elsewhere.

In my case I had none of the above idiosyncrasies, at least I didn't evidence any, so the process of focusing frustrations began its natural selection.

Alan, the director, was too nice to be a candidate; and anyway he hung out with people and alternately scolded and cuddled his dog in such an endearing way that the gossip about him centered around his "dog-man" relationship, automatically making the pickin's slim.

Mike Flowers, company manager, responsible for the stage crew, hotel accommodations, paychecks, and traveling, was—in everyone's judgment—fair, courteous, kind, and commendably easy to deal with. Except that he was movie-star gorgeous and no one could figure out his personal life, there was nothing to complain about where he was concerned.

I could see the problem in rehearsals. Which one could people focus on? In the absence of a definitive candidate, they turned their feelings on each other.

Camps began to emerge. There were camps within the ranks of the musicians. There were camps among the gypsies, involving a few role players from the wardrobe department.

Pete Menefee, the costume designer, had been with me for fifteen years. He was a retired gypsy and knew the gypsy mentality backwards. "You have the best dancers in the business," he said correctly. "That means you also have four divas."

And why not? However, divas can be biting and sometimes cruel with each other. Since they practically live in one another's laps in their dressing rooms, emotions build from lack of privacy and a wealth of combustible talent. Those with the penetrating wit and self-centered authority prevail. The others fall by the wayside. And yet gypsies are such sensitive, smart, intuitive human entities; in the end, if they deliver on stage, they all survive.

I watched the drama unfold. One of the girls began palling around with one of the guys, sparking entertaining gossip that they were having an affair, which everyone agreed would end as soon as she reached a city where there was really good shopping and he went broke.

A few of the musicians were having trouble with the conductor, who played a significant role in their discontent because he never gave them a downbeat.

The head of wardrobe was a bright young man who teased that he would rather wear my costumes himself than put them on me. Roger's domain was the basement of every theater where he and "his ladies" sewed, gossiped, repaired, and made decisions as to who would be the recipient of small and big favors. Mike was smart in that he ordered delicious food between rehearsals and made sure that people were happy in their assigned rooms.

As opening night approached, I was pleased that my tensions were not too deep. I actually enjoyed our hotel and the sweet city of San Antonio.

Larry and I had a few meals together at which we discussed our lives and the interplay in the company. I hadn't realized that he had been through his own camp-clique problems, which he weathered, as indeed all of us had to.

Buz didn't come with us to San Antonio, because he had a benefit to do at the White House with Barbara Bush and literacy. I didn't feel it was very literate of him to be missing. We had worked together many times, and Larry and Buz had worked together for twenty years. One of the mysteries of show business people is we never really know one another as well as we think we do. Of course, we're in the business of game playing. But the game playing is fundamentally competitive. Even with the extraordinary degree of personal honesty and sharing that takes place during the creative process, we are always thrown when one of us acts unpredictably and without understanding.

From my point of view, such was the case with Buz not being there. The show was set for the most part; but without a writer aboard, I felt isolated, even though I'd often make my own changes and rewrites according to the audience reaction. I missed Buz. So did the others. One of our most important "team" members had something more important to do. Buz's absence, therefore, was good for a day of gossip, but it quickly faded in anticipation of our opening.

I worked with Mary every morning in our hotel suite. My body felt pretty good. My voice was holding its own. And I guess you could say I was ready for the moment when the houselights would dim, anticipation would mount out there in the darkness, and it would be up to me to deliver. Thank goodness my recurring nightmare had three weeks of rehearsal to counteract it.

The musicians took their places on the bandstand. I entered in the dark and found my mark, waited for my cue. Then the musical chord sounded and the spotlight hit me. I was blinded. The audience erupted in applause. I couldn't see a thing. I had forgotten the impact and the isolation of the spotlight. It shocked me. The applause was loud and long. You'd think I'd been away for a lifetime, instead of only six years. I wondered how their perceptions of me had changed since I was last on stage. Had my books and "New Age" philosophy confused them?

Still blinded by the spot, I could only rely on my ears. So I listened to the applause, waiting for it to die down, hoping my eyes would adjust. I looked out over the audience. Everything was black, except for the stream of light rays trained, it seemed, directly into my eyes. I couldn't find the horizon in the blackness and began to feel disoriented, as though I would lose my balance. Even the exit signs had disappeared. I saw no human faces, although I could hear people. The edge of the proscenium dropped off into darkness.

I inched my way downstage, afraid I would step over the line, remembering that Marlene Dietrich had once fallen into the orchestra pit and broken her arm.

The applause subsided, and I heard the musical vamp emerge from the orchestra behind me. When there was silence in the house, I began to sing the lyrics to the opening song. I was wearing a body mike in a choker around my neck, designed to look like a piece of jewelry.

As I sang my lyrics, I realized I couldn't hear myself. I sang louder. I still couldn't. I reached up and touched the mike. Where I should have been concerned only about how to play the number, I was completely distracted about whether the audience could hear me or not. I couldn't ask the sound man because he was located upstage, off stage right, and I couldn't see him. The conductor was looking down at his music, not yet familiar with the show. I felt absolutely isolated, trapped in the spotlight with no support system to tell me whether I was coming across or not.

I finished the number, tense and miserable, singing

blind and deaf about how much I loved being on the stage again.

For the entire first act I could have phoned in my performance as far as I was concerned. I couldn't hear myself at all. The band was too loud. The musicians couldn't hear me either. I finished the first act with "Rose's Turn," and after the blackout I left the stage for my dressing room and intermission.

I clawed at the microphone around my neck. What was going on? If performers can't hear themselves through their own stage monitors, there is *trouble.* Stories abound about such troubles. Some sound crews are fired on the spot. Sound guys for Engelbert Humperdinck had T-shirts made up that read "I survived Humperdinck—again and again." Other performers put earpieces in their ears until the sound people got it right.

The balance of sound on the stage is twofold. The audience and the performer do not hear the same thing. There is a sound mixer out in front mixing audience sound and a mixer offstage mixing performance sound. I was learning that using omnidirectional body mikes was a problem, because they pick up all ambient sounds on the stage. In other words, the band was leaking through my mike so badly that I couldn't be heard. It was better in the house than on the stage, but what matters to a performer is what *they* hear. And I was drowned out. When that happens you force, you push. It's an automatic response, guaranteed to make you lose your voice.

I tried to stay calm in my dressing room as I simultaneously dried off and warmed up my legs for the dance number in the second act. I thought ahead. How could I use a hand mike without destroying the effect? It would be too much like Vegas, and mine was a theatrical show, not a saloon show. Besides, I did three long acting sketches where props and costumes were necessary. How could I hold the mike while acting with props and costumes? I couldn't find a solution in between pliés and hamstring stretches. Mary put me through a fifteen-minute warm-up before we heard the band take their places again.

I was wearing a leotard for the second act, which contained the battery pack for the microphone in my crotch. I hoped it would survive the splits. The microphone itself was nestled in my bosoms, lifting them even further. I had to laugh at the preposterous glamour we performers presented on stage, while actually being connected and wired and screwed and glued into every sophisticated mechanical device known to the audio business. Which still didn't produce results.

I wondered if sweat from my crotch would leak into the battery pack and electrocute me. A show biz first.

I found my way back to center stage and began to warm up at the bar constructed around the bandstand. I lifted my leg in a stretch that I knew was impressive to the audience, but really to test whether the battery would fall out—and was not reassured. Nothing to do but get on with it. I lowered my leg and did a few pliés.

The number began. Being heard was not an issue during the dancing; staying upright was. I was working with new shoes. Suddenly the snap across my ankle strap came undone. I didn't feel it—I saw it. In that intuitive way dancers have of knowing that doom is impending, something told me to look down. If I hadn't seen it, my shoe would have flown off.

Instead I bent down and resnapped the shoe. During the bend the battery pack came loose. I reached up under the backside of my leotard and positioned it. Jesus. Who said once you're out there everything works?

I finished the number, happy to have survived in one piece, and went on to the next hunk of material. I had no idea whether the people in the audience were enjoying themselves or not. The music, the lights, the salty sweat in my eyes, the stretched muscles, controlled breath, wet hair, precision movement, and the last wrenching steps that brought the twenty-five-minute dance number to a close were finally over. It *had* come together somehow.

The dancers took their bows and left the stage. I quickly changed into a silver and black beaded gown over my soaking leotard. It weighed a good twenty pounds. But not for long. As I stood regally in the subdued spotlight, having earned the right to some quiet moments with the audience, I felt something on my sleeve. A line of sequins had torn loose, and the dress was coming unraveled. The more I pulled, the more it unraveled. Perhaps this was symbolic of things to come. Holding a handful of stringed sequins, I finished the show, which the audience seemed to like in spite of everything. How could one prepare for this in a rehearsal hall? Only by remembering that audiences love to see that performers are just like they are—participants in the fall from grace.

On top of the problems with the sound, which would certainly have to be solved, I had decided to travel without a personal assistant this time. I wanted to be responsible for what went on around me, and I never did like people who hovered. That meant I would have to get up early the morning after the last show and pack myself. We traveled on our day off, in order to open the next city the following night. Since I slept on a magnetic mattress I had brought with me, I couldn't pack it the night before. Mike Flowers would collect the luggage in the hall in front of our rooms by nine o'clock. Falling into bed at three o'clock in the morning (we were all on that schedule now) wouldn't leave much time to sleep. I was beginning to see some of the attendant hardships that touring would involve—no day off, really, following two shows a day on both Saturday and Sunday.

As I woke on Monday, the last morning in San Antonio,

my body felt as though it had been hit by a truck. I slipped into an Epsom salts bath and tried to stretch and relax.

I found myself ordering chocolate truffles and waffles and pancakes for breakfast, just as a consolation–reward I suppose. Besides, I needed the carbohydrates to get me going. My voice was shot from the pushing during performance—the room service operators asked if I had a bad cold. They weren't far wrong. The cold happened as soon as we opened in Dallas. And, of course, it started with a sore throat. Again I couldn't hear myself during performance, the band couldn't hear me, so I shut my throat down.

I was miserable—wheezing and coughing and stuffed up. I found it metaphysically interesting that the problems I was having related to communication. I couldn't communicate properly. No one could hear me. I wondered what that was really saying to me. Yes, I was concerned about being understood, relative to confusion that might have developed as a result of my writing. But would that concern actually translate to a manifested reality on the stage? Of course it would, but I couldn't see that until later. I just blamed it all on the sound guys and their unproductive equipment.

I found something else happening to me that was probably relevant. The Hotel Crescent Court had set aside a presidential-looking suite for me. But I didn't want it. It had nothing to do with the expense (we had an extraordinary discount). It was about coziness and convenience.

I just wanted one bedroom like everyone else had—one room, no living room–dining room suite, no kitchenette with a refrigerator expected to house cold champagne and caviar, and no running from room to room to answer the phone. All I wanted was a bedroom that was quiet with color TV and a window that opened.

The manager of the hotel was subtly shocked, as though

I would suffer needless inconvenience. But I had long since learned that when you travel alone, you want to be near the front door when room service comes, able to drag your telephone with you as you open it. I also suspect I needed to feel more in control of my surroundings. I had no control on the stage, so at least I wanted it where I slept.

The manager had trouble with my pragmatic point of view but nevertheless found me a small room with an open window and a long telephone cord. I was happy.

Despite the sound problems and my bad cold, opening night went quite well.

The Texas audience response was bombastic. They gave me a five-minute standing ovation, which people said was unusual for subscription opening night audiences. I was thrilled. Maybe we'd be all right after all. The critics were a different story.

Since I had said that my show was a work in progress, because I was touring until I reached New York, I guess they felt called upon to be creatively helpful. They saw it as a Vegas show with legs, flashy dancing, and energy. They didn't like the sketches in which I played Sousatzka, Ouiser, and Aurora from three of my films, charging that it was self-serving of me to act these characters on a stage when one could easily go out and buy the real thing in a video store. Accusations of self-celebration always bothered me, because I knew it related to my philosophy of "love yourself before you can love anybody else."

The sketches were actually very well done, with costumes, hair, and makeup that were almost exact replicas of those in the movies. The audiences seemed to like them, always applauding as soon as they identified a costume, even before I launched into the character. Audiences seem to appreciate the celebratory aspects of a performer's life. They come to see you because of who you are and what you've done. The critics somehow have a problem with performers having a good time with themselves (reflection on their own thwarted creativity?). Were the critics reflecting what audiences secretly felt but were too polite to express? Surely not. You can always tell when an audience is "in the cellar." It worried me.

My creative team left right after the opening in San Antonio, figuring the show was set. The critical reviews resulted in extended telephone conversations that continued when we played in Dallas, all of a personally defensive nature settling to the view that critics don't know what they're talking about anyway. Nevertheless, tempers flared and creative defensiveness lurched into full swing. If I cut out the acting sketches, I wouldn't have a long enough first act. The "people" loved them. Why should I be affected? And then finally, "Let's wait and see what they say in Denver," which was our next stop. I agreed.

But the sound problem still had not been solved, and no end seemed in sight. After each show, there was a technical meeting about dials and new microphones from Germany and other mechanical wonders I couldn't understand. With the escalating frustration of the sound on stage came problems from the musicians, which served once again to amplify how each department in a live show is dependent on every other.

Our conductor was an excellent musician who had expertly programmed the synthesizers with sounds that replicated a thirty-piece orchestra. He was a very laid-back individual, Oriental, and with his stoic personality, one could never tell what he was thinking.

I could see the musicians were longing for more fiery leadership. In that respect our drummer, Cubby O'Brien, took charge. Someone had to do it. However, the focus of leadership then became diffused. I knew the conductor was not entirely familiar with the music yet, so his creative freedom and experimentation had not yet emerged. Live performers love to feel harmonious musical risks coming from the band, since each member is basically a soloist. This wasn't happening. They were having trouble simply playing what was expected of them, because they couldn't see any directive arm movements, which, in fact, may not even have been there.

I asked myself whether I should call in my old conductor, Jack French, who was a real leader and creative too. Jack knew very little about synthesizers, but the new man had already accomplished that transition.

I was now faced with firing him, going to hand mikes instead of body mikes, cutting the acting sketches, and eliminating the intermission, which had given me an opportunity to warm up my body for the twenty-five-minute dance number in the second act. My team was helpful, but I knew the decisions would ultimately be mine.

Just as we were going into the double-show weekend, I came down with the flu. I couldn't believe I was doing such a thing to myself. But I did. I could hardly breathe. I lost my voice, which was hard enough to find on stage anyway. My joints and muscles ached. My anxiety mounted, and I wondered what the hell I was doing in show business. I'd rather drive the Wonder bread truck for a living.

Every four hours I sniffed warm salt water up my nose. It's very healing. It's guaranteed to clear up nasal congestion the natural way. I soaked in Epsom salts every chance I got. I drank enough water to sink a ship and took vitamin C until I had heartburn.

I mentioned my problem with the conductor to Mike Flowers. He had worked with him before and couldn't understand the change in how he was with the band. I knew that once I said anything to anybody else, regardless of how discreet

I was, the word would get around. Our business is so small that all it takes is one musician in Dallas to tell another in Los Angeles, and everyone on both coasts knows there is trouble. And the news is guaranteed to move faster if you insist on keeping it a secret.

Then just as I was ready to let the conductor go, he suddenly took charge. It happened on the last double-show day in Dallas. With his improvement, I felt it would be unfair to fire him. Mike, in the meantime, had arranged for Jack French to meet us in Denver.

Because of the flu, my fading voice, and my discomfort in general, I took off my body mike and went with a hand-held. That meant breaking the proscenium immediately, but I would make it work somehow. I had a long conversation with Otts Munderloh, the leading sound man in the country who did all the Broadway shows, and he said I was foolish to ever expect a sound balance as long as I had my band on stage behind me and used body mikes. The decision was clear. With a little rechoreographing, I could do it.

The only problem would be what to do with the acting sketches. I couldn't do them and hold a hand mike. It would destroy the illusion, and besides I'd have to redo them without props and without changing costumes. It seemed that the decision to cut them out was being made for me. But I still wanted to see what the critics in Denver would say about the acting sketches.

I decided to use the hand mike for the songs and the original body mike for the sketches. Finally I could hear myself when I sang. The band could hear me too, so we could relax about that.

The microphone remained sewn into my choker necklace for the acting so that I could change costumes without brushing up against it. Some women have the mike sewn into their hair if they are wearing wigs. I couldn't because of the perspiration from dancing. The problem with mikes in the hair is that the audience can see the wires from the mike to the battery pack cascading down the back. If a woman's hair is long enough it's okay, but I had short hair. So the wardrobe man sewed the wires underneath the backstraps of my costume. During the acting sketches I couldn't move my head in any direction because the sound changed, calling attention to the location of the body mike. Illusion is everything on the stage. I wanted to retain it as much as possible.

I dragged myself through the final Dallas weekend, packed up my mattress and clothes on Monday morning, and moved on to Denver, where we would open the following night.

I thought a lot about the performers who do one-night stands and travel and sleep in buses. The buses are like luxurious hotel rooms with double beds, wet bars, and TV; but I could never do that. I remembered going to a party years ago when I walked into the host's bedroom and put my coat on top of all the others piled on the bed. Someone moved underneath. A small dark-haired woman smiled up at me. It was Margot Fonteyn. She was in town with Ballet Theater and that was her night off. I wondered if I'd ever be able to discipline myself to sleep and rest in those conditions and still perform.

I left the Hotel Crescent Court in Dallas with fond memories of my comfortable little room and the specialties I had come to love from the room service menu. My favorite there had been their homemade bran muffins. In San Antonio it had been the tortilla soup. All the favorites in a traveling show business company are consumed at around one o'clock in the morning. A company wouldn't last one week without twenty-four-hour room service.

We'd be going from eighty-degree sun in Texas to snow in Denver. High altitudes necessitate oxygen masks in the wings and chromium pills just before each performance. Chromium helps explode the oxygen in the bloodstream. I had often taken it in Lake Tahoe and Mexico City.

When altitude sickness hits during a performance, you feel it first in the extremities. The fingers, lips, and feet begin to tingle. That's the warning. From that moment on it's up to the individual how to handle it. Taking deeper breaths can cause hyperventilation, which brings on fainting even faster. I usually decrease the muscular intensity with which I work. I don't do the steps quite so full out. I don't sing with quite as much diaphragm force. I've never fainted on stage, but in Mexico City I once fainted *after* a show. Still, I think that was due more to an irregular diet than anything else.

I noticed that when performing so many shows, the most important foods were protein and carbohydrates. Fats were a killer, and dairy products produced phlegm while singing. So I lived on bread, soup, meat, fish, vegetables, and fruit. On my day off, I sprang for ice cream and chocolate.

The most difficult performance I ever gave in my life was in Las Vegas one night after my company and I had stuffed ourselves on a homemade Mexican meal. The refried beans, cheese, meat, onions, and salsa came up and met me with every step. I felt I couldn't get off the ground, and even when I did I was afraid to hit bottom again.

When performing live, everything about your life has to be policed and regulated. One stupid day of throwing caution to the winds can result in heartache, heartburn, and injuries. There is no such thing as running wildly in the rain, or abandoning yourself at a disco, or drinking a bottle of wine with a seven-course French meal. You'll pay for it in spades in the middle of a number.

And sleep? You need eight hours. The first thing you do in a hotel is take the receiver off the hook on the telephone so the operator won't mistakenly put calls through your "do not disturb" order. You cherish your Do Not Disturb sign hanging on your hotel room door; and if you're a light sleeper, like me, you take a white-sound sleep machine with you everywhere you go. Its constant whir deflects and overrides all the other sounds around, whether it's traffic below your room or a couple having a lovemaking fight next door.

You live in a constant state of emergency, free of projected anxiety for only a few hours after you wake up each day. From three o'clock on, your life and orientation are directed toward what you will be doing for only a few hours that night. It seems absurd on the face of it, but every live performer experiences the same thing. This state of being isn't so intense on a film, because there are many ways to deal with desired perfection. On the stage you have one crack at it per night. Your life depends on it somehow. In films it's the director's life on the line.

So the Rocky Mountains loomed below us as we circled Denver. It looked crisp and invigorating. I had friends in Denver and was looking forward to seeing them again. Perhaps this engagement would be a bit more normal. Perhaps I'd be able to feel like a real live person who could enjoy little things like a walk in the park or a shopping spree or even a hamburger and a movie.

That was not to be. What no one had mentioned was we would be dancing on a cement stage. Shinsplints are common as a result of dancing on cement. And other bone problems and muscle injuries occur. A cement floor is a dancer's nightmare.

As soon as I walked into the theater, called the Auditorium, I felt my back and legs freeze up. Your muscles remember what cement has done to them in the past. Mine remember only too well, and they rebel from the first instant they come in contact with cement.

Well, there was nothing to be done. Not only was the stage cement, it wasn't flat. It was raked, and that floor was sheer hell. Pain rippled down our backs and across our shoulders. Our shins were jabbing, skin against bone. Beyond that, the conductor went back to not giving downbeats because the sound was malfunctioning—which also meant I couldn't hear myself sing again. My props were misplaced, and to top it off, my shoe broke as well.

I came off the stage after the first act, threw my arms up against my dressing room wall and screamed, "I really hate this. Hate. Hate. Hate."

Mike Flowers, who was the witness to my tirade, looked shocked. He knew how expectant I had been of having a good time on the tour, and it obviously wasn't happening. He tried to comfort me. If I quit, everyone would be out of work.

I tried to warm up for the second act, but my anger and negativity were out of control. I was in a furious temperamental snit, born out of the fear that everything was conspiring against me to humiliate me in front of the audience.

"I'm not going back out there," I yelled. "I hate it. I hate the floor, I hate the acting sketches, I hate my material, I still hate the sound, and that excuse for a conductor–pianist thinks he's Liberace!" (Actually, he was a good accompanist but not for me. How could anyone have been good for me at this point?)

Mike looked at me, stunned. I had never behaved like this before. This was spiritual? This was an enlightened human being? I clearly needed to study one of my own books but the adrenaline high that usually supports an entertainer turns on you when you're in trouble, and, with me, it had all been transformed into anger.

I flounced and crashed around my dressing room for the

entire intermission, giving a better performance backstage than I had presented for the paying audience.

"What can I do to help?" asked Mike, trying to be loving but more appalled than anything.

"Who do you have to screw to get out of this business?" I yelled. Mike didn't know whether to laugh or not. I glared at him as though it was all his fault.

"Oh, I don't know, Mike. I don't know," I said. "I have so many changes to make in this show just to get through it that I don't know where to begin. I need Jack French, but I feel guilty about firing the guy we have. He's a good conductor but apparently not for me. He's used to Vegas performers who have no nuance in their performing. He doesn't need to conduct them 'cause it's one song after another. I'm different. I don't know what I am, but it's not what he's used to."

"I know," said Mike. "Jack has arrived, but he can't go to work for another two weeks. Can you hold out for this engagement and then through the next one in Seattle?"

I shrugged.

I changed into my leotard knowing I would go back out there, even if I got a broken neck from the cement stage.

"Let's see what the critics say here," I said. "If they have the same complaints as Dallas, I'm going to change the show and take out the intermission."

Mike looked at me blankly. "You're going to dance without warming up?"

"Yes," I said, patting powder on my nose and calming down. "I'll have to."

"So will you wear your leotard from the top of the show?" he asked, seeing the problem right away.

What he meant was that I would have to underdress from the top of the show, wearing the dancing leotard from the beginning. That would require a new costume that would blend into the leotard top, cover it, and work for everything up until the dancing.

"Can you design a costume with Pete Menefee on the telephone?" asked Mike. "What about a fitting, and will it go under the costume for 'Rose's Turn'?"

"Yes, yes, yes," I said. "We can do it, and we have three days because I want to change the show for the weekend."

"Okay," said Mike. "I'll get on it right away." He stopped at the door and turned around. "Remember, you said you didn't want to do this again unless you could have fun."

I looked at him. "I sure did, didn't I? I wonder if that's ever going to happen."

I left the dressing room and walked back out onto the stage.

I remembered a saying my mother often quoted to me as a child: "You cry because you have no shoes until you meet a person who has no feet."

What right did I have to complain about my piddling problems when so much suffering was occurring in the world? It was ridiculous. But everything was relative, I guess. To me, the most impressive human quality was the compassion a person could have for even the smallest difficulty that another human soul was going through. No feeling was insignificant—none more important than another—because all troubles occurring in a human life were occurring for a reason. Lessons were to be learned and accumulated. Knowledge would come from hardships. And all of it furthered self-enlightenment. I knew from experience that I had always learned more from adversity than from success. What were my lessons now, and how was I participating in erecting obstacles for myself?

The day after the Denver opening I woke to medieval pain in my body and newspaper reviews that said I should cut out the acting sketches.

From yet another bath of Epsom salts, I had a long-drawn-out conference call with my creative team. They didn't understand the critics and wanted me to keep the show as it was. I balked. The reviews were hurting business. We should have been sold out and we weren't.

I knew it was inevitable that I'd have to cut the sketches, cut the intermission, and have very little time to warm up. I faced the music, bit the bullet, designed the new underdress costume on the phone with Pete, forfeited twenty thousand dollars in discarded wardrobe, and prepared to do twenty thousand more pelvic tilts than originally planned every morning—one for each dollar down the drain.

I had a talk with the conductor. He wasn't happy with me any more than I was with him, mostly because he felt he couldn't satisfy me. It was true. We agreed that he'd leave after Seattle and Jack would take over. The musicians were happy about that decision.

Pete put a roomful of "busy fingers" to work in Los Angeles, sewing on sequins for a new opening costume. And I tried to eat less so there wouldn't be quite so much of me landing after every step on that damn cement stage.

In the middle of the week in Denver, my agent, Mort Viner, came to my hotel room to have a talk. Mort has represented me since the first day I arrived in Los Angeles from New York. Of course, there were more senior agents at MCA at the time who oversaw everything, but Mort and I grew up together in the business. He was the one who drove me to the Hollywood sign as soon as I got off the plane and said something like, "Today a sign—tomorrow the world."

He had shepherded me through films, television, and stage. He had also educated himself in book publishing so he would know the world of books. He claimed he hadn't read a book since *Black Beauty* and wasn't sure he understood that.

Where my books were concerned, he only knew a lot of other people must have understood them because they made money.

The PR man at Bantam, Stu Applebaum, had tried on many occasions to get Mort to write a book about Hollywood and some of his clients. Mort refused, of course, citing fiduciary relationship, but said that he at least could deliver a great title, *Hollywood and Viner.* It didn't much matter what followed.

Mort and I had been through many things together. Agents and stars often form very close relationships when there is a mutual trust. Such was the case with us. He saw me and Dean Martin (whom he also represented, among others) as his children whose lives were up to him to protect and run.

He had been married a few times (I always thought there was one more wife than he did), and never had children because he didn't like the idea of getting up in the middle of the night tending to whooping cough and croup, and whoever he fell in love with understood that his theatrical family came first.

Mort had booked our "phantom tour," as he called it, before I had agreed to do it. "Balls in the air," he would laughingly say while waiting for me to either commit to it or read a movie script I liked.

Mort never saw much point in doing anything unless you enjoyed it. When they made him Executive Vice President of ICM, he only accepted the position provided his official picture in shirt and tie could be taken while wearing his tennis sweats on the bottom half. Mort loved jokes but was as shrewd a businessman as he was a human observer. Living through forty years of Hollywood chicanery is a great teacher. He was also very sensitive to other people's feelings.

He sat on the edge of my bed sipping orange juice (Mort didn't smoke or drink). He looked at me for a long beat. Then he said, "You're not having any fun, are you?"

"Not much," I answered. "I don't know what's wrong.

Maybe I've outgrown it all. Maybe I'm too old to dance. Maybe it doesn't matter to me anymore."

"Why?" asked Mort. "What is it, do you think? When you get out there do you enjoy it?"

I couldn't find the answer. "I don't know. I used to, but maybe I was just as anxious then as I am now. Why am I drawing all this trouble to myself?"

Mort had learned to accept and tolerate and even seriously employ some of my metaphysical philosophy. He certainly didn't pooh-pooh it. Many of his own friends were into it too.

"Well," he said. "It takes time for a show to shake down. It doesn't matter what business you're in, adjustments and stuff have to be made. But what concerns me is even when the shakedown is accomplished, will you enjoy getting up there in the spotlight?" Again I could say nothing.

"Do you get a kick out of it when they applaud, when they laugh, when they give you a standing ovation?" He was asking all the right questions, but I couldn't answer.

"Screw the money," he said. "It's not worth the aggravation. We'll find another way to pay the bills."

My mind wandered the stages of the world where I had cavorted and brought some joy not only to others but to myself as well. Why wasn't that happening now?

"You love seeing people in different cities who come back and take you to dinner, right? I mean you still love to travel?"

"Yes."

He waited a moment, choosing his next question judiciously. "What happens to you," he asked, "when you're standing in the spotlight and you know they're loving what you're doing?"

Mort was so smart. He had hit the nail on the head. Yet I wasn't sure how to answer him. I hadn't figured it out myself.

"Well," I said, "at first I'm scared. Then it's okay. But then maybe I feel like a fraud, because I know what it takes to make the magic. It's all a trick. I don't like tricks."

Mort looked confused. "But all show business is a trick. It's an illusion. You know that and so does the audience. So why does that bother you?"

"I don't know," I said. "It seems like I should be doing more to contribute to the raising of their awareness than tricks."

"Well, you could always run for President, but that's being more of a trick than anything."

"Yeah," I said. "Funny."

"Come on," he said, "you like tricks; you love magic. You always have. What's changed?"

I paced around the room eating a piece of bran muffin left over from breakfast. I wasn't certain what I was feeling.

"Maybe I find a conflict between surrendering to the natural flow of things and needing to take total control of a stage and an audience in order for the magic to work. I'm contradicting what I advise everyone else to do in their own lives. 'Surrender to the natural order of things,' I tell them; but if I surrendered to a cement stage, and body mikes, and a conductor with no downbeat, my show would fall apart. So what am I doing in show business since all of it is about control?"

Mort blinked. "You lost me on that one," he said. "At least I think you have. But wait a minute. Isn't there a way to do both and not call it contradictory?"

"Sure," I answered. "That's easy for you—you're a Republican."

"I don't have to be," he said. "Not if it makes me unhappy."

He shifted his position on the bed. I could tell *this* kind of show business conversation was new to him.

"So you're telling me," he said, "that you always have to tell the truth?"

"Well, yes."

"Fine. Tell the audience they're stupid for buying a ticket, because you hate what you're doing. Tell them how much your legs hurt, and how offbeat the conductor is, and throw in the fact that you can't hear what you're singing. See how much they'd love to hear that. See how much truth they really want to hear. Audiences come to a theater because they want to be fooled. Don't they? I mean if you fall on your face and get up and make a joke, they don't want to know that you broke your nose. Do they? I don't know, maybe I'm crazy."

I laughed.

"The bottom line," he went on, "is if you're not enjoying yourself, you should walk away; screw it. It's simple."

I guess it *was* simple really. But *why* wasn't I enjoying it?

"Do you still enjoy making movies?" he asked.

"Oh, I don't know."

"Oh?"

"Yeah, oh."

"Why?"

"I don't know that either. It's sort of like I can't wait until they're finished so I can go on to things that matter to me."

Mort's expression changed. What I was saying was serious now. He sat on the edge of the bed, his face deeply troubled, and yet maybe we were getting to the heart of the matter. Then a humorous smile flickered across his face. He threw up his arms.

"Maybe you've outgrown show business," he said. "Maybe you don't get a kick out of it anymore, because you have to be a kind of a kid to stay in it. Maybe you should just do your metaphysics and do seminars and write books."

His face was filled with understanding, even though I'm sure he had never thought such a thing was possible for me.

"Well," I said, "every time I do an interview or get into a long conversation with anybody, it's this metaphysical–spiritual psychological stuff that interests me. I love investigating behavior and beliefs in people and discussing the connections they make in their lives that might never occur to them otherwise. That's what I get a kick out of. I get bored with show business talk, but what I can't understand is why I still insist that everything about my show go right. If I'm so bored, why don't I leave it alone?"

"Because you're a perfectionist. You're a professional. You've never sloughed off anything."

"Right," I answered. "I still don't know what I'm talking about."

Mort searched for me. "Did you enjoy your seminars, talking about metaphysics for eighteen hours every weekend?"

"Yes."

"And you never got bored?"

"No."

"Did you get bugged if things didn't go right?"

"Things always went right."

"Well, there must have been some things that you found lacking."

"I didn't notice."

He got up and walked to the window and looked out over the town square of Denver. The bell in the middle of the square chimed two in the morning. He turned around.

"You were working with Mike Nichols, Meryl Streep, Dennis Quaid, Gene Hackman, and Richard Dreyfuss. Right?"

"Right."

"That's the cream of the crop in my book."

"Mine too."

"And still you didn't really get a kick out of it?"

"Oh, I guess so."

"Did you ever enjoy making movies?"

"Maybe I just thought I should, because it all happened for me so fast. But I was always counting the days. Seems like I've always counted the days, and only now am I realizing it."

I hadn't intended for the conversation to sound so alarmist, but I was being as honest as I could. Was my present mind-set affecting my perceptions of the past? Was I even being correct in the assessment of my feelings? Here I was telling my agent that I really hadn't derived much pleasure or satisfaction from the profession I had been in for nearly forty years. Was that really true? Had I entered the world of make-believe because I enjoyed creating my own magic, or had I done it because it was expected of me? My mother scampered through my mind again. Then my father stood over me, berating my attempts at self-expression. I felt as though I was on a treadmill of making magic in order to please other people.

If a good movie script came up I'd do it, forgetting that around the third week into shooting I'd be looking for my days off. If a good play date was arranged for my show, I'd take it because I loved to travel, not remembering that what I really enjoyed was to come home to a hotel room and be by myself and think and write or watch a movie.

Was I basically a recluse? Did I want to do nothing? I seemed so extreme—out there in front of masses of people, then the quiet solitude of just me. I adored being by myself for weeks and months on end. Once I hadn't even left my house in the Pacific Northwest for three months. I had a rich

—WHAT A GREAT OREO COOKIE—FRENCH AND ITALIAN.

A GENETIC PHENOMENON, WHICH IS CUTE BUT SOMETIMES HARD ON SACHI.

(ALLAN GRANT, LIFE MAGAZINE © TIME WARNER, INC.)

SACHI AT TWO LEARNING TO SWIM.

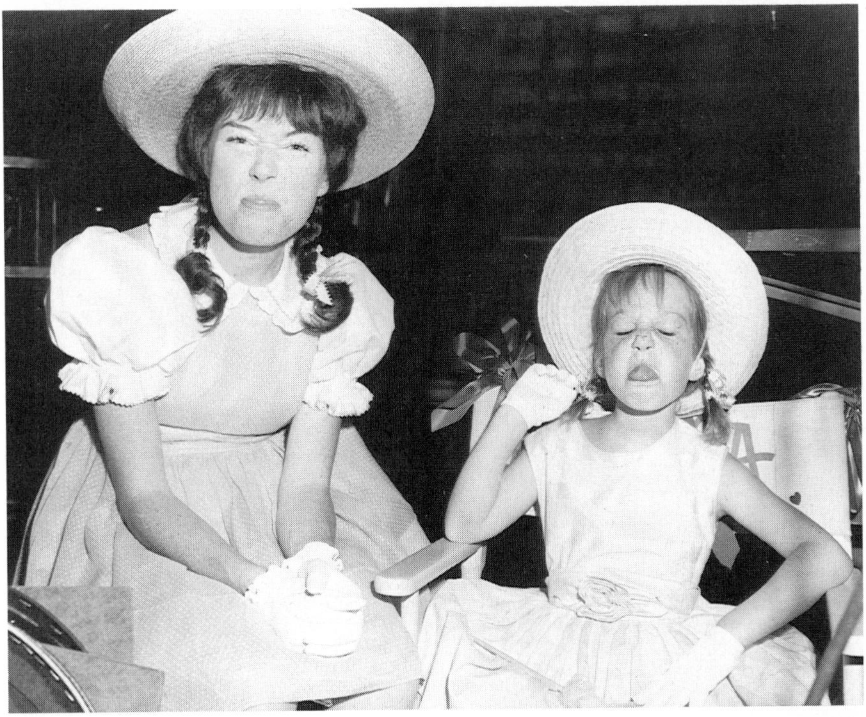

—Sachi at three learning to mimic.

— Sachi in Japan.

Sachi and me learning to love.

Khrushchev said, after my *Can-Can* performance, "The face of humanity is prettier than its backside."

J.F.K. as a cultural minister of movie stars.

Indira Gandhi when she was cultural minister of India.

I liked Queen Elizabeth II. She understood how hard we worked on the stage. So did Lord Grade (next to her), who was my employer for a time.

(Doug McKenzie Photographic Services Ltd.)

ROSALYN CARTER AFTER MY PERFORMANCE ON BROADWAY...A TRUE STEEL MAGNOLIA. (RICHARD BRAATEN)

TWO FELLOW SOUTHERNERS. (OFFICIAL WHITE HOUSE PHOTO)

I DIDN'T KNOW THEN I WAS SITTING NEXT TO THE FUTURE BUTCHER OF TIANANMEN SQUARE. (OFFICIAL WHITE HOUSE PHOTO)

—WITH GEORGE MCGOVERN AND PIERRE SALINGER, CAMPAIGNING IN THE SNOWS OF NEW HAMPSHIRE. (DONALD K. DILLABY)

—BELLA ABZUG LEARNING HOW TO ACT ON A MOVIE SET.

—FIDEL CASTRO SPEAKING NONSTOP ABOUT EVERY-THING.

Steel Magnolias. Daryl Hannah was out getting a pizza.

I was trying to figure out how to handle Debra, personally and in the part. (Photofest)

Jack and me at N.Y. Film Critics luncheon, where we both won for *Terms.*

Of course, because I was the real dancer, they cast me as the housewife who gave it up. Anne Bancroft played herself. (Photofest)

Maybe I started character acting ten years too early. Anyway, it was fun slumming into the future with John Schlesinger. (Photofest)

When you're down, you don't bother fearing a fall.

DEBBIE REYNOLDS AND ME IN OUR KARMIC "SKIP THE FLOWERS" RELATIONSHIP. (AARON AMAR)

MERYL AND ME DISCUSSING FIGURE PROBLEMS.

FOSSE, GWEN, AND ME AT MY BIRTHDAY PARTY ON THE *CHARITY* SET.

BOB FOSSE GAVE ME THIS PART. NOTHING LIKE HOLDING UP THE STAR WITH YOUR BACKSIDE. (*PAJAMA GAME*) (PHOTOFEST)

Kick up your heels and die! (Syndication International)

After a first dress rehearsal you wish you had someone else's feet. Alan Johnson agreed, but not his. (Jean Guyaux)

A self-portrait right before Thanksgiving dinner.

My favorite photo of Mom and Dad.

Sachi's favorite photo with them.

Warren focused this and took it with one long arm!

Me and my little brother.

— Sachi and me at the Academy Awards the night I won.

(Wide World Photo)

— Latest picture of the three of us at Sachi's birthday party. (Scott Downie, Celebrity Photo)

internal life somehow, not seeming to need people and parties and action. Yet when I ventured out into the world, I was more gregarious than anybody—the first to come and the last to leave.

Maybe I was just noticing these contradictions in myself for the first time. Perhaps I was using films and this show to mirror parts of my basic motivations in life. Mort finally broke the silence.

"Remember how we tossed that coin of chocolate in London over whether to extend the run at the Apollo?"

"Yep."

"Let's treat this the same way. Whatever you want to do is no big deal. I can cancel the tour. Legally we'll have some problems, but so what? Your life and happiness are more important than anything. Whatever you decide is okay by me. But I've gotta tell you something. I think that when you get on a wooden stage, cut the show like you want it, get Jack French back as conductor, and get to your house by the mountain, you'll feel different. Maybe I'm wrong, but knowing you, you probably just need a rest."

I laughed. He knew me pretty well. He had heard apocalyptic talk from me and others more than once in his life. Maybe I was overdramatizing. Depression is a powerful distortion trap. Maybe he was right. I'd wait.

Mort left and I tried to sleep. Was I really toying with the idea of leaving the world of entertainment before it left me? Were advancing years creeping up on me so rapidly that I was getting defensively ahead of myself? I didn't seem to be able to fully lose myself in the moment anymore. I was projecting too much into the future and that was what was causing the anxiety. But even if I was only five minutes ahead of myself, I was ripping off the joy of the present.

Show business, and live entertainment in particular, is an

art form that requires immediacy in the moment. The joy of it dissipates when one thinks too far ahead. Yet I seemed to have a lifelong habit of putting the cart before the horse.

I was always thinking too much into the future, and perhaps I was now doing it on the stage. Perhaps I had even experienced the whole tour already on some existential level that wasn't clear to me. If I believed that we each should take responsibility for everything in our lives, then I needed to take responsibility for everything that was happening to me. Perhaps it was all a lesson in enjoying every moment and not taking anything too seriously.

The next day the new opening costume arrived. It fit pretty well, and I liked what it looked like. The weekend of double shows arrived. I cut the sketches, *and* the intermission, and did the show my way. It worked. A critic who had had reservations on opening night came again and gave it a rave. But by Sunday night's second show, I was ready for a rest home. So were the dancers.

My home near Mt. Rainier beckoned, the thought of it sustaining me through waves of fatigue. When the phone rang at seven in the morning I knew it couldn't be good news. No one ever calls me at that hour when I'm on the road. It was Mike, who takes care of my house. He was sorry to wake me, but all the power was out in the house—no lights, no hot water, no stove. Maybe I should stay in a hotel.

Life was getting to be a bitch. Maybe I should just put my electromagnetic mattress on an ocean wave and float out to sea.

When I arrived in Seattle, I went to the Four Seasons Olympic Hotel. I stayed overnight, got up early to do a press conference, and then drove home in a rented car. I didn't care about the power. I just wanted to sleep in my own bed and play with my dogs.

The mountain, the river, all my trees spoke to me as soon as I arrived. I walked among the flowers and fed the fish in the pond. I romped with my dogs and told them my woes. I watched the moon come up over the mountain, and for a few short hours before I fell asleep I was in paradise.

The next day I drove to the Paramount Theater, which only took an hour; and after a sound check, which was pretty good, we opened. It went very well. I talked about loving to come to work in my beloved city and meant every word of it. The reviews were excellent and I was feeling comfortable with the show for the first time. I guess I was meant to perform without an intermission; the pacing was smoother, the energy built and sustained.

I called Alan and Buz and Larry and told them what I'd done and that it worked. The orchestra was happier because I was. In fact, I really felt that Seattle was my lucky charm. The show jelled there and we all knew we had it right. I loved the long drive after the theater at night, and so many members of the audience were people I knew.

I was tired and my body was still in pain from the Denver stage, but I began to see the light at the end of the tunnel. Maybe Mort had been right.

Before the Friday night show I made certain that I warmed up for an hour or more. I wanted to be prepared for the marathon weekend. Then we were scheduled to have a week off before San Francisco.

When I walked out onto the stage, I knew I'd be all right from then on. Everything came together—the sound, the lights, the band, the dancing, the audience. It was thrilling. I let myself have a wonderful time. It was magnetic.

Then came the big choreographers' dance number. I finished the first section—a tribute to Bob Fosse. Big hand. Some people stood up. Then came the cancan and the tribute to

Michael Kidd. Our skirts were flying, our legs were over our heads, the audience applauded every kick and trick. Then, heading down the homestretch of sixteen pirouette turns and inside circular turning kicks, I grabbed for my skirt because I thought the hem had come loose and I didn't want to catch my heel in it. I made a slight adjustment in my hips as I was turning, and suddenly I heard a loud snap like a handclap. I tumbled to the floor.

I couldn't get up. I was so stunned that I didn't feel any pain. I didn't know what had happened. I tried to rise to my feet, and my right knee buckled under me. I couldn't put any weight on it. In a flash I knew I'd either have to stop the show or rechoreograph everything for myself on the left leg. I was constitutionally incapable of quitting, so I rechoreographed, and the dancers, thank God, were skilled enough to adjust. They all knew something had happened.

At the end of that section, they asked what was wrong. I had to say I didn't know; it sounded as though I'd broken something, and I couldn't put any weight on my right leg. I finished the rest of the number. I didn't really know how.

Then, as I finished out the last half hour of singing and telling stories, I felt my knee seize up. I couldn't turn around. The audience sensed something was wrong, but I didn't say anything, didn't offer any explanations, and no excuses.

After the show I collapsed. Someone lifted me and carried me to the dressing room where a doctor was waiting. He diagnosed a dislocated right kneecap and proceeded to snap it back into place. "You won't be able to walk on this for a while," he then said, "much less dance."

Those were dreaded words I had always been sure I'd never hear. *Me* not dance? Why, I had danced on sprained ankles, broken ankles. But a knee? That was different—and I knew it.

I got very angry. I cursed myself, my stupidity at falling, the stage (could I have gotten my heel caught in the crevice of the extension over the orchestra pit?). I seemed to want to blame something or someone. It was hard for me to accept that *I* had indeed injured *myself.* My injuries had all happened when I was much younger. In the last twenty years of performing I had never missed a show, and I didn't want to start now.

Bags of ice surrounded my knee, above and below the injury. My dance captain, Damita Jo, knew all about dislocated kneecaps, because she had been through the same thing herself. She tended to me while Mike Flowers and the doctor talked quietly about what this would mean. The promoter of the Seattle engagement, a sweet man who was about to be married and saw my run as a week of having a good time, walked in the door. His face went white as he instinctively understood he would have to contact over ten thousand people that weekend to say I couldn't perform.

I apologized. I was beside myself. For the first time in my privileged life, a circumstance quit me before I quit it.

An old friend and previous assistant of mine had been in the audience that night. He saw me fall, came backstage after, and offered to drive me home. "It happened for a reason," he said. "Now just calm down and figure out what it is."

Back home I iced my knee again (ice is a dancer's best friend) and climbed like a cripple into bed. I was wracked with guilt—*guilt* at doing this to myself, the promoter, and the audiences. I had heard that several bus-loads of people had come from Vancouver for the next day's matinee. It was too late to stop them. I could see their faces as they got off the buses to discover there was nothing to do but turn around and go home.

I couldn't sleep at all. Over and over I relived the moment I went down. It was during a high-kicking turning step. What did that mean? Why that? If everything had a meaning, and I believe it does, what did that step signify?

Metaphysically there are intricate explanations for such things. It's amazing how much sense these explanations make when you learn them.

For example, feet represent the first chakra issues of fear, fight or flight, and grounding—footing, so to speak. When you lose your footing (or your basic security), you are basically dealing with issues of confidence. My confidence was in the process of reaching a turning point from negative to positive. I went down in the middle of turning.

Knees are representative of flexibility (as are ankles), and they carry hidden anger. It made sense that I was angry over all that had gone on and pissed that at the point of turning my show into a happy experience, I had aborted it. Evidently there was more I needed to stop and look at. I was angry at much deeper issues. I needed time to confront them, so I had arranged an enforced vacation for myself by going down. A dislocated kneecap meant I was dislocating the fear that I had held there.

Sometimes an injury has hidden benefits. It stirs up hidden pain. It requires reflection. It certainly forces you to stop and take stock of yourself. There's nothing like an injury to promote growth!

I knew that nothing in this world happens, regardless of how tragic it may seem, that doesn't carry with it a positive reflective learning process. I hold that belief regardless of how serious or life-taking the tragedy is. Of course, my belief comes from the understanding that our physical lives are only moments on a magnificent canvas of time in the cosmic scheme of billions of learning experiences.

I no longer believed death was real; death was a *belief* even though fear of it dominated everything we did and felt. How extraordinary to harbor and nurture a conviction with such negative connotations! So even an injury was felt as a mini-death, because it served to remind the injured one of his or her belief in mortality.

But if the belief in mortality could be viewed as a *limitational* belief, rather than an actual fact, it changed one's attitude toward "tragedy." The same applied to anything "bad" that happened to us. Things happened for a reason; certainly there are no accidents. But also events don't just "happen"; *we* create them. Whether we do in fact learn then depends on our attitude.

Some of us create more pain than others. Much of the world has been taught that suffering is necessary to self-enlightenment and certainly the stressed search for personal power, money, status; the greedy and callous trashing of our home planet; and the overall drive to militant "solutions" to the world's political problems indicate a hunger to fulfill the teaching that we need to suffer.

But suffering was a belief too. In fact, our reality was always a question of what we perceived it to be. If I didn't want to perceive an event as a tragedy, it was my choice. I could thereby alter my reality, because I could consciously alter my perception of it. We all know individuals who can perceive the happiest event—the birth of a child, say—with dire foreboding. Our reality is up to each of us, and how we chose to perceive it would either destroy or improve our lives.

We have become accustomed to believe that disease and death are tragic. But so many of my friends who were diseased and dying from AIDS were teaching the rest of us that there were mystical dimensions of great peace and understanding attached. When dying people reach the state of "peace that passeth all understanding," it is beyond beautiful. Many of them seem to innately know that they are not dying but rather going on to another level of understanding. When that state is reached, the body pain subsides. But if a person fights death out of fear of it, the result is pain-wracked suffering.

I had seen that "peace" with my father and with several other close friends. In fact, one of the great gifts my father gave me was the happiness of being with him while he was dying. Those months were among the most peacefully fulfilling we had had together. He had finally accepted himself, his foibles, his failure. He talked only of love. He talked of visiting his mother and father, teachers that he had loved, and relatives that were long gone. The doctors thought he was hallucinating. I believed he was in touch with other dimensions, because he was in the process of giving up his body.

Everything he said related to love. He said there was nothing more important in the world than love and God and that we all needed to learn that. I always felt that he lingered as long as he did, hovering between the two worlds of "life and death," because he was teaching his nurses, doctors, friends, and members of our family that love and God were all that mattered.

That was why it was so fulfilling for me. I didn't even recall his harshness, his cruelty, his unaccepting disappointment in himself. I couldn't remember any of it, seeing him only as LOVE personified. As a result, I didn't feel his slow passing as tragic. I saw it as the grand communication in which the blissful silences of understanding between us were unspoken lessons in surrendering everything that had hurt us to love.

For some people, hanging on to life and fighting against death are defined as courage and the "will to live." But in my Dad I saw his magnificent courage as that of the act of surrendering to God, which he claimed was in everything. He said it was a shame that it took dying to finally understand that.

* * *

The next day, Mort Viner arrived and met me at the hospital with his suitcase. "Isn't this a little extreme?" he joked. "I could have gotten you out of this tour in an easier way!"

Then he looked serious. "How do you feel, really?"

"I'm okay," I said. "It only hurts when I laugh."

"Well, you're going to do what the doctor says, and I'm going to make sure he's conservative."

I nodded as the nurse took me into a lead room and injected my knee with dye so the doctor could take x-rays; arthrography, they call the procedure.

I could feel the liquid mush circulating in my knee, which they said would be uncomfortable for a few days; they also said that I shouldn't engage in any activity. The pictures showed that there was no actual tearing of the ligaments or tendons or muscles away from the patella (kneecap).

"If you had to have an injury," said the doctor, "this was the best kind." He sent me to a physical therapist who put me through exercise for the ankles and thighs, which lose their strength rapidly without use. He said I shouldn't dance for a week or two. Maybe he had his own guides.

I felt relieved that nothing serious had occurred, except for the adjustment I would now have to make with the time on my hands. And then I recognized that that was a gift to myself.

Chapter 9

~ Reprise

WHEN I AM ALONE AT MY house in the Pacific Northwest, it is a healing. I wish everyone could have a little spot with tall trees, water, open clear skies, and time. I never understand the importance of it until I'm in those surroundings again.

Nature is the grand teacher and the trees the tallest instructors. The idea of cutting them down simply for profit is a grave misunderstanding of what real profit is. They speak, they listen, they understand, and they heal. Yet they too are vulnerable, which is so evident after an eighty-mile-an-hour windstorm. As I walk among the mountain paths, sometimes stepping over one of the proud fallen giants, I wonder why this tree instead of another. Perhaps it has completed its own cycle of learning and its consciousness has gone on to another understanding.

The seasons of the wild flowers could always be trusted to follow in rhythm and harmony, and the accompanying insects were busy daily reminders of the creative reproduction of birds and bees and life.

This time I experienced six climates in a single day. The morning shrouded in a mist gave me a feeling of enveloped protection. By noon the sun gleamed through, accentuating the glistening moisture on every single leaf and bud like so many sparkling diamonds displayed on green velvet trays.

Then a breeze came up, chasing the liquid diamonds until the unseen movement churned into a wind blowing the clouds at a speed faster than the plane flying above them.

The air suddenly turned crisp and hauntingly silent, no movement in the leaves, until a hailstorm of crystal ice rained down, bouncing off the emerald-green carpet below.

The sun emerged again, a master lighting designer, painting a circular rainbow over Mt. Rainier. And then the miracle, a gentle fall of snow, the great wet flakes melting on the tops of the bushes and pine cones before I could confirm that each one was indeed a different shape.

It was a cavalcade, a show of natural beauty so awesome that I stood transfixed, unable even to pull out my camera. This happened the day after I hurt my knee. It was worth it.

For the next two weeks I sat and moved about slowly in my house. I was essentially alone. I wanted to be. I needed to be. Mike shopped for me and cleaned; but otherwise I just sat looking out at the mountain, writing, talking on the phone every now and then, thinking, and doing my therapeutic exercises.

San Francisco was down the pike a way. I would be ready for it somehow. For now I needed to reflect.

My injury seemed like a mini-death to me. It made me

more compassionate of people who were *really* in trouble—really dying. I was trying to learn from them. There were so many who were dying these days. What were they going through? I had tried to understand whenever I talked to them before. Now I really *cared.*

Each friend who was dying was engaged in his own program of assessment. What had life meant and why?

And in every single dying friend, the principal concerns were with parents. There was the desperation, confusion, and compulsion to work out the conflicts with their parents before leaving. Nothing and no one seemed more important. Even if it meant attempting to do it though the parents had passed away, they tried to reach into the grave in order to understand. And in every case, they felt their sickness had either been motivated or exacerbated by low self-esteem generated, to a large extent, by the parents.

"My parents didn't love themselves, so I never learned how either."

"My parents didn't love me, so how could I love me?"

There was always the understanding that the parents had been children of parents who suffered the same self-loathing and fear. The apple never fell far from the tree.

With my problems now I found myself thinking more and more about my father. I remembered when he was dying (he hung on for six months longer than expected), he spoke constantly of his parents and their parents. He became obsessed with his mother's side of the family, trying to figure out how she came to be the way she was. His father's passivity was a source of great pain for him and was probably, in the final analysis, the most difficult aspect of his childhood to understand. The tyranny of the passive was elusive, rendering one profoundly guilty if anger over it was expressed. So my father's obsession became the Family Tree.

At the end, he talked constantly of the talent that Warren and I possessed. It was a mystery to him. Where did it come from? He never saw himself as the source of any of it. "Must be your Scotch–Irish genes somewhere way back there," he'd say. And then he'd pull out another book on our family lineage.

I found it so symbolically touching that he died of leukemia—a blood disease—blood symbolizing the family. His heart and lungs were strong—heart symbolizing the soul (the masters believe the soul resides in the heart chakra) and the lungs symbolizing the belief in God (God being in the very air we breathe).

No, my Dad had damaged blood. His parents had let him down and given him a hard lesson to understand. Their parents had done the same thing. It was a never-ending lesson in finding one's self-esteem. I knew my grandparents and had even witnessed some of the dramas between them. But the emotional hooks weren't there for me. My emotional hooks were with *my* parents, just as Daddy's were with his.

I watched his sister, Ruth, at his funeral. She sat ramrod straight, the image of their mother. There was a kind of pioneer resilience but no tears. She had come from stock where there appeared to be little joy and no expressed sorrow. Life must go on. Individual pain and suffering were part of it, simply to be endured. She and my father had never made peace with each other either.

I never understood what their problem was. Sibling conflicts can only really be understood by the individuals involved. I wondered if my daughter would ever be able to fathom the intricate dance of deep sibling love and rivalry that went on between Warren and me. *We* could barely deal with the profound sensitivities of our feelings for each other. Much of that was because we couldn't see our parents clearly.

And now one of them was gone, taking with him some of the clues.

I always wondered what kind of weather we'd have on the day of my father's funeral. It rained—a cleansing, peaceful rain.

The doctors from Johns Hopkins spoke. They said they each learned from his humanity, humor, and talent for friendship. They praised him as a great teacher and educator; but more than anything, they admired his twinkle and spunk as a human being.

Mother didn't cry. She was as resilient as Ruth. She couldn't sit up as ramrod straight, but the steel in her backbone was not bent by much.

But when Daddy was buried in the ground, Mother broke down. "We can't just leave him out here alone in the rain," she cried. "The dear old soul needs me."

That had been true for the fifty-five years they were together.

Mother was proud there had never been another man in her life and believed, probably correctly, that Dad's flirtations were all bluster.

They had choreographed an intricately patterned dance of life for themselves, literally shutting out anyone else who might even come close to understanding their rhythm. Their arguments were legendary, and each of them said, "At least it prevents boredom." I remembered hearing someone describe boredom once as unenthusiastic hostility.

I remembered the afternoon Mother finally came to see Daddy in the hospital. She had put it off, because it was too painful for her. He never asked her to come. They communicated through the nurses, never even through Warren or me. Their dance continued to the end.

She leaned down to kiss him. He responded by lifting his

head mischievously. I snapped their picture, which I still have—a memento testifying that they were central in each other's lives. They were the costars in their drama. The children, and in fact other relatives, were supporting players waiting in the wings.

When Mother turned to take a chair and tripped, she nearly toppled the IV machine. Daddy screamed, "The woman is trying to kill me. Get her out of here before she succeeds. She never was any good with goddamn machinery. Don't let her back in here. I want to stay alive."

I shrank up against the window. So did Sachi. The stars were acting out their dramatic comedy.

Mother said nothing at first. Instead she pulled herself up and, as though nothing had happened, smoothly rounded the edge of his bed and sat down.

Having gotten no rise out of her, Daddy rang his little bell for the nurse, who arrived immediately. "Get this woman out of here," he ordered. "She's too damned clumsy to be around sick people."

The nurse looked over at Mother in sensitive confusion. Mother just smiled. Crossing one leg over the other and tapping her foot against the foot of his bed, she said, "Ira, I tripped over Sachi's purse, that's all. There is no damage done."

I looked over at Sachi. She was holding her purse. I surreptitiously looked under the bed where Mother had tripped. There was nothing there.

Oh God, I thought. This was the dance I grew up with. Could I possibly execute my own steps with the same dexterity as these two? At least when I tripped, I didn't blame it on anything!

As soon as Mother left, Daddy's eyes filled with tears and he said, "I just love to open my eyes and see her face sitting at the foot of the bed." It was George and Martha, straight out of *Who's Afraid of Virginia Woolf?* I'd probably play Martha someday as a way to figure them out.

Daddy once asked me if I thought death would be like taking a flying leap at a marble wall. The image was so funny to me that my metaphysical answers paled in comparison. He went on to say that he had been taught many things in his life except for the most important. "Nobody ever taught me how to die. I want to do it correctly, but I don't know how." I was stunned at this self-judgment even in death.

Then he turned around and eloquently described his certainty that God was in everything. He said he could see the colors around our heads and bodies, around the flowers and plants in his room. He said he didn't believe in a separated heaven or hell—that everything was with us *now*.

Another time he asked Mother to sit and read "Invictus" to him. She cleared her throat and, adopting one of her subtle performance modalities, held his hand and spoke: "I am the master of my fate; I am the captain of my soul." He squeezed her hand and tears slid from under his eyes.

As if on cue, his nurse had walked in. Daddy looked up at her. "The piss brigade is here," he said. "She's going to take my piss bottle now so I can contribute to the sewer system of the town."

The nurse laughed, evidently used to his broad-country humor, and handed him some juice. He took a sip.

"Do you have a moose tied up outside?" he asked.

She looked confused. "No, why?" she asked.

"Because this juice tastes like moose piss, that's why."

Now she blushed and put her hand under the sheets to retrieve his urine bottle. Daddy looked up at her with sadistic glee.

"You find it," he said. "You probably know more about

taking it out than I do." She blushed again. "I want you to line this bottle with fur," he said, "so I'll feel right at home."

My father's bathroom sense of humor was even more basic than what I'd heard from Himalayan mountain people.

"There must be a man out there with a mighty sore pecker," he'd say to one of the nurses.

"Why?" they'd ask. "Why?"

"Because there's at least four pregnant nurses running around," he'd answer.

That kind of humor drove my mother round the bend. "I don't think it's funny at all, Ira," she'd say. "You are vulgar and repulsive."

He'd counter by saying he was never going home, because she had ripped his little handle seat off the toilet. "When I sit to take a dump, my goddamn balls dangle in the water. You could at least wait until I die. Then you can do whatever you want with my balls. I never used them anyway."

It went on like that—the constant sexual vaudeville. Once when Sachi brought her fiancé home to meet Mother, Mother wouldn't let him stay in the house. "The neighbors will talk," said Mother.

"About what?" I asked.

"About your daughter sleeping with a man she's not married to."

"How will they know?" I asked. "Maybe they'll sleep in separate rooms."

"The neighbors will know by the way she walks," said Mother.

I suppose her rich sexual fantasy necessitated her conservative attitudes. Anyway, Sachi and her fiancé had to go to a motel. Mother never relented.

"It's my tradition," she said, "and I'll never change. I don't want to. So stop trying to make me into one of your Californian loose women."

She wasn't posing either. She meant it.

"I have to hang on to my traditions," she said. "I have nothing else left."

I could see her point.

A few days after Daddy's funeral, it snowed. The fresh flowers on his grave froze.

I went for a walk in the snow. I headed for the neighborhood around the school where I grew up. As the snow crunched under my shoes, I could feel Daddy with me in all his wicked, funny splendor.

"Your mother is fragile," he'd say. "She doesn't know a goddamned thing about machines. She doesn't know about much of anything."

He used to say they had a bargain that she'd go first, because then he'd be the lonely one. But it hadn't worked out that way. He had tried to hang on and live up to the agreement, but maybe they both knew *he* was the one who couldn't have been left alone.

I walked to the school where I had first gone out for track. I remembered how much I loved the broad jump and high jump. I had had an appendicitis operation just before the track meet. I was back on the field in a week, which upset Daddy because he was worried that I would tear muscles and not be able to dance.

Now, as I walked in the snow, I slipped my hands in my pockets. I had put one of Daddy's pipes in there. He had a huge collection of pipes, which we would now wrap carefully in old cigar boxes and store. He had once written a small essay on his reasons for loving pipes. His father had smoked a pipe.

He loved the rich mellow smell of the tobacco. His dad wouldn't even let him hold a pipe, so Daddy took to smoking his toothbrush. When he was old enough, he graduated to the real thing and couldn't collect enough of them.

Then he said he graduated from pipes to pens. He had pipes and pens collected from all over the world. They represented so much more than what they were, which I suppose is what motivated him to write essays on their importance. I was struck, when I read them, by the pitiful awe these objects held for my father. Why couldn't he want more than a new pipe or a new pen?

He loved watches too. He owned about thirty of them when he died. His father had been a watchmaker and perhaps Daddy needed to be close to what his father had been close to, an object-link to substitute for the imperfect emotional link.

The reverence with which my father appreciated any small gift brought from an exotic place was a joy to behold. He would turn an ivory statue, or a Russian icon, or a mosaic from Tunisia over and over in his hands, appreciating its beauty, its human craftsmanship, and its cultural expression.

He'd hold small cuff links up to the light, examine them for hours, return to them later, wax eloquent on their exquisiteness, then put them in a drawer and never wear them. He was "saving" them, he'd say.

I remembered he told me that his parents had strapped a money belt underneath his clothes when they sent him off to college. The world was cruel; people might steal. He would always have protection if he needed it.

He was such a sensitive, fragile man, using his humor to bluster his way through any given situation, cracking jokes to cover his own uncertainties—and yet the first to notice someone else's discomfort. But he would tie the tails of a dog and cat together just to see them fight.

I continued to walk. There was the drugstore where I used to slurp a cherry Coke while waiting for my boyfriend to walk me home. No one was on the street now. A blanket of snow silenced the air, muffling the cries of children somewhere in the distance.

My father had just died, and children were laughing. The tears froze on my cheeks. I could see him climbing from his old Lincoln Continental, dapper in his plaid sports jacket and tan slacks, his hat placed squarely on his head like a Russian general secretary.

He'd sidle up to the school fence to observe how I was running or jumping. If I was engaged in "love talk" with my boyfriend, I'd hear about it later at the dinner table.

"I can understand screaming in the halls," he'd say, "screaming until someone paid attention. I can't understand holding hands and necking."

That was about the gist of it too. Desperate frustration was familiar to him. Peaceful love was beyond his comprehension.

I trudged in the snow down to the creek, which had been the scene of adolescent excursions into lovemaking for me and many of my friends. Where were they all now? Did the death of Ira O. Beaty mean anything to anybody else? How could a man like that, with so much rich and important talent for contradiction, be ignored?

I thought of Willy Loman in *Death of a Salesman*. "Attention must be paid." If no one else paid any attention to him, I would bring him to life in the pages of my books and in the conversations of my life. He would not go unnoticed regardless of his reluctance for recognition. He was half the reason I was who I was. It was because of him that I needed to tear away the shackles of my own insecurities and grow up. He might have initiated those insecurities, but I was going to break the pattern.

He had given me a gift—a catalyst for insight. And I was going to unwrap it and hold it up to my own light for examination. It would never go back in a drawer. I would use it and savor it and hopefully understand the spirit in which it was given until I was more clear of my own contradictions.

I walked for an hour or two, feeling my father with every breath I took. Attention would be paid. I'd see to that. I didn't know then how far I'd go.

When I returned to the house, Mother and I had dinner. We didn't speak of Daddy. We spoke of trivial things. Underlying our meal was the understanding that I had to leave. I had miles to go and promises to keep.

I went to my room to pack. I looked over the bed to where my father's picture hung. It was gone. When I looked behind the bed it was on the floor, having fallen off the wall somehow. Perhaps he was removing himself from the house so we could get on with our lives.

"I will always be sitting next to your green chair," he told Mother. "Just when you think you're the loneliest for me, look over to the rocking chair. I'll be there watching you, listening to you, loving you."

Mother had gently laughed so that she wouldn't sob. "Your Daddy can be so touching and sweet," she said later.

He had wanted her to come and lie down in bed next to him. "I know," she said. "He's been trying to get me to do that for years. It's nothing new." She went on, "You can bet when he starts that lovey-dovey stuff that he has something up his sleeve, and I'm just not going to fall for it."

I retrieved the picture from the floor and put it back on the wall, knowing Warren wanted it there. It had fallen down once before, and Warren feared someone had taken it.

I stood, looking at the rest of the room. This was the bed

I had slept in for most of my childhood; my recurring dream had started in this bed. I had brushed my hair one hundred strokes per night at this dressing table and had opened the closet many times resolving to clean it out and throw the past away. Somehow I had never been able to do it. It now hung with clothes Mother kept. Some I had given her from Hong Kong, from Paris, "from all the great capitals of the world," she told her friends. Others I remembered her wearing when she was forty.

I squeezed the pineapple knobs of the four-poster mahogany bed. A mound of snow fell from a tree outside the open window. Oh, how my need for open windows had disrupted our family. I couldn't breathe in the claustrophobia of a room with tightly shut windows. In my bedroom, regardless of weather, I was allowed to have them open—in the heat of summer and in freezing winter.

I breathed deeply and looked around, not knowing when I'd be coming back but certain that when I did, I'd be overwhelmed by entering the home my father would never be a part of again.

Slowly I left my room and walked through the living room. I passed the Wedgwood bowls, crystal glasses, and the George Mason wedding breakfast table. These were items deeply treasured by Mother—by Daddy too. But suddenly, for me, their worth and meaning had been put in proper perspective.

Gypsy, Mother's red-haired cat, scampered across the carpet. "I don't want a cat, Shirl," she had said. "If I learn to love it, what would I do without it?" Maybe it was true that every time we love we die a little.

I gave her the cat anyway, and it was now going to be her solace. She had a couple to take care of her; but in the long lonely hours of the night without Daddy, Gypsy would curl up against her cheek and remind her that she was loved and needed.

I went to Mother's green chair. She sat alone, as though waiting for her execution. My departure was going to be painful for her, and I didn't know how to begin to make it any easier. She looked up at me. Her eyes were a milky-gray color as she looked deep into mine. Then her face twisted in anguish, and she reached up and clutched at me with her fingers.

"I don't want you to go," she sobbed. I kneeled down and gently put my arms around her. Mother held me tightly for a moment, and then she pulled away and looked at her watch.

"I don't want you to miss your plane either," she said. "You must go and do your work." Tears still flooded her eyes, but she straightened herself up.

"I love you, Mother," I said. "I love you more than I can say."

"I know," she answered. "I'm sorry I was cranky with you the night the wind blew the trees so hard. I'm sorry."

I tried to hug her again, but she wouldn't even lift her arms in return. I felt her detach herself. She would handle this the only way she knew how.

I slowly stood up and walked to the door. Just as I was about to leave the room, I turned around; perhaps I should stay another day. But she waved good-bye as though I had already disappeared into thin air.

I had cried silently all the way to the airport.

The ice-and-gold days of recovery and remembering in Washington were over. I returned to Los Angeles a few days before opening in San Francisco to take voice lessons and to work with

Mary and Damita Jo. My body had lost a lot of strength and I was concerned about my stamina, but my knee seemed to be progressing nicely.

I was in my apartment in Malibu doing my exercises before Mary and Damita arrived, feeling good about my progress and doing a few pliés to warm up. I went into demi-plié and made a slight turn to the left, a barely perceptible turn. My knee went out again—and something tore in the back of my knee. I buckled to the floor, the pain excruciating. I couldn't believe what I'd done, and began to curse out loud and talk to myself.

Just then the doorbell rang. It was the two girls. Thank God they immediately realized what had happened. I popped the kneecap back into place, and in a mad rush they raided the icebox freezer and applied the lifesaving chunks of frozen water to my knee again.

Now I only had three days to heal. Damita explained that she had had her own knee injury for years now. It was something she was very much aware of all the time and now, it seemed, I would have to become aware of mine for a long time to come, maybe the rest of my dancing life.

She went on to explain that during rehearsals she had to rechoreograph in her mind everything that Alan gave us to do, in order to imperceptibly alter the position of every step so that she could accomplish it without pain and to prevent her kneecap from popping out. She said neither Alan nor the rest of the dancers ever knew or noticed that she had such a problem. I certainly didn't. She then began to show me how I would have to take the show from the top, and with every single movement of the body I would need to reposition myself so that I too would be safe.

The next day we went into a rehearsal hall, and for three days we analyzed every move, every step, and every position so that I could work around the kneecap injury. It was like learning the show all over again.

Some of the singing numbers were more treacherous than the dancing, because the movements were seductively subtle. I had never realized the intricacies involved with body movement in such a refined way. I had been free about it before, so attention wasn't necessary. As I worked, I had to concentrate on every shift from one leg to the other, every slight turn of balance; and, of course, every harsh and athletic move. But the danger points were the subtle ones.

I relearned the show from a handicapped point of view. It was an experience that was to be ongoing.

I went to Dr. Leroy Perry, a sports chiropractor, scientist, and inventor who runs the International Sportsmedicine Institute in Los Angeles. We talked about my training program with Mary. We tried to figure out what was going wrong. He treated me with ultrasound and ionized electricity, which he administered to many of the injured Olympic and professional athletes he takes care of.

My biggest fear now was fear itself. I didn't know how I'd react to performance energy, the bright lights that affect your sense of horizon and balance, and the quickness that always accelerates when you have to mentally be a few beats ahead of the music and the audience. The need to be careful would slow me down, make me tentative, cause me to hold back, and possibly make me look like I couldn't dance at all.

Perry bandaged my leg using a figure-eight East German technique, which insured that the kneecap would stay in place. I knew I would be favoring the right leg, so I needed to build up the strength in my left one with weights and exercises.

Then Dr. Perry and I tried to figure out why I really went down. We concentrated on my shoes. A dancer who is strong, as I was, should be able to correct an imbalance in mid-movement. I had not been able to do that. Perry wasn't satisfied that it was an accident. He said there is always an explanation for what happens, and he was determined to find it.

He examined the orthotics that I wore in my shoes when I danced. They seemed fine, yet perhaps I had corrected my body alignment enough with my exercises, therefore possibly did not need the orthotics. Perry wondered if perhaps I was overcorrected now. That was a possible explanation.

He called Dr. Arnold Ross, sports podiatrist, to reevaluate the orthotics. The corrections were made. Dr. Perry felt that as a dancer I was nothing more than a high performance athlete, and all body movements—posture and muscle development (biomechanics, as he calls it)—had to be analyzed and corrected as soon as possible to ensure a safe yet maximum performance. He understood I was an athlete and that I could become my own worst enemy by overcompensating.

He treated me for three days in between rechoreographing, and then I went to San Francisco. I knew I would have fun there, where I had many friends, and the people usually liked my shows.

We loaded in the equipment, and I went on the stage to try the floor early. I walked every inch of it, adjusting once again to the extension out over the orchestra pit. I remembered this Orpheum Theater from six years before. After about a week, the extension begins to sink. For us dancers, it was like dancing on the Burma Road. As I examined it, I scrutinized it from the Seattle stage point of view. Had my heel really gotten caught in the crevice of the extension as I believed?

Some of the dancers began to arrive. I hadn't seen anyone since Seattle. They were worried about me, saw my bandage, and said they'd be there to back me up regardless of what happened.

Gypsies are really in their element when there is a crisis.

They have a crisis mentality. They had also had a long rest and were longing to move again. After much discussion, they and I determined that I had been dancing too far upstage for my heel to have gotten caught. It was something else.

We redid some of the harder, more athletic steps so that the visual effect wasn't disturbed but they were also not so difficult to execute.

I had forgotten some of the lyrics; but when I got out of my own way, my lips seemed to form the right words involuntarily. There was muscle memory in the lips, as well as the legs and feet.

We ran down the show and that night we did a preview. It went fine. I tried to conceal my bandage but knew I'd have to dance on it for a few weeks. The TV news cameras panned down to the bandage, naturally, and that was the story.

The next night we opened. It was wonderful. I favored the knee, but I don't think anyone noticed. The reviews were good and I was set to have a fabulous run, having learned a lot in the meantime.

Then it happened again. Only this time it wasn't my right knee. In the middle of a number, I turned my left ankle and sprained it! The pain shot through my foot so I couldn't finish the number the way it was choreographed. I sort of stood in the middle of the dancers and waved my arms around. They covered for me.

After the show, I couldn't walk. I tried to put weight on it, but I absolutely couldn't. I only had two legs. Which one was I going to favor now?

I called Dr. Perry. He was appalled. "Something's not right about all this," he said. "There is some reason these things are happening; send me a pair of your shoes again."

I sent a pair by Federal Express immediately. He went over them again with the orthotics doctor. Then he called the shoemaker. To the eye they looked fine, but Perry wasn't satisfied. He related the conversation with the shoemaker to me:

"Listen," he said, "is there anything about her shoes that's different from what you've always done for her?"

"Only the sole," answered the shoemaker.

"The sole?" asked Perry. "What do you mean?"

"Oh," he said. "I thought they looked too clunky when we lowered the heel, so I beveled the sole to make them more cosmetically beautiful."

"You beveled the sole?"

"Yes," said the shoemaker. "It looks beautiful, don't you think?"

Perry hesitated. "A beveled sole? That means she rocks back and forth, side to side, doesn't it?"

"Yes," said the shoemaker

"Well, how much less control of the floor does she have as a result of the bevel?"

"About seventy percent less, but as the shoe breaks in she will have more contact," he answered.

Perry exploded. "You're telling me she's out there dancing with only thirty percent control of the floor under her?"

"Well, yes," said the shoemaker. "Does that matter?"

"Matter?" said Perry. "She's out there dancing on ice skates. It's the same equivalent. She only has the center of the sole to rely upon. No wonder she's injuring herself. Her feet are continually looking for one hundred percent control of the floor. You can't do what she does *without* one hundred percent control of the floor under you!!"

"Oh," said the shoemaker. "I'm sorry. I didn't know."

So now we had it. Perry instructed him to put a wedge on the bottom of each shoe to even out the balance. I could feel the difference immediately. One of the benefits of working with Dr. Perry is that he relates to me from a doctor/coaching point of view and demands that his athletes have efficient biomechanics of good posture. Correcting the shoes would enable me to perform more efficiently. The problem now was that I had to wear an ankle brace and a knee brace. I looked like a veteran from the Long March.

I went into a series of exercises for my left ankle, knee, and back. Dancers can't exercise or stretch too much—we must stay in maximum shape, yet maintain flexibility. My San Francisco run seemed to consist of exercising both sides of my body during the day. I used the Perry-Band, an elastic band exercise system used by athletes around the world, to keep my muscles strong; and another Perry product, the Orthopod, a forward inversion exercise device to keep my hamstrings, buttocks, and back stretched out while keeping my inner thighs and abdomen strong so that I could look captivatingly balanced every night. I always keep the Orthopod outside my dressing room door to remind me to stretch.

I had given myself the final lesson. Ankles were not only about flexibility and support. They enabled one to stand on the toes, lift the head high, and take command of looking up and over life. When one's footing was sure, that was possible. When one had only thirty percent surefootedness, it wasn't.

I had not been one hundred percent sure of myself and my show. I had been thirty percent sure of it. I had gone down while attempting to "turn" it around. In that act, I had learned what I had been reflecting from the very beginning, that I had drawn all of this to myself to mirror my own insecurity. Perhaps my insecurity had come from not totally committing to the belief in myself. Would I ever overcome the conditioning my father had instilled in me? He might have died peacefully, having become love, but his face and twisted insecurities had been etched on my consciousness forever.

After San Francisco I gratefully returned to my home in

the Pacific Northwest. Needing time to reflect again, I took careful walks in the fields around the house; not that I could yet climb the mountains or visit my beloved river, but peace lived in that place and some of it would seep into me. I wondered how much more the beavers had expanded the pond below. Which trees had succumbed to the latest cleansing windstorm? Had mischievous teenage boys burned campfires, endangering the wildlife?

I could feel the weather change. There had been less and less rain every summer for the last seven years. I remembered the scientists at the Davos Conference on Economics the previous year warning the CEO's of the world of the global warming already in effect. They predicted that within ten years the temperate zones around the planet would resemble desert climates and the northern latitudes would be temperate.

As I walked the fields in the first week of April, it was eighty degrees—unseasonably warm. I was more sensitive to the imbalance occurring in nature because my own personal balance had been thrown off. Because of what was happening to me I was more aware of the misfortunes of others.

We and our planet were in trouble, and the awareness we needed to put ourselves back on track was not particularly high. Death seemed to be lurking around every fork in the road, whether from disease or from economics, famine, drought, or crime. I was becoming more and more acutely aware of what was happening in our world. I felt it personally. It began to frighten me. Relationships were in trouble, marriages crumbling, parents and children unable to communicate, teachers and students living two different realities.

We all seemed to be walking contradictions. None of us really, really knew what we were doing or why. So, of course, we couldn't really understand anyone else—governments out of touch with those they governed; police becoming as violent as the criminals they arrested; church and state corrupt; disease outstripping medical knowledge. I could see why the prophets of doom and gloom abounded.

I reckoned, as I walked the fields of green grass and wild flowers, that none of the answers would come from the outside anyway. I was in effect trying to go within myself to establish a real and lasting support system. My injury had forced me to. I would go as deep as I needed to, to understand what had brought me to this point. Only then would I be in charge of where I was going.

I stopped to peer out over a hill at Mt. Rainier, which was emerging from behind cloud cover. I stepped up on a rock to have a better view. As I did, I felt a painful twinge in the back of my knee. It had become a voice of warning to me. I stopped the pain by bending my knee. "It isn't quite healed," I thought. "I need to be cautious, vigilant—not let my guard down." It was good to have the time to feel a twinge and not be panicked that the audience would see me go down again.

Chapter 10

~ L.A., L.A., L.A.!

IN ANOTHER WEEK I returned to Los Angeles to prepare for my big opening in the city where most of my friends lived. I felt good, strong, and rested. I had been through my tunnel of demons and had come out the other end.

I chuckled to myself at the idea of two psychics and one channeler who had told me that my playing L.A. looked murky and probably wouldn't happen. "Of course," said they, "your individual consciousness can change any dynamic; but from what we see now, your playing L.A. is doubtful at this time."

When asking advice from psychics and teachers from spiritual realms, it is understood that one's consciousness can change destiny. And I *had* changed my consciousness, which would therefore alter the prediction. Of that I was certain. L.A. was on, my ankle was more flexible, and my knee didn't feel as though it held fear. I was going to play the City of the Angels, and more than one of them would be protecting me.

The first event I got through was my birthday. A few close friends of mine gave me a little party and we celebrated. The cake was beautiful with about ten candles on it. When I made a wish and blew on them, two candles remained lit. It caught me by surprise, because I have strong lung capacity. I had to blow several times before the flames were snuffed out. I wondered what that meant.

Sachi, now completely recovered from her surgery, was previewing the play she was in, so she didn't join us until after dinner.

As sanguine as I was about being fifty-six, I was not so at ease about having a party. Unbelievably, I am shy; and when the introductory testimonial speech had been completed (which was touching but difficult for me), I was mercifully saved by a Mexican trio who followed the toast with folk songs and South of the Border joyful noise, even though I felt unfulfilled that I hadn't had time to acknowledge the precious friendships of the people there. I was glad I had taken the time in the afternoon to do my projections for the following year. It put me in touch with people I loved, rather than social appropriateness.

I did my projections every year on my birthday, since I knew that I *owned* the exact moment I was born. And because that energy was mine forever, I wanted to utilize it to create with. It is said that if you visualize what you want in the coming year so acutely that you can taste, feel, hear, see, and love its truth, and accompany that vision with an oral declaration of purpose three times (one for mind, one for body, one for spirit), then let it freely go—the vision will materialize. I had done it every year for the last seven. More often than not, my visualization manifested. And when it didn't, I knew it was because I didn't trust it.

I was becoming more and more aware now that we all need to be more careful about what we think. The positive and the negative are amplified these days and, from what I'm learning, will continue to be as we journey into the nineties and the next century and millennium. The energy of the earth itself has accelerated, and its impact on human consciousness is profound. We are in a speed-up process, whether we admit it or not. The negative is speeding up, as well as the positive. So the old adage "Be careful what you think" rings with truth more now than ever.

Over the years, with each progressive birthday, I am struck by time marching across the faces of my friends, enveloping their bodies, working its influence on their memories and body rhythms, and in general reminding me, through them, that we're all just passing through.

I see my face and body every day in them and in the mirror. The crinkles and loose-fitting flesh creep up on me, sometimes surprising me as though overnight folds belonging to someone else decided to make a frontal assault on my stomach and drip down over my hips. Where did the love handles suddenly come from? What could I do to prevent them? And would it be worth it?

Sagging skin was hard for me to look at. It represented deterioration to me, the incapacity to control time and gravity. And I could never understand, or rather wouldn't understand, why older people who continued to exercise vigorously still suffered the same vanity-stricken fate. Ballet dancers, for example—why did their skin have to sag, even when they continued to dance every day? It seemed unfair. Such physical discipline should be rewarded by the gods.

And the memory loss! How could it be happening to me?

My mother at eighty-six, okay. But *me*? There were times now when I forgot who I was calling. My attention span seemed to extend to no more than twenty seconds sometimes! If I didn't make written notes, I wouldn't remember my schedule for the next day. My car keys? I forced myself to put them in the same place when coming home and leave them there till I left again. I was lucky I remembered what they were for when I found them.

Sometimes I'd wake in the middle of the night and sit up in bed with panic as I tried to remember whether I had taken my vitamins. My mind often wanted to float—cruise—wander—idle in neutral, responding less and less easily to my stringent commands to snap into discipline. I could see myself with very little effort living a quiet, almost reclusive, life—allowing nature to take its course and my body and mind to hover wherever they wanted to be. Perhaps I continued to dance because I knew how fundamentally lazy I could be.

It always amused me that people saw me as a whirling dervish of disciplined overachievement, when in truth, more and more, I preferred doing nothing. Of course, doing nothing for me was feeling so completely blissful in the "moment" that it never occurred to me to address myself to the future. More and more I liked the feeling of channeling time. I remembered how much I loved the philosophical thought that time runs through us, rather than we run through time.

So once again my birthday brought me in touch with my sense of time and bodily mortality. Maybe it was my knee injury that caused me to think suddenly so much about age, for I was well aware that age might have caused the injury. It was not a pleasant thought. I didn't want to admit it. My body had served me like a workhorse. I was not about to put it out to pasture. And yet—and yet.

* * *

The night after my birthday my telephone rang at three-thirty A.M. I heard a voice drawl a kind of comedic cheery hello. It was Debbie Reynolds.

"Well, my dear," she said. "Happy Birthday or whatever."

"Thanks, Debbie," I said. "Happy Birthday to you a few weeks ago. Did you get my flowers?"

"Of course I did, my dear," she said. "I always get your flowers. I got your flowers when you began the picture. I got your flowers when you finished the picture. I got your flowers on opening night with *Molly Brown*. I got all your flowers. I'm here to tell you one thing, though."

"What's that, Debbie?"

"From now on skip the flowers, just send me those wonderful notes."

"Oh," I answered. "Okay."

"Did you know Groucho, dear?"

"Yes, a little. He made me laugh because he was a sexual put-on artist."

"Yep," she said, "that he was. Well, he used to say skip the champagne, skip the caviar, just give me a call! I say to you skip the flowers, I just want to hear what you have to say when you write." She hung up.

We were scheduled to open Tuesday, May 1, in the theater where I had only been once—to see Debbie Reynolds in *The Unsinkable Molly Brown*. That seemed like a good omen.

I went into the rehearsal hall Friday, April 27, with Alan and the dancers. We had been off for three weeks (a long time for a dancer not to wrap the body around steps). Alan wanted to give them notes and change a few things. So they danced in the morning, I the afternoon.

It was glorious to be back. My body felt strong. I had

been thorough with my workout program; and even though I felt the famous twinge intermittently in the back of my knee, I was so happy to be back with my show, knowing that I could depend on it regardless of what happened to the world or the rest of show business, that I found a way of working with the weakness that allowed movements to be altered slightly so as not to aggravate it. The rehearsal went fine.

The crew loaded into the Pantages the next day, Saturday, while we did another brush-up rehearsal in the rehearsal hall. We were scheduled for a dress rehearsal on Sunday and a preview on Monday night.

Alan altered a few steps to make the choreography easier for my knee, just in case. The dancers were coping with their own injuries (hamstrings and lower back).

The windows were open. The sun streamed through. There were honey graham crackers on the table, along with bottles of Evian water. The jokes flew, our bodies whirled, we found new acting attitudes in the steps, and we were having a wonderful time.

Dancers need to dance. We had been off long enough. We were doing the acting section at the end of the choreographer's number. Keith and Blane and I were fooling around, finding new nuances in our interplay.

I did a double turn into Blane, came out of it, and brought my right foot down in a modified fifth position to prepare for the lift. It was a routine step—in fact, it wasn't a step, it was a preparation for a lift. Blane supported me as I sprang into the air from a demi-plié.

Then it happened. The TWINGE became a full-blown tear. I had never felt pain as I did in that moment. And the "moment" seemed to go on and on. It grew. I screamed in midair.

"Oh nooo!" I screamed.

I heard myself scream over and over. Blane gently brought me to the floor, and I tried to lie down. The pain didn't stop. I couldn't believe what was happening. A full two minutes of pain ensued. Nobody knew what to do.

"Ice. . . . Ice. Get some ice." The dancers' eternal cry. "Get ice!"

Keith ran out of the room to find ice. Damita bent over me and asked me to describe the pain, which I did. All the time I thought I was dreaming.

"Is this a bad dream?" I asked the dancers. Alan looked into my eyes. He knew what I was talking about. If we all create our own reality and life is a dream we create through which we learn, then what was going on?

I slapped my thigh, hoping it would wake me up. "Someone tell me this is only a bad dream I've created for myself."

"It's real," said Alan. "It's not a dream. You really hurt your knee."

"What day is this?" I asked, confused about time.

"It's Saturday," said Alan.

My mind raced like a computer. I could skip dress rehearsal the next day, maybe even skip the preview on Monday so that I'd be ready to open Tuesday! I simply couldn't afford to cancel my opening—not after Seattle and San Francisco. People would really think there was something wrong and I was unreliable. I didn't want them to say that I was too old to dance anymore. I tried to move my knee. Regardless of the position, the pain was excruciating.

"Get Dr. Perry," I said desperately. "Tell him to come right away."

Blane rushed to the telephone. People began to make suggestions—maybe the paramedics, maybe an ambulance. In the meantime, all I could think of was getting on that stage at the Pantages regardless of what it took.

The pain began to subside a little. I tried to visualize what had happened inside my knee. The pain was coming from the back of the knee, not the top. It was coming from what had been the "twinge." The whispers, I thought—I hadn't listened to the whispers. Even if I had listened, what could I have done?

Someone moved me to the office where there was a telephone. I called Dr. Perry's wife. She said she'd be hearing from him soon.

The paramedics came with blood pressure equipment and a stretcher. That was definitely not for me, but the young men were sweet about my refusal. They wished me well and said they hoped I'd be able to dance. Oh God, I hated to hear those words.

Mike Flowers had been in rehearsal earlier and had left to go to the theater. He returned, shocked, knowing what this new problem really meant.

I waited for about an hour for Dr. Perry to call but we couldn't find him. Rehearsal was obviously at an end.

Damita took me home and I managed to limp to my car, already finding ways to maneuver my body around the pain.

"Do you think I'll be able to dance?" I asked her in that way of wanting reassurance, even if it wasn't legitimate.

"I don't know," she said. "The important thing is that you get well and don't dance on it too soon. That's all." She was right, but that didn't matter to me.

I put ice on my knee as soon as I got home and waited for Perry. All manner of demonic thoughts rambled and scrambled in my mind, but the heart and core of all of them was the inescapable question: Was this really the end of my dancing career? I remembered a friend of mine coming to see me at the Statue of Liberty Centennial Fourth of July Celebration in New

York, because he believed that was the last time I'd dance. I wondered if he was right.

Of course not, I thought. I've already danced for two months. Did I have some strange muscle dysfunction that prevented me from sensing an injury before it occurred, which had always been the case? Would I have to learn how to sing better, because I'd soon have to take the dancing out of my act? Would the people come? Were they only coming now in order to see if someone my age could still kick?

Maybe I could learn how to act every song ever written so that people would come to hear and see the true meaning of lyrics. I thought of Julio Iglesias. He was a sportsman, as I recalled, and because of an accident he *had* to sing.

Dr. Perry arrived in the middle of my paranoid speculation. "What the hell happened?" he asked. I told him. "Torn meniscus [cartilage]," he said, seeming to understand what had happened right away. "It's probably part of the original injury. We need to do an MRI [Magnetic Resonance Imaging]. Where is your arthrogram from Seattle?"

I told him I'd get all that. What I wanted to know about was my immediate future. Perry was honest. He didn't know. "But I doubt," he said, "that you'll be opening Tuesday night."

I stared at him. "Really?" I asked.

"Really," he answered. "You don't want to injure yourself any further. This should have been taken care of in Seattle."

"What do you mean taken care of?" I asked.

"I don't know. We'll see. We'll know after the MRI. You should have had one done with the first injury. They didn't read the arthrogram properly in Seattle. But then maybe it didn't show the full extent of your injury. We're speculating in the dark now. Have some patience. Remember that previously I told you to go back to work and not give up, as you'd never be able to live with yourself?"

"Yes."

"Well, now I'm saying *don't* go back to work until you are really certain that you won't hurt yourself."

I said nothing.

He taped my leg. "Keep the tape on," he said. "I've put a felt material next to your skin. It draws the heat and inflammation out."

"Can I have a massage?" I asked. "Bonnie is coming. I'm so tense. Every muscle in my body hurts."

"Yes," he answered. "I agree with massage."

I thought of my shoemaker. The man never even realized. I thought of Mary and how she had assured me that I would have a pain-free tour. Pain? I'd settle for a little pain if I could just dance without injury.

Dr. Perry left when Bonnie came. He said he was going to arrange for an orthopedic surgeon to look at me the next day. I needed an MRI and another opinion besides his. A surgeon? "Are you kidding?"

"No," he answered calmly. "First we need to see what's wrong. If orthopedic surgery is necessary, we go in there and see what's going on."

He went on to tell me of all the athletes and dancers he had treated who went through surgery and were more active than ever afterward. I had never been injured before, at least not to the extent that required surgery. I didn't know how to relate to it. Perry nodded in reassurance and left.

As Bonnie began to massage my muscles, my wrapped leg began to throb. The wrapping was on too tight. Impetuously I ripped it off.

"Maybe you can massage the ligaments into shape?" I asked Bonnie.

She nodded. "I can help," she said. "I know that."

While she worked on my knee, I visualized the ligaments and cartilage to be healed. I was determined to get up and dance. Bonnie was insistent that I be cautious, not so much now but for the future.

"You don't want to force yourself now and then screw up your longevity," she said. My longevity? How much did I have left anyway? I never thought I'd be thinking in these terms, but I was.

Bonnie plied and kneaded and gently pummeled my leg from the top and bottom. I felt that I had been correct in removing the bandage tape so she could do it. I was now involved with the fragile dance of instinct. Did I know my body and its requirements better than the doctor? I couldn't answer yes or no. It depended. For tonight massage was, in my opinion, a better idea than the bandage.

While on the massage table, I got manic about the audience who expected me to open. I called Alan.

"How are you, honey?" he asked. "What goes?"

"I'm not sure yet," I answered. "I've been thinking. What about cutting the choreographers' number and putting in some stuff that worked from one of our old shows? Maybe it's time I started thinking about cutting my dancing down anyway."

There was a silence on the other end. Then, "That's possible," he said. "What have you got that we can put in in one day?" I gave him a rundown of material that I knew worked.

"Okay," he said. "Let me get back to you."

I called Mort and told him what I was thinking. He hadn't yet informed the Pantages management of what had happened.

"I knew you'd think of anything to get yourself up on that stage, but let me tell you something. First, I told you before there is nothing worth risking your health for the future;

and second, when people buy tickets to one of your shows they expect you to dance. So *no,* you can't cut the choreographers' number. You just don't open, that's all—not now. Maybe later. Okay?"

"Okay," I said, totally unconvinced.

When I woke up the next morning, my knee felt like a chunk of seized meat. Stiff wasn't the word—seized from the inside. I couldn't put weight on my leg without pain. Perhaps it was just "morning after" trauma, I thought.

I got in my car and drove to the Pantages Theater, where dress rehearsal was scheduled to take place at one o'clock. As I drove over Malibu Canyon and into town via the Ventura and Hollywood Freeways, I tried to project whether I would be making this drive every night for the next five weeks. I couldn't see or feel the answer. Again I thought of the psychics and channelers who had told me L.A. looked doubtful. What was going on? Was everything already written on the wind, or did we create it?

I knew the answer. It's just that when you're involved with the transpiring of events, it's difficult to see your participation in their reality.

I drove up to the stage door of the theater. Slowly I got out of my car. A man rounded the corner, stopped his car, and watched me hobble toward the stage door.

"Hey, Shirl," he yelled good-naturedly. "Are you going to be able to dance?"

I don't know who that man was. But I didn't like him. I'll never forget him. He really pissed me off. I shot him a look in lieu of a bullet.

"Yes, you idiot," I said curtly and turned on my heel, which produced a sharp pain. I hobbled toward the stage door and into the backstage area.

The musicians were warming up. The spotlights were

being focused. The floor had been laid and the costumes were hanging, ready for rehearsal, on my little mannequin center stage.

I didn't know whether the musicians knew, because the dancers hadn't arrived yet. I was scheduled to have a music rehearsal. Gary was there waiting for me, because he wanted to go over the vowel placement in some of my songs.

But people in show business, particularly live theater people, have noses like bloodhounds. They sense trouble out of thin air—all having to do, I think, with keen survival instincts that could spell loss of a job.

The musicians and stagehands saw that I was limping. I couldn't conceal it. But I elected not to discuss anything just yet. I had an appointment for an MRI the next day, and for now I was going to concentrate on the music.

I went through everything. I thought I sounded really good; even the musicians remarked about my voice. "At least something on me works," I answered with sarcasm that was genuine.

I could feel the rhythm of the stagehands and crew accelerate in that supportive way that show business people have of being there for each other in every department when crisis lurks.

The light cues were perfect, the sound (hallelujah!) incredibly pure, and the stage itself felt like a theatrical paradise with sight lines available to every seat in the theater, a sense of intimacy even though seating capacity was three thousand or more, beautiful decor, and an ambiance of theatrical vibrations that seemed to hang in the air from bygone days.

Oh, I wanted so much to play this theater. Why couldn't I have been more certain a few weeks ago? Maybe none of this would have happened.

Alan stepped on the stage from the wings on the left

carrying his dog in his arms. "So?" he asked. "What do you think?"

I told him about the MRI I was going to have on Monday. And by way of making a point, I told him I was going to go through with the opening night regardless.

"Well," he warned, "why don't you get it fixed once and for all; and if it means postponing, then that's what it means."

I turned away from him. If I couldn't accept what seemed to be going on, how would I be with a really serious calamity—like cancer or some horrible car accident? Would I be in the same kind of denial? Or was it positive thinking? And when did positive thinking end and denial begin?

I began to go over some of the dance steps. I could hardly move, but I still insisted. I heard Alan say, "This is a really bad fall waiting to happen."

Dr. Perry arrived. He saw me dancing and raced across the stage. "You shouldn't do this," he said. "You'll really make it worse. I'm telling you. Wait till we find out what's going on."

I didn't listen. Dr. Perry, meantime, arranged for me to have an emergency MRI right away. I wasn't dancing hard or even working into the pain; I was experimenting with the body movement and necessary choreography changes, but I *knew* in my heart that I couldn't go on. I knew that performance energy would be dangerous. Once you get out there, it's as though you're wound up with a ticket on an express train. You don't stop till you pull into the station and it's over.

I made one turn too many and felt another twinge; my leg started to buckle.

Perry yelled at me, came onstage, and grabbed me by the arm. He said, "I've arranged for an emergency MRI and we are going now before you get injured worse!" So I turned in a 360-degree circle, registered everything around me, and wondered how the theater management would react to yet another cancellation.

The MRI is a long tube of a machine. They insert you into it, and it takes pictures of the soft tissue that x-rays can't pick up. I had seen it advertised on *Meet the Press* with a little boy and a teddy bear.

The boy asks his mother, "Will it hurt and can I take Sam [teddy] with me?" The little boy comes out fine and so does Sam. So I wasn't worried.

What they failed to advertise is that such high-technological equipment (to promote good health for Americans) will cost you $1,800 for one set of pictures. To me that was fine. To Mr. and Mrs. America, they have to stay injured.

I was inserted into the tube for eighteen minutes (that was $100 a minute). They put hi-fi music earphones on my ears and told me not to move. That was like saying, "Meditate and whatever you do, don't think of a white elephant." I heard thumping sounds that interfered with the music enough to keep me still.

Dr. Perry was waiting for me when I was finished. We then sat with the diagnosticians at the MRI Clinic.

Their conclusion: I had a severely torn medial (inside) meniscus (cartilage), which was now floating and migrating. I had bone damage to the knee, which they considered far more serious than the torn cartilage, and there was damage to the anterior cruciate, the ligament that controls stability and movement.

"I told you," said Perry. "Someone did not read the arthrogram in Seattle correctly. You danced in San Francisco on pretty serious damage. It's a good thing you were taped."

There was no hope left for me to open on Tuesday. It still hadn't really sunk in. There was the invited preview to consider, plus all the people coming to the opening and party afterwards. Well, I'm having a humbling experience, I told myself, while feeling that what I really wanted to do was crawl into a cave someplace. I could not bear the idea of failing everyone, quite aside from being robbed of the joy of that opening.

Old gypsies like me prided ourselves on "being there." We were beings of reliability, completely dependable, would always come through in a crunch. To deny and defy that would either crush my spirit or make me grow.

The next morning Perry arranged for me to have a consultation with a surgeon who was available for emergency problems. We knew we would seek several opinions. But we'd start here. His name will stay our secret, because he belonged on a TV series instead of in an operating room. He was gracious enough to see me right away, but I sort of wished he had been too busy. His personality wasn't designed to inspire the greatest of confidence.

Mort and Perry went with me. Mort had been an athlete in college and had gone through his own series of football injuries.

Dr. X was a man who was chained to his moveable chair on wheels. He never rose to make a point or walked to demonstrate. He did, however, apparently feel the need to race around on his chair, talking constantly. A scriptwriter would be hard-pressed to capture his manner and dialogue.

First he rode all over the examining room on his chair with wheels, going to his wall telephone to take a call from his nurse, who was evidently instructing him in something he was to do. When he finished the conversation, he rode back to me sitting on the examining table and said, "You girls are certainly smarter than we are, aren't you? Now, let's see that beautiful leg of yours."

I was fascinated to hear such an opening line from a man who was a surgeon, and apparently a pretty good one.

"I really enjoyed you in *Can-Can*," he said, endearing himself to me even more. "Do you still do that kind of kicking? I can see why you fell down!" He laughed uproariously. I was thinking Ed Asner would be good to play him in the TV series.

"Well, pull up your knickers," he directed me, "and let's see what you've done to yourself. At least there's no blood. I keep them laughing in the Emergency Room," he said. "It's just the way I am."

It sure was.

I pulled up my slacks as he wheeled himself around in front of me. I looked at Perry. He rolled his eyes. Mort was already looking out the window. I knew he was going over other surgeons in his mind.

Dr. X squeezed my right knee. His touch was worse than the pain. "How's that feel?" he asked. "Does it feel like you'll ever dance again?"

I wanted to kick him in the crotch, but he wasn't standing.

"I guess my dancing again depends on what you tell me to do," I answered, opting for playing straight in lieu of what the alternative could be.

"The decision is yours," he said, looking up at me with a smile on his face.

"Mine?" I asked.

"Well," he went on, "I'll bet you're good at making decisions, except for how to keep yourself from falling down." He laughed again, overcome with enjoyment at his natural "comedic" talent for relieving tension.

Dr. Perry moved right in to try to salvage the situation, since he was responsible for my being there.

"We've done an MRI," said Perry. "Maybe you'll want to talk to the diagnosticians at the clinic who've read the pictures. They are concerned about bone damage, which is clearly more serious than a torn medial meniscus. We were wondering how serious the bone damage is."

Dr. X wheeled himself to the wall phone again. He picked up the receiver above him. "What's their number?" he asked. Why a surgeon asking for someone's phone number seemed so inept, I didn't know. It just added to what was a budding maniacal mistrust on my part.

Perry gave him the number, which he gave to his nurse. He wheeled around a few times, no doubt in deep surgical thought. Mort never cracked a smile. Perry crossed his arms as though he was either disgusted or protecting himself from a body blow. Granted, I wanted to throw one, but not at him necessarily.

The call came through. Dr. X introduced himself and went on to listen to the results of the MRI. He talked some medical–surgeon talk with them but not without a parting shot.

"Well, the little lady's sitting right here; she'll decide." He hung up. He wheeled himself back toward me. The thought occurred to me that he might actually be a paraplegic. Maybe he *couldn't* walk.

He felt my knee again. "Well," he said, "I use a general anesthetic during surgery, so which do you prefer?"

"What do you mean you'd use a general anesthetic? Why not a local?"

He smiled. "Because you might move and that would be bad."

"Why?" I asked, feeling that I was on a sadistic roll with him.

"Well," he said, seeming to need the "well" prefix before

every sentence he uttered. "I use instruments, and if you move I might make a bone indentation which would be worse than what you've already got with your bone."

"It is really serious, this bone thing?" I asked.

Dr. X cocked his head. "Well, you've been using these beautiful knees of yours for many years. There's bound to be some grinding down of the bone if you've danced on it for as long as you have. We all get ground down sooner or later."

I told him that I hadn't been dancing for twenty years before I decided to go back on the stage at forty. There was a twenty-year gap with no intense athletic activity. He didn't hear me.

"So after you've danced for fifty-six years, you have to expect some damage," he insisted.

Oh well, I thought. Maybe just being alive this long pounding cement pavements can cause damage.

"But," he added, oblivious to anything I seemed to be saying, "it's your choice."

"What's my choice?" I asked.

"The kind of anesthesia you want," he answered.

"So you're saying I definitely need surgery?"

"Sure," he answered, as though the knife was the solution to everything. "How's ten o'clock in the morning?"

"Tomorrow?" I asked, hardly believing that I was continuing to play this ridiculous charade with him.

"Yep," he answered, "and I promise I won't move if you don't!"

I looked over at Perry, who was so nonplussed he sat down.

"Dr. X," said Perry, "give us your reading on this bone problem. As you heard, one of the clinical diagnosticians wasn't as alarmed as the other. What's your position on it?"

Dr. X looked over at Perry, who was now at his eye level. "You could always do a bone scan. That would tell you more. You might even find more hot spots in the body."

"What's a bone scan?" I asked.

"You have radioactive isotopes injected into the bloodstream. Where there are hot spots—showing damage—the isotopes register."

"I'm going to willingly have myself injected with radioactivity in order to find out how sick my bones are? The radioactive isotopes would make me sick, wouldn't they?"

"Maybe," said Dr. X. "But you drink a lot of water, and it doesn't last long."

"Can you arrange the bone scan immediately, should we elect to do it?" asked Perry.

Dr. X said he could arrange it at the hospital just next door. "Just walk across the street, and you can do it within a few hours."

I jumped off the table. "Let's go talk," I said. "Thanks, Doctor, you've been very enlightening. I thank you for your time, your expertise, your humor, and for proving to me that the TV networks in this country know what they're doing when they use hospital characters like you to pull ratings. You must be very popular with your patients and staff, because I know you'd be a big hit on TV."

Dr. X sprang from his wheels. "Do you think so?" he asked. "I know I can always keep them laughing in Emergency. That's probably harder than TV, don't you think?"

"Yes, I think," I answered. "I think, therefore I'm going now."

"Okay," said Dr. X cheerily. "Let me know what you decide. Remember, if you don't move, I won't move!" He laughed us all the way to the elevator.

I was now a full-fledged member of those American citizens increasingly dependent on the idiosyncratic expertise of the medical profession. It didn't matter if you were a celebrity or not. In fact, perhaps I would have been spared his humor if he hadn't been compelled to perform for a performer.

On the street outside, I stopped to retrieve my crutches from the trunk of my car. Standing in the sunshine, Mort and Dr. Perry and I had some decisions to make.

First of all, a press conference had been called in the lobby of the Pantages Theater to welcome me back to playing live in Los Angeles. It was now clear to me that I wouldn't be opening. I had to decide how to handle that, plus whether to go through with this bone scan idea or not.

"How about Dr. Finerman?" asked Mort.

Perry agreed. "That's just who I think we should call. I'm sorry about this guy upstairs. He does good work in Emergency, which is exactly where he should stay. Finerman is excellent . . . UCLA orthopedic surgeon, head of the Orthopedic department. Doesn't care about publicity . . . understated. In any case, we should get his opinion next step. I need a telephone."

The three of us made our way to the bone scan lobby and sat down.

"The press conference is in forty-five minutes," said Mort. "I told Stan Sieden [manager of the Pantages] it didn't look good, but who's going to handle telling the press?"

"Okay," I said. "I'm not going to do the bone scan until after I get Finerman's opinion of what's happened to me. I'll eat anything but not radioactive isotopes, unless I have to. I'll go over to the Pantages and tell the press myself. I don't want any *National Enquirer* mystery speculation about what's 'really' wrong with me."

I pulled out my compact and applied my makeup as we sat in the lobby and made plans for what to do with the company if I had to have knee surgery.

Perry returned. "You have an appointment with Dr. Finerman tomorrow morning at nine," he said. "He said it sounds like you'll need surgery."

I asked Dr. Perry to attend the conference in case there were any technical doctor-type questions, and he agreed.

Mort fetched my car so I wouldn't have to walk. He and Dr. Perry followed me to the Pantages.

I parked the car in the space that was allotted for me, slowly climbed out, hobbled to the trunk, retrieved my crutches; and as I made my way into the backstage area, I was more than a little self-conscious that I was making an entrance more befitting Elizabeth Taylor than me. This kind of stuff just didn't happen to me.

My company wouldn't come until one o'clock for a rehearsal. It was now eleven-thirty. The managers of the theater watched me swing toward them step by step on my crutches. Their faces were long and caring, their words sparse, because they really didn't know what to say.

"I'm so sorry, guys," I apologized, "but I'll make it up to you."

"No. No," said Stan. "The only thing that matters is that you get well." He took my arm and led me to the lobby where the press waited. "You know," he said, just as I was about to round the corner, "those guys are going to think these crutches are a joke."

There was total silence as I walked into the room. The cameras whirred and the flashbulbs popped. I stood in front of them having prepared nothing to say. No one asked me a question, so I began to speak.

I said that I had hoped we would discuss my excitement at returning to the L.A. stage, but for now that wasn't in the cards, because I had sustained an injury that would probably require arthroscopic surgery. I went into more detail about the nature of the injury and concluded with saying that mine was a typical athletic injury, and I would probably be able to dance in six weeks.

Someone asked me what I felt about what happened, and I said something about doing it to myself because apparently I needed to take the time to stop and smell the roses, reflect on life, and do what was necessary to insure that I'd still be dancing when I was ninety.

There were really no questions. The journalists either were reflecting on what I had said or didn't much care. They wished me well, and our little get-together was mercifully over.

I went to my dressing room and checked over my costumes while Mort and Stan went away together. An hour later they returned. Stan happened to have five more weeks available at the Pantages, from the end of August till the end of September. They made a deal on the spot. I wouldn't cancel—I'd postpone. The ad would go in the paper the next morning, and no one would lose any work because of me. In fact, because of the later date, we'd probably be able to make a date in Japan.

"Maybe you're guided to do all this," said Mort. "How come it always works out with you, even when there's trouble? Do you know how rare it is for Stan to have a five-week cancellation that perfectly fits your schedule?"

I wasn't surprised. But I did need to look more closely at the harmony that was unfolding.

The musicians and dancers came to my dressing room. Mike Flowers announced the dates for the summer tour after I recovered from surgery. He then added L.A. in September and Japan after that. I was concerned whether everyone would stick with me, so I wanted to assure them that they'd have work.

It was Jack French's birthday, and we celebrated with a

cake and champagne in plastic glasses. The opening night party food had already been ordered, so everyone was invited to come to the party anyway. People began revising their schedules so that they could best use their time off. I could see several of them comparing what work they were guaranteed with me and what they might have to turn down in order to wait.

I asked them to wait if they possibly could, because we were all really a family now. I said I would understand if they couldn't—sort of.

We had a good time saying good-byes, teasing Blane about causing my injury during the lift, and joking that each one of us had created this reality in our lives in order to have the time off. What we each needed to do now was figure out why.

As each person said good-bye and left my dressing room, I thanked him or her for understanding. Cubby O'Brien, our drummer, was most concerned about which hospital I would be in so he could send me flowers.

"Skip the flowers, Cubby," I said. "Just make sure you're waiting to go back to work with me when I get out." He chuckled, but I noticed he didn't say absolutely.

After everyone left, I sat in my dressing room for a while, contemplating surgery and six weeks of rehabilitation instead of the smell of the greasepaint and the roar of the crowd. I quickly called Sachi and we decided to go to a movie.

The next day I had my diagnostic appointment with Dr. Finerman at UCLA.

UCLA Medical Center is an exercise in bureaucracy. If you don't have your "blue card," you can't get through any door, regardless of who may be waiting for you on the other side. Rome could have burned while they fiddled with my blue card. It took nearly half an hour. It didn't matter. Finerman was an hour late himself.

He was a nice, balding, white-haired man—detached, stooped over (from surgical procedures I presumed), and experienced. He looked at the MRI pictures and manipulated my knee. He was gentle and yet no-nonsense. I liked him and I sensed his reputation was accurate.

"I'm not worried about the bone damage," he began. "These MRI pictures are too clever by half. You, and many others I have seen, do just fine with your bones in such a condition. But I *am* worried about your anterior cruciate. That ligament is partially torn and floating, and we may have to cut away half of it. That means you won't have the stability and control you're used to when you land on your leg. But you can live with that, I think. This arthroscopic procedure isn't much. What you should have is a cruciate reconstruction, because you have a laxity [separation] between the femur and the tibia. That means you have an unstable knee and can use all the ligament you can get. But that would mean open-knee surgery, which would keep you off your feet for a year."

"A year!" I gasped.

"Yes. That's a serious reconstruction. But afterward, you wouldn't have any problems, except for the laxity. This way you're fifty percent guaranteed."

"Will it get me through the summer?" I asked.

"I think it's possible," he answered.

"Possible?"

"Yes. You'll have to train hard to build the quadriceps above the knee and the calf and inner thighs. Deflect the pressure on the knee by building up the muscularity around it. Let muscles do what ligaments used to, and you'll probably be fine."

"Can I dance in six weeks full out?" I asked.

He hesitated. "If you pay attention to rehabilitation, you probably can."

I could see he was covering himself all over the place. Dr. Perry was nodding in the background that I could do it.

Dr. Perry demonstrated for Dr. Finerman the Perry-Band exercise device he developed for joint rehabilitation. He was familiar with it and liked it. I felt like an athlete getting ready for the main event.

"When can you operate then?" I asked. "The sooner the better."

"Have you eaten this morning?" he asked.

"Yes."

"Okay. Then sometime tomorrow morning. We'll work it out. Do all your lab work today, and my office will let you know what time tomorrow."

"What kind of anesthetic do you use?" I asked.

"We'll give you a local, and you can watch it if you'd like."

"But what if I move?"

He looked at me like I had two heads.

"Well then you move," he said. "I can move too." Is that what I had heard before?

Finerman straightened up, as though to dismiss Perry and me.

"I'd like to be in the operating room if I could, please," said Dr. Perry. "If I am going to be responsible for her rehabilitation, I want to make sure we don't miss anything, and I understand exactly what her situation is."

Finerman hesitated. Then he said, "Okay. We'll work it out. You'll find it interesting."

That was it then. I'd get my lab work done now and come in the following morning. What I didn't realize was that if you didn't have an injury before working your way through the bureaucratic maze in the hospital, you'd be guaranteed one afterward.

I held on to my precious blue card. I was like a soldier who was told, "When crossing a stream, you may drown; but save your rifle."

I went first to the outpatient surgery department, where they would instruct me further. A nurse took my blue card to register me, while soon after another nurse said I should go immediately to the blood count department.

I began the trek to the blood count floor and got lost. A nice intern took pity on me and directed me correctly. When I arrived at blood count, the room was teeming with people.

I sat down. Several people began to ask for autographs. I knew if I did any that would be it, but everyone stared at me. One guy shrugged; a blond mother smiled. I decided to go to the nurse behind the glass-walled office.

"Yes?" she asked.

"I'm here for my blood work to be done," I said. The roomful of people were now intrigued about what blood problem I might have.

The nurse didn't look up. She reached out her hand. "Your blue card?" she demanded.

"Oh," I said. "The nurse on the sixth floor has it."

"Well, we need it," she assured me.

"Oh. Okay," I said. "I guess I'll have to go get it."

I crutch-hobbled my way back across the floor between screeching kids and open staring faces.

"Someone is supposed to be accompanying you," she said. "Why aren't they?"

I didn't know what to say. Was it somehow my fault that I was alone? Dr. Perry rescued me. "I don't have my blue card," I said. "I'm on my way to get it back from that nurse on the sixth floor."

"I'll get it," he said. "Wait here."

The nurse left. I went back to the teeming room. A buxom, kind-faced nurse came to get me. "We had the same problem with Richard Chamberlain," she said. "Come with me. The last thing you need is autograph hounds. It would be hard for you to write while you're trying to hold yourself up, wouldn't it?"

"Yes," I said gratefully. Just then a male nurse, whom I recognized from the sixth floor check-in, walked up. "You forgot your blue card," he said. He handed it to me.

"Dr. Perry went back to get it for me," I said. "Could you tell him I have it now, not to worry?"

"If I see him I will," said the male nurse.

The buxom nurse led me to a blood-taking booth. There were people and needles, and blood and records, and kids and mothers, and syringes and helpers all over the place. It reminded me of *Soylent Green,* a movie made years ago about overpopulation.

A black male nurse came up to me. "Hi there," he said. "Can I have your registration papers, please?"

"What registration papers?" I asked.

"The ones they were supposed to give you on the sixth floor," he answered. I pulled my newly returned blue card from my pocket. "Will this do?" I asked.

"Not enough," he answered.

"Oh. So should I go back and get the registration papers?" I asked.

He thought a moment and said, "What kind of surgery are you having?"

"Arthroscopic on my knee," I answered.

"Which knee?"

"Right."

"Okay," he said, "here." He handed me a small plastic

bottle. "Let's do the urine now, while I call up to the sixth floor." I thought about Perry, who was now probably frantically looking for my blue card.

"Just around the corner to your left, then right, then left, you'll find the bathrooms," he said.

I set out with my crutches. But I got lost. I hobbled until I returned to my point of origin, where the black nurse took a look at my empty plastic bottle and said, "You couldn't go, huh?"

"No," I said. "If I had had to go, I'd have been in big trouble. I couldn't find the left, right, left doors. I got lost. Where are they?"

"A lot of people have that problem," he said. "One day we'll get it marked out here."

"When?" I asked.

"Well, they're building a bigger wing. Should be finished next year."

"Bigger?"

"Yeah."

"Is that really the answer?" I asked.

"I don't know," he said. "What're we gonna do with all the people?"

I shrugged. I had just purchased Paul Ehrlich's latest, *The Population Explosion*—it was clear what we were all in for.

"Here, let me show you where those bathroom doors are," said the male nurse. He took me part of the way. I, like some old lady in a nursing home, finally found the unmarked doors. I opened one and went in.

With my crutches, it was very hard to turn around. I dropped one. In trying to retrieve it, I dropped the plastic bottle in the toilet, which didn't have a lid. Standing on one leg, I picked the bottle out of the toilet water and wiped it with some toilet paper, which was so thin it kept tearing.

Finally in position, with my crutches placed snugly up against the wall, I unzipped my slacks and did what I had to do into the plastic bottle. When I was done, I wished I had a daisy or rose or something to add the finishing touch.

There was no back on the toilet, so I had no place to put the full bottle while I zipped up my slacks and retrieved my crutches. On my good leg I did a grande plié to the floor, while keeping the bottle steady. My slacks slowly receded down my bad leg. I couldn't pull them up, because I had no free arms.

I finally made it by sitting on the toilet again, placing the bottle on the floor, standing up, zipping up the slacks, sitting back down, retrieving the crutches in one hand, clutching the bottle in the other, standing again, maneuvering one crutch to the other arm, opening the door with a now-free hand, and hobbling out to the hallway.

It was then that I realized I couldn't maneuver the crutches and hold the bottle of urine at the same time. There I was stranded in the hallway of the UCLA Medical Research Center, about to be prepared for surgery so that I could go on with my bombastic, free-spirited, athletically proficient career in stage dancing, and I couldn't even carry pee and walk at the same time.

My male nurse spotted me, rescued me and my bottle, and led me back to the blood-taking cubicle. My registration papers had arrived, but Perry was apparently still searching for my blue card.

The orderly took my blood, quickly and painlessly. I just hoped he put the right name on the vials. He then directed me to the elevator that would take me to the x-ray department. He said he'd redirect Dr. Perry to me when he returned.

I stood in front of the x-ray check-in desk. "I'm here for x-rays," I said.

"Let me have your packet," said the nurse.

"What packet?" I asked.

"They gave you a packet on the sixth floor which is necessary for you to present before an x-ray."

The sixth floor was now my idea of hell. Nobody had given me anything, and I would not return to it for anything. I told that to the x-ray man. He was chewing gum and listening to someone else's phone conversation. I spied the x-ray rooms.

"I'm going on in there," I announced, "because there'd be no reason to x-ray me if I go up to the sixth floor again looking for a packet. There's already enough troops running around looking for stuff."

I maneuvered my way into the x-ray department. An attendant met me. "Please remove all your clothes and jewelry," he said, handing me an open-backed hospital robe.

I hobbled into the changing room and, balancing carefully on the crutches, reached up and tried to undo my necklace. Why I needed a chest x-ray when it was my knee in trouble I couldn't figure out. But rather than argue, I struggled to remove the interfering necklace, an opal I associated with my father. There was a security catch on the chain, and it was too small and too high for me to see. I struggled and struggled.

"Are you ready?" asked the attendant.

"Well almost," I answered, and, abandoning the problem of the necklace, disrobed to emerge dressed in the hospital gown.

The outside door opéned. It was Dr. Perry. He looked at me and shrugged. "I've been on a safari to the sixth floor. I take it you got your blue card."

"I did," I said. "But now I need this packet thing, whatever that is, to have an x-ray."

"What packet thing?" he asked.

"I guess they'll tell you on the sixth floor."

"Okay, I'll get it," he said and kindly turned to make the trek again. I stopped him first. "Lee, could you undo this necklace? I can't."

He sweetly reached up and undid it for me. Without him, I probably would have checked out of the whole process.

In the x-ray room, I tried not to move when the pictures were being taken. It was difficult, because by now I was hyperventilating.

From the x-ray, I was directed to the EKG on another floor. They were nice but sharp with me. As I was strapped with electrodes to a table, the nurse said, "This is an EKG. You're supposed to be relaxed. Why are you so tense?"

I just laughed and said, "What I really feel like is having a coronary arrest, just to see if I have the proper papers to be taken care of."

She seemed to understand and didn't say a word as she went on with her work.

After the ordeal of the surgery preparation, I went home and tried to relax. As nighttime approached, I could think only of the audience who would have been filing in for my opening night. Instead, my company was at the theater eating the pre-ordered goodies and having a party, as they looked forward to a six-week vacation.

Then, at eight o'clock, I pictured myself at the theater about to do my show. I would be perspiring in demi-plié after one hundred repetitions, the straps of the underdressed leotard digging into my shoulders.

I would be swigging down gulps of water and sucking on a Halls cough drop, which was good for clearing the throat.

I would peek around the corner of the bandstand and check the patches of maroon fabric in the audience, which would indicate empty seats. I would "will" them to be filled.

I would make my rounds of the gypsies and the musicians from our entrance positions backstage, asking how their day went, but not really hearing the answers because I didn't want to break my concentration. If one of their stories got too detailed, I'd move away with a warm-up step, longing to be left alone.

Eight-ten . . . the first musician (drummer—Cubby) would make his entrance, followed one by one by the others. Then would come the dancers dressed in rehearsal clothes, and finally me.

Eight-twelve . . . the spotlight would be hitting me, and over the vamp I'd begin to sing of how I was nervous about live performing.

I puttered around in my kitchen in Malibu. I had to eat before midnight. Nothing allowed after twelve, so as to prevent nausea from the anesthesia. I hated anesthesia. It always made me sick, even if I didn't eat for a whole day before I had it. I remembered an operation for an impacted sinus I had in Bombay, India. They gave me sodium pentothal, and I cried for hours afterward. Tomorrow it would be Versed, a derivative of Valium.

Eight-thirty . . . while eating a salad, I silently went through my hooker-victim medley. I'd be wrapping the red feather boa around me in an attempt to change the look of the basic costume without having to go offstage.

Hooker-victims—why had I inherited so many of those tarts with hearts of gold? Was there an aspect of me that spoke to that identification? Had I seen myself as a victim in those days, and was I simply reflecting my own self-image in my work?

And now I had made a transition, with age, to playing parts that were not only not victims but more like victimizers—women who could be extremely difficult, commanding, and demanding . . . women who saw to it that things were done their way or not at all.

And I had felt as comfortable with these women as with the victims. As a matter of fact, the older I got the more cantankerous I was becoming. If someone didn't do something "right," I didn't even bother with the pretense of patience and understanding anymore. I said what I thought, and I no longer cared about getting more flies with honey. As someone said, "Who need flies?"

In my professional associations, I tried to maintain a level of diplomacy; but it was becoming more and more difficult for me.

In my private life with everyday contacts, errands, and casual relationships (grocery shopping, tradesmen at home, fans, answering service people, secretaries, airline stewardesses, etc.), I was fine and happy until I tangled with people who didn't give a damn about how they did their job or how slow they were at doing nothing. That kind of attitude drove me crazy.

I found myself turning into some of the characters I'd been playing lately. I was becoming "Ouiserfied" (Ouiser was my curmudgeonly character from *Steel Magnolias*) in some respects, and I wasn't about to change.

Eight forty-five . . . I'd be launching into "Rose's Turn"—the number that best exemplified a mother who had done everything for her children and was bitter about never having had her own turn. I couldn't find anything in me to identify with in those feelings, but I did find myself expressing emotions my mother would have felt.

This was the hardest number for me—to sing about my mother, pace my breath, climb stairs, at the top of which I jumped up on the piano, and throughout the number, thinking about how to warm up for the choreographers', which followed it.

Nine-ten . . . I sat down to eat my dinner and massaged my knee. I would be dancing now—carefully aware of each body movement, wondering when the powerful hand of destiny might strike again.

How would I really be after surgery? Was Dr. Finerman pessimistic or accurate about the "possibility" that I could dance again? Was it all basically up to me?

Nine-thirty . . . I'd be heading into a story about Peru and seeing a great master who would give me a mantra that sounded like Jimmy Durante's theme song. I would make fun of myself, my beliefs, and my books.

Did some people resent that, while others appreciated the "don't take it all so seriously approach"? What were they all really thinking when they watched me sing and dance and tell stories after having heard the umpteenth Johnny Carson joke about me the night before? Were they searching themselves, or did they not care about anything but just having a good time that evening?

Nine fifty-five . . . show over, applause, standing ovation (they were common for anyone these days), spotlight off, backstage empty, audience gone . . . magic in limbo till the next night.

I loved having my traveling show. To me it had always been something I could depend on when nothing else seemed to be going right. For all the anxiety and hassle, ultimately the immediacy and vitality of the living connections to dancers and musicians, the expertise with choreography, staging, lighting, sound—the whole complex creation that climaxed in the overwhelming vibrancy of a live audience—this was what I loved. I didn't want to be prevented from doing it. I was finally beginning to understand how much it meant to me and how I really *did* want to do it. Yet, I had tried to prevent myself in every conceivable way. Did I need to construct a format of disaster in order to learn? I seemed to have been conditioned to feel familiar with negativity—obstacles to overcome. Perhaps I really identified myself more with the spirit of overcoming than the spirit of balance and serenity.

My physical body would reflect that consciousness. If that was true, I needed to shift the emotional values by which to measure my identity—how to do that when you've been in the habit of expecting trouble? That was the nub of the problem.

My mother and father had lived their lives in anticipation of the worst scenario, and I had inherited the habit. Money was to be saved for possible future troubles. Life today must be sacrificed for the future, because one never knew what tragedy might come.

I remembered giving my mother $1,500 on her eighty-fourth birthday. She refused to spend it, claiming she'd put it aside for her old age!

My father never wore the cashmere sweater I gave him. He also was "saving" it until sometime later when he might "need" it more. A sweater to enjoy wasn't part of his emotional equation. A sweater to "need" was. He wore his moth-eaten wool sweater until he died, never once enjoying the cashmere.

I was much the same way, in fact. I possessed some finely tailored clothes made of exquisitely woven fabrics, but did I wear them much? No. I was saving them too—saving them for a time that might never come. I would choose something from my closet that I should "get some wear out of" until it fell apart.

And did I throw anything away? That was as difficult for me as allowing myself to buy anything new that was really expensive.

Mine was a truly middle-of-the-road mentality, at least where money was concerned. I came from middle-class values and would probably always read the menu right to left and order something in the middle. I didn't deserve the best. Nor did I deserve nothing. I was somewhere in between.

My parents were not unaware of their retentive value system—on the contrary. They spoke openly about how afraid they were about letting anything go, because they had been through the Great Depression. Such an experience was not insignificant, and I knew it. The prospect of material poverty rendered them paralytic. Perhaps their fears about so many other things stemmed from that, so that they could never really relax and be happy. Trouble or potential disaster was only a "stone's throw away."

This kind of thinking meant that I was also "moderately" prejudiced against things going well. Sometimes, if I found myself overcome with a sense of peace and satisfaction, I'd wake in the morning focused on a small imperfection going on in my life and magnify it until it became so explosive it needed resolution. I suppose that is the definition of a perfectionist. I was beginning to see it was also the definition of institutionalized turmoil.

Perhaps my turmoil was more mild than most; but with the evolution of my spirituality, I should have given it up altogether some time ago. I couldn't simply "accept" that this was the way I was anymore. I had to change, if for no other reason than having only two knees!

I couldn't keep doing this to myself, using such physical adversity to point up what was unresolved in my desire for happiness. I had refined pulling the rug out from under myself to a fine art. So fine that most observers would empathize with the "accidental" troubles I was having.

No one seemed to notice that I had gone out of my way

to create everything myself out of a deep longing to confront the obstacles from childhood and solve them once and for all as an adult. I had drawn the shoemaker to me. I had attracted the sound problems in the beginning. On some level, I knew the stage in Denver would be cement, contributing to the wear and tear on my knees. I had chosen to fall in Seattle, so I could recuperate in my home. And I was sure, in some way that was positive, I had prevented myself from playing L.A. until the time was right.

Why, I couldn't quite grasp. But the spiritual guides had picked it up. Everything that happened was for a purposeful good. Even *I* understood that. I just had to make the decision whether I wanted to continue to work out my problems through adversity or finally give it up. How much longer would I need to undermine my footing, so much that I had no other choice than to ultimately stand on my own two feet?

I faced the surgery the next day with a spirit of everything happening for the best. I needed to trust the bureaucratic incompetency of the hospital staff. Thank God it was only a knee operation.

Sachi and her best friend, David, came with me—plus Dr. Perry. Some form they had given me insisted in each paragraph that I was only to have *one* person with me in the waiting room. They put me in a chair that was meant to be comfortable; but instead, because it tilted back of its own free will, it actually contributed a great deal to more "torquing" of my knee.

I was told by a nurse, whom I was never to see again, that I should take my clothes off and be ready in my hospital gown for the stretcher people who would come by shortly. She didn't know what I was having done.

I elected to wait until the stretcher people arrived before

I sat around in the drafty holding room in a little, thin open-backed gown. I was right. They came three hours later. The nameless nurse had also expressed a preference that I wait alone with no relatives or friends (because of noise), but I told her my lonely screams would be louder than our conversation. She let me talk with my group.

Another nurse came by who instructed me on how to walk with crutches. It was scientific and useful, although intended, of course, for someone who had never ever used crutches. I asked her what kind of rehabilitation therapy I should do after the surgery. She said, "That's not necessary. Just learn to use your crutches properly, and you'll be fine."

I looked over at Dr. Perry. He deadpanned an eye roll. I wondered if Dr. Finerman knew what the nurse was recommending. I wondered if they had a rehabilitation department at UCLA.

As I waited in my tilting chair hour after hour, I was so grateful for Sachi's and David's and Perry's presence. I would have gotten very nervous had I been alone. I thought of all the people in the world who endured really serious maladies without the love of anyone standing by. Nurses can be sweet and attentive, but they have too much to do and too many people to do it for.

I remembered a doctor telling me once that one should have a personal friend attend a hospital stay twenty-four hours a day just to keep an eye on the nurses' dispensation of medicine and instructions. He said they don't always read the patients' charts correctly; and in many cases, the patients themselves catch an error. If they're in shape to do it.

I thought of the nineteen thousand deaths in New York City in one year alone that had occurred through hospital inefficiency. I knew the medical profession itself was sounding the warning signals. There just were not enough nurses and doctors to fully operate a hospital, and not nearly enough money. Our government had trillions of dollars committed to killing enemies but not enough to save its own citizens.

Never mind, I thought, as I chatted with Sachi and David and Dr. Perry. I must trust that everything will be fine. You get what you expect. You draw to you what you're afraid of. I was not going to accept fear anymore. I was going to expect the best.

The stretcher people finally came; and, just like movie directors, wanted to know why I wasn't ready. I always felt guilty keeping anyone waiting. Then one of them said, "What are you having done?" I told him. He seemed disinterested.

I kissed Sachi good-bye. She looked into my eyes, patted my hand, and said, "I love you." David cocked his head and said, "You know everything will be all right." And Dr. Perry came with me, because he was going to attend the surgical procedure.

As I was being wheeled into the elevator, I suddenly had to go to the bathroom. But it was too late now.

The elevator seemed to go to the basement . . . I don't know. And when they wheeled me from it, the corridors seemed more narrow. People were walking around in green surgical outfits.

Another nurse leaned over me. "What are you having done?" she asked. I told her. I was beginning to wonder if anyone knew what I was having done. Would the surgeon ask me too?

I began to lose my sense of consciousness, although I can't remember having been given any sedative. Dr. Perry appeared with a surgical mask on his face.

I didn't remember seeing Dr. Finerman. The anesthesiologist appeared. "Are you allergic to anything?" she asked. "Codeine, I think," I answered. "What are you having done?"

she continued. I told her. "Which knee," she asked, "right or left?" I was really worried now. We had talked the night before, and she had asked me the same questions. Why was everyone so uninformed?

I was on the operating table in the operating room, which was gray and antiseptic and impersonal. The anesthesiologist was beside me. I know I had an intravenous drip, but I can't remember how or when it happened. As I drifted off, I only hoped they'd operate on the right knee.

Coming out of the operating room I was awake enough to know that I was nauseous. I vomited. Some nurse was upset because I had vomited during the surgery also. She said I had moved around a lot because of lower back pain, so the anesthesiologist had given me more anesthesia (Versed) than she thought would be necessary.

I don't remember dressing to go home. I don't remember leaving the hospital, except for standing on my crutches in the sunshine almost asleep. I don't remember who drove me home. (It was Sachi.) I *do* remember vomiting about nine times during the trip in the car. (I had a plastic dish on my lap.) I was in a time warp—a lost weekend.

My knee was covered in a bandage that kept slipping around, and I was wearing an elasticized white stocking that held the swelling down. I don't remember who was with me or who helped me into bed. I only remember that Dr. Perry said I should take three things for my nausea—vitamin B6, chlorophyll tablets, and Coca-Cola syrup.

Someone—Sachi? David? Yvonne (who works for me)?—gave me those remedies, and in five minutes the nausea was gone. The nurse at the hospital had given me codeine tablets for pain, even though I told her I was allergic to codeine. "You should have told us," she said. I said I had.

I have since learned that the hospital's idea of double-checking its procedures was for all personnel encountering the patient to question what the problem was and how it was supposed to be solved. I could understand the checklist procedure, but *I* felt the *least* capable of understanding what needed to be done, and it produced a decided feeling of anxiety.

With the nausea gone, I was able to sleep. When the anesthesiologist called to ask me how I was feeling, I gave her the "vitamin B6, chlorophyll, Coke syrup remedy." "It might help others who vomit all the way home," I said. She thanked me, said she'd never heard of it, but if it worked, fine.

Dr. Perry was on the phone bright and early the next morning to insist that I get up and move around on my crutches. "You can't let yourself rest on this type of injury," he said. "The surrounding muscles will atrophy quickly, in a matter of days, and besides the knee itself needs to be worked."

Thus began my rehabilitation period. Sachi stayed with me, relieved by Yvonne—who took care of my apartment and the apartment building—and Bonnie, who came to give me massages.

I used crutches for one day, hardly worth the lesson I was given in pre-op. The second day, I began weight-bearing walking. The third day, walking and exercise, which consisted of Perry-Band bicycling movements. The fourth day, walking, bicycling movements, exercise with weights, and yoga.

Perry brought his muscle stimulator machine to me, which I was to use at least twice a day. Electrical impulses surged through the muscles, providing deep muscle stimulation.

And, of course, ice. "Ice is your best friend," said Perry. "And it will be for a long time to come. Whenever you dance, you must ice immediately afterward."

Perry came to see me every night. Sachi made us dinner.

And then for four nights in a row we watched the restored videocassette of *Lawrence of Arabia*. It was a study in emotional, physical, and spiritual endurance. I knew I was going to need all three. And in the coming days, my capacity for balance in each of those areas was to be tested.

Because I felt no connection with Dr. Finerman and was not even sure where to call him, Dr. Perry became the expert I trusted in postoperative matters. Since the surgical bandage continued to slip down my leg, I took it off the second day. Then I removed the Band-Aids that covered the fine and expert surgical work Dr. Finerman had done.

Perry brought me the video of my operation; and after heralding it as the best movie I had ever been in, he explained what I was looking at. It could have been a journey to the center of the earth as far as I could see.

Wafting pieces of flesh floated in disturbed motion, as the microcamera recorded the adventure. Torn flesh looked more like a crimson sea anemone. The blood encrusted in the torn cruciate indicated that the original tear had occurred in Seattle, not in the rehearsal hall in L.A.

Dr. Finerman hadn't understood how I could have danced on it in San Francisco at all. Perry said he mumbled something during the operation about my being a wise old gypsy, because I knew my body.

A stainless steel instrument that looked like a cross between a pair of pliers and a pincer gobbled at torn flesh within my knee and pulled away the excess torn ligament, which would never repair itself and the torn cartilage. My knee was indeed a universe in which an earth-oriented scientist wielded his detailed technological expertise. Ten years ago, this operation would have been open-knee surgery requiring a year before weight bearing was allowed.

The colors of my knee-universe were pastel pinks, with

harsh strokes of crimson where real damage had occurred. The plier–pincer gobbled away at the ligament and cartilage until what was torn was gone, and I was left with half a ligament and half a cartilage.

"Enough to dance on," Perry reassured me. "The ligament is a major knee stabilizer. You'll just have to build up your muscularity around the missing ligament. You will have to keep your thighs, knees, calves, and ankles very strong. You'll be rechoreographing all the pressure points when you dance, but that's what any athlete does when he's injured. You'll be fine. In fact, you'll be great. But you need to work harder."

The next day (day four) I went into the International Sportsmedicine Institute to begin my workouts in the pool.

Dr. Perry had a remarkable technique of hydrotherapy rehabilitation he invented. He strapped twenty-five to fifty pounds of weight, hanging from rubber ropes (the Perry-Bands), around my waist. The weight hung down in the water, producing a hydro-traction and decompressing my back. I was strapped into a life vest with a few flotation bananas around me to keep me afloat, as the weight pulled my midsection down.

Then he strapped a four-pound sand weight to my ankle, which I would lift intermittently. It took fifteen minutes for me to become seaworthy. And then something hit the wrong pressure point underwater; one of the leg weights fell off.

I returned to poolside and restrapped myself. Then out to deep water again. I bicycled for an hour underwater, with the flotation devices keeping me afloat and the weights decompressing my back and knee.

"You want to regain your flexibility as soon as possible," said Perry. "I know it's uncomfortable, but do it."

Uncomfortable was not the word, but I did it. I thought of Ron Kovic in *Born on the Fourth of July*. I thought of Mary

Hite, who had been through seven years of this kind of painful therapy in order to regain control of her body. I thought of Dr. Perry himself, whose entire left knee had been crushed by a moving hoist. Each of them had endured much more rehabilitation than what I was going through.

Thus began my associations in Dr. Perry's pool with other people from "real life" who were rehabilitating injuries much more serious than mine.

One man hadn't been able to sit for seven years because of a compressed vertebra in his lower back. A music teacher, who stood beside her piano students all day, had to quit her job because of a back injury. She lay on her back for five months before someone told her about Dr. Perry and his water technique. She was now able to sit up and even stand for a few hours, where every other doctor had said surgery would be required to make that possible.

When I heard about the man who lost his footing while working on his roof, and fell off and broke his neck, and was told he would never walk again, I wondered what the finger of destiny was telling him. Then I heard the rest of the story. His wife was dying of cancer. After she finally passed away, he died too. Perhaps he gave himself the fall in order to join her more quickly.

As I listened to the litany of injuries ("I just woke up one morning and haven't been able to walk since"), I couldn't help but wonder what else there was underneath each person's tragic dilemma. In the pool we exchanged theories. There was a lesson for each of us; that was clear. But what whispers that we had each ignored had preceded the final blow?

As we examined our lives we could see, if we were honest with ourselves, the inevitability of needing to slow down. Simple wear and tear would demand that. And equally, most of us would want to deny that inevitability and attempt to ignore it. So what was it each of us was supposed to look at? What mysteries of our own consciousness were we failing to unravel? Each of us would have a different answer to that; and if we allowed ourselves free time to *feel* into what the answer might be, we'd see it.

Even the most confirmed believers in "accident" were moved to modify such a belief when they really honestly looked at what had preceded the "accident." On some level we each of us had created and participated in our personal "accident," because that was the only way we felt we could see underneath our conscious behavior.

As we paddled and bicycled in the therapy pool, we discussed these ideas. We needed to take full responsibility for our lives if we were going to get well, and the first step toward taking responsibility was to admit our unconscious participation. That put us back in control of our own empowerment.

The theory of accident disempowered individuals as to how they were creating the reality in their lives. It might be painful to accept the responsibility for creating whatever the disaster was, but the disaster itself was the real pain. That was the bottom line. It was our task to unravel the detailed implications in between.

In my case, I began to think more deeply about what I had done and why.

My injury occurred to my right knee, my masculine side, controlled by the left hemisphere of the brain. Symbolically that was tied to the father in one's life, the masculine authority figure.

Of course, I remembered that he had told me years ago that I should never strive to be anything but a dancer; but that I was not even very good at that. And, of course, I knew that he had found my acting aspirations childish pipe dreams and my singing not even discussable. Yet, in the end, he had been forced to go along, no matter how reluctantly, with my ambitions. I thought I had resolved that lack of support and integrated my understanding of it into my own need to achieve and overcome adversity. But no, there was something else going on now that did not have that much to do with show business.

I remembered now that the real respect and praise that my father reserved for me came long after my childhood, in the realm and arena of human thought. He loved what I was investigating in my books. He, being a teacher, had been more impressed by my books than by anything else I had ever done. Some kind of intellectual snobbery never allowed him to acknowledge or even, perhaps, to recognize that any really good teacher first uses a certain theatrical quality to grab attention, and then to get the point across. Teachers—*good* teachers, like my Dad—and *good* actors have much in common.

I could see the actor in him. What he saw in me was an innovative investigator and a dispenser of the knowledge I had accumulated about metaphysics and paranormal phenomena.

Before my father died, he saw himself as having passed the mantle of investigating the mysteries of life over to me. I had accepted it and enjoyed what I could pass on to others.

When I organized my seminars and spent long weekends in the give-and-take of teaching and learning, I felt my Dad was always there with me. He finally approved of what I was doing! I wore his opal at every seminar, I felt he helped me orchestrate what I said, how I taught, and how to be sensitive in bearing a student's confusion.

I felt his energy in my opal, as though he spoke to me invisibly through it. When I was stuck as to how to proceed on a complicated metaphysical point, I'd touch the opal at my throat, and instantly the correct words would come to me.

I had not been comfortable in calling myself a teacher, however. I preferred to be called a "sharer." I felt I didn't know enough to teach—all I knew was my own experience. I was a fellow student of life.

So what did this have to do with my right knee injury? Well, one of the conflicts as I put together my new show was whether I was a teacher (a lecturer) or an entertainer. How could I be both? Did I have the right to be both? Didn't my father respect my teaching more than my performing, because that was what *he* had done?

Then I remembered something that had dominated and haunted my father all his adult life. His Ph.D. dissertation on musical theory composition had been turned down at Johns Hopkins University where he taught. He had never gotten his doctorate; and he had said it was because his professor, a Dr. Bamberger, had failed him as a friend.

She was an older woman who "destroyed his ego," according to Mother. She "caused" him to fail in his future aspirations, because she didn't believe in him enough to accept his dissertation. Her turndown of his Ph.D. work influenced the rest of his adult life. It was a rejection that confirmed the terrible lessons in fear of his childhood.

She had disastrously reinforced his disbelief in himself. He lost his will to succeed and make something of himself—again, according to Mother. He was a truly great man who denied his own greatness. He wanted to contribute to humanity and knew of no other way than to teach. Yet without degrees and titles and years of study as an imprimatur, he never really saw himself as qualified.

Some years later, the Bamberger turndown was rectified, because Johns Hopkins gave him an honorary doctorate in the humanities. He was thrilled and felt compensated. More than anything, I believe my father wished to contribute to the betterment of the human race. He saw education as the way to do it.

So toward the end of his life, he viewed me more as an investigative teacher than a performer, regardless of my success in show business. I was venturing into areas of human speculation that he had always longed to question himself. As he lay dying nothing was as important to him as why we were here and where we had come from. I felt much the same way. Yet, I also loved to perform.

Since his death, the conflict between the two forms of expression had become more pronounced for me. Should I devote myself to the "deeper" questions in life and continue my search, my seminars, and my writing, and perhaps help people investigate their own mysteries, or should I indulge myself in bringing pleasure to people with my little songs and dances as I pranced around the world enjoying being "perky" in my advancing years? It was a puzzlement. And still at my age, having looked quite deeply and resolutely at myself, I had to admit the long arm of my beloved complicated father had reached from the grave, and I had allowed my perceptions of his wishes to sweep me into a fall just as I had reached a turning point. I apparently had not resolved what I wanted to do.

It occurred to me that perhaps I had allowed the unconscious conflict about my father to pull me to my knees—literally. I had had a typical "knee-jerk" reaction to my father's hidden wishes. I was unable to stand on my own two legs, because I felt the pull from him to take up the mantle of his calling—teaching.

Whether he actually wanted me to do that—I don't know. That doesn't matter. What matters is I *thought* he did, and because I didn't want to defy him—I went down. I hadn't even speculated on such a thing until now. It hadn't occurred to me when I fell in Seattle. I had gotten well, I thought. But no, I'm never well unless I understand the reasons for sickness.

I was beginning to understand now—for the first time—that I wouldn't have realized my long-buried conflict if I hadn't injured myself. I made it impossible for myself to go "on" without understanding what I needed to resolve.

During the weeks of rehabilitation, I had felt compelled to wear my opal. Now I understood why—I needed to clear out the conflict with my father. I knew he knew and was probably doing everything from his vantage point to get the point across to me.

We were cooperating with each other. How else would I stop to take the time? A knee injury was a small price to pay for understanding the conflict I still had left to resolve in myself about who I was and what I wanted to become.

Of course, there were people who would say that none of my metaphysical musings were necessary. I had simply fallen and damaged a knee—an accident not worthy of elaborate hidden meaning. But I knew better. There was no such thing as "accident." Cause and effect was the fundamental agenda of all events. I was beginning to get to the bottom of mine.

As my rehab continued, I'd hear from members of my company every now and then and also from people I had not had contact with in years. My living room looked like a gangster's funeral, there were so many flowers. Many people who had had the same arthroscopic surgery called to give me tidbits of help in getting well.

As I focused myself on being physically disciplined, I became more and more aware of how age was affecting my body. My bones seemed to creak at unpredictable moments. The joints in my hips, ankles, wrists, and fingers were becoming stiff.

Water . . . I knew I needed to continue to drink at least eight glasses of water a day. I didn't much like water, but there were many things I didn't much like that were necessary to include in my life now.

At times my mind seemed to slow to a dream rhythm. I was thinking and feeling underneath my thoughts now, instead of always being ahead of myself. I was physically stronger than I had ever been (I was on the stage again, and I noticed that I was rarely out of breath). I had become more scientific and focused in my workout program than ever before.

But I found that everyday activities of movement were more difficult for me than what I did on the stage. That was because of the unpredictability factor. On stage I knew just what was going to happen and how. In life I never knew who would dart out in front of me while crossing a street or yell to attract my attention, which caused me to wheel around and wrench something.

Life was making me feel older than entertaining did. I couldn't rehearse life. I couldn't tailor it for myself and my needs. Life went on with its own rhythm and natural ebbs and flows, whether I was out of sync with it or not.

More and more of my friends were dying. I had finally come to the point in my life where death was a constant. I loved George Burns's remark. He said he was so old that each day he read the obituary columns to find out if he was still alive. If he didn't see his name there, he knew he'd have a nice day.

I visited with Jill Ireland two days before she died. I was overcome with admiration at her sensitivity to others in the midst of her own pain. She was fully aware and caring about other people's problems. She was peaceful; and while angry at her cancer, she was ready to go.

I wondered how she had reached such a place of acceptance. Was such peace reserved only for the dying? My father had evidenced the same beatific state of being before he died. Why couldn't we *live* in that state of consciousness?

Was that what I was after? Was I looking to "follow my bliss," as Joseph Campbell said. If so, where was it?

Many of my friends in show business and the world of dance were dying of AIDS. There was a funeral every week. Many were unable to care for themselves and needed attention, clothing, and food. Projects and organizations were formed to attend to those living with AIDS, as well as those dying with it.

About twenty people that I had worked with closely had left their bodies with AIDS. And about five really close friends afforded me the opportunity to be there with them every step of the way, which was in some cases more horrible than I could have imagined. I tried to understand the suffering, the slow death, and the lessons inherent in their experiences. I was having trouble with a stupid injury. They were losing their lives.

When Sammy Davis, Jr., was diagnosed as having throat cancer, I gave up even the sparse social smoking I did. I never inhaled, but what difference did that make? It was his throat that was infected, not his lungs.

Sammy's sickness affected me a great deal, as it did all of his friends. Sammy tasted the feast of life as though it was his last meal. There seemed to be nothing that he left untried—booze, women, drugs, cigarettes of all kinds, impressions, instruments, voices, dance steps, drama, comedy, musicals, cars, houses, jewelry, and several religions.

I wished I had had the freedom and spontaneity to try, without concern for the future, everything he tried. He lived completely in the present, expanding it to the fullest until it became the future. It never occurred to him that he was overdoing anything. Life was to be lived, to be loved, to be laughed at.

Sammy told me he was going to recover. I had arranged for him to undergo voice building with Gary. Gary believed that his technique could help Sammy's voice after his therapy because he had worked with radiation patients before. Sammy's attitude was optimistic, as he appeared on late-night talk shows and posed for picture magazines.

But when we sat together backstage at a benefit somewhere, his eyes warned me that death lurked behind them. He never spoke of the fear—quite the contrary—but he couldn't hide the truth. His frail body had been a wiry miracle to me, and his energy came from a source that no one else seemed able to access.

Sammy was a man who would do anything to be loved, and we all knew it. Whatever his excesses might have been, he was greedy in giving and taking.

I thought of his life as a child. He had been cultivated and nourished in the spotlight since he was three years old. He was only at home when the spotlight was on. So his sense of his life was BIG and theatrical, because that's what was real to him.

I remembered Frank Sinatra, when we were doing a picture together in the fifties, taking me to see Sammy. His show defied the logic of the saying "Jack of all trades and master of none." He was the master of everything he touched on the stage. And after the show, when we all filed into his dressing room backstage, I felt I had always known him—he had a quality of such instant, eager rapport with people because of his need to identify with others. His dressing rooms were always full of his collection of characters—some savory, some not.

In England, he'd speak with a British accent—in Paris, French . . . and so on. He was a superb imitator, because he wanted to *become* the identity of another; such was his conflict in the search for himself.

When I was making *Two Mules for Sister Sara* in Mexico, I'd go up to Mexico City and watch him perform on the weekends. We'd talk long into the night about the tricks of the trade of live performing. When we made *Sweet Charity* together, we talked long and deeply about the Rhythm of Life, inspired by the jazz gospel song he sang. Soon after that he began his search into different religions.

Sammy had a way of making show business enter your living room. Many a time he'd get me (and others) up on the stage with him, because he made performing seem so intimate. When I went into live performing for the first time, I sought the advice of Frank, Liza, and Sammy. Frank said, "Don't worry. Remember, you change the room by showing up." Liza said, "Do it because you have something to say." Sammy said, "Don't hold back; pull out all the stops."

Over a period of forty years our paths crossed many times, and each renewal was a living, continuing experience, as though no time had elapsed in between. So when Dean and Frank and Liza and I had dinner the night before Sammy's funeral, even though all of us had known the inevitable for some time, the feeling was very much that an era had ended.

We reminisced about old times (the Clan performing at the Sands in Vegas). Our bunch was never known as the Rat Pack. That was a previous group that revolved around Bogie, much earlier. The Clan came out of the film we made together called *Some Came Running*. Sammy hadn't been in that one, but he was in many subsequent films with Dean and Frank.

Over the years, our relationships have held. I'm not sure why. I think it has more to do with mutual respect for talent than anything else—plus a shared sense of irreverent humor. The practical jokes abounded. Life with Clan members was a theatrical party, where sleep and taking care of oneself were secondary to the FUN. In fact, I wondered in those days if fun wasn't more important than having discipline and caring for one's health.

Now as I sat at dinner with the Clan, reminiscing about Sammy's life, which ended at only sixty-four, my depression and ennui returned. I wondered whether the priorities of the past shouldn't have been different.

Except for Liza, who had made the choice of discipline and sobriety, I was sitting with friends who suddenly seemed to me to be old men. Like a reflection of oneself unexpectedly encountered in a mirror, I was seeing them, and hence, myself, with unwelcome vision. Their dialogue was repetitious and forgetful, their body movements hesitant and halting. Stories were repeated, and the reliving of events in the past seemed to be clearer to them than what was happening at the moment.

What was becoming of us? Was I showing the same signs of age? Was a live show business era coming to a close, where lyrics and love songs and lush orchestrations and blue-ribbon endings were no longer appreciated, abandoned in favor of athletic movement and relentless marathon MTV musical drive with no meaning, no nuance? Was rebellion and antisocial behavior more "in" than romantic communication?

At this moment, I was feeling more and more like a matron icon myself, as I survived year after year in a business that swallowed its own young and spit them out. I treasured my accumulated wisdom, but right now I didn't feel I fit in anywhere anymore. I didn't want to be old, but I didn't want to be young either. Everything seemed transient, without longevity. The present became the past before it had a chance to survive the future. Sammy's death put a point on the transition.

I tended to spend more and more time alone with my inner thoughts and my writing. I no longer understood the slang and "argot" of the new dialects of show business "English" as spoken by most of the tribes of rock and roll players. I retained a youthful spirit, yet it was tempered with a sigh of experience. It was as though I wanted to sit in my favorite chair, gazing at the frenzy of the world passing before my eyes on CNN. I didn't feel much like keeping up with the new styles in clothes and behavior. They wouldn't last long anyway. I felt somewhat suspended in time, waiting to "get with it."

The competition in the world and in our business depended on so much "hype," as though overpopulated numbers of people out there needed to be stimulated in any way possible. Product needed to be sold. I felt beleaguered by the greedy, back-stabbing merchandising techniques I saw around me. It all seemed perfectly acceptable to everyone, since the spoils were so worth it. But not to me.

Studios went about making "hits" now, instead of films. They were often agreeable to exposing their own magic tricks in an attempt to draw a bigger audience. They were more in the *business* of show now than in presenting that inspired abstract—the show that is believable and moving because it reveals, whether comic or tragic, a truth about life. Instead, in a desperate attempt to give the audience a sense of authenticity, the money moguls *show* the violence, *show* the sex, producing profits by catering to shock effect.

Of course there were those dedicated creative talents who managed to cope with the hype and cutthroat show biz politics to produce innovative, honest statements on film. I was thrilled that Kevin Costner forced through *Dances With Wolves* with his creative passion. Dick and Lili Zanuck proved that authentic casting could make money with *Driving Miss Daisy*. There were always those artists who didn't succumb to the hype and "requirements" for the big opening weekend. But for the most part, our business had become more about money than not.

And through it all, I wanted to hang on to my own identity *while* I was involved with the seeking of it.

I wanted to feel the experience of being free of monetary concerns and competition and show biz hype. But it was too complicated. I guess I was unhappy settling for just going along.

I thought of becoming an eccentric writer who ventured out of my retreat once every few months, only to return to reclusion for the sake of sanity.

Sometimes I even daydreamed about not staying in show business. The negative aspect to being in the spotlight was that to be any good you could not escape the self-centered "me-first" infantilism basic to the human psyche, which was constantly reinforced and even justified by the demands of a "watch-me" profession. It was all so ironic. I was on a self-search, but I didn't like thinking about myself all the time, or at least I didn't like thinking about what other people thought of me.

I wondered if I would be happy down the pike some years with a large family and a farmhouse somewhere . . . lots of grandchildren running around to play with and teach. I don't know. I'd probably get bored with that after a while, although I was looking forward to children that Sachi might have someday.

So where was I? At times I felt I was floundering; then at other times I reveled in giant leaps of understanding.

I was feeling the world whirl at a faster pace. It was as though sixty seconds' worth of experience in any given minute was now one hundred twenty seconds' worth. It was hard to keep pace. There was an energy of some kind accelerating the very air we breathed and the soil we trod upon. The energy was invisible, but its presence pressed in on all living things as though to say "Hurry—Hurry or you'll be left behind. Hurry and keep pace with the acceleration that's taking place. Hurry so as not to be discordant with the harmony of the symphony of life."

Or could it simply be, in an aging world that now included me, "Hurry, because the time is getting short?"

In any case, *how* did one become harmonious with the music of the universe? With the lives we led, it was hard to hear anything but the clanking of the systems we had each become willing partners in building. We had destroyed the natural harmony to fit our material needs. We had defied the laws of nature, and nature seemed determined to cleanse herself of our pollution by fighting back.

Drought, floods, global warming, fruit flies, snow in summer, heat in winter . . . Mother Nature and Father Time reorchestrating their symphony to include players who were not willing to play and respect the natural laws of harmony. They would nourish us only if we would respect them. And that was how it should be.

So perhaps my ennui was an acknowledgment that I, and most everyone I knew, was going through a transition of cleansing so that true harmony could result. Yet I seemed not to be moving fast enough, or slow enough—as the case may be.

I took time during my rehab to go to the Pacific Northwest to be alone and do nothing, hoping that a revelation would occur. Nothing of the sort happened. But I seemed to enter a phase, some kind of plateau of healing, perhaps. I became reluctant to even project expectations of changes in myself. I felt that I was almost on hold, like a telephone button waiting to plug into a revelatory conversation.

When I meditated, I fell asleep. When I hugged a tree trunk, I no longer heard the voice within it. The inner conversation in nature had shifted, and I could no longer decipher it. I felt oddly restless and abandoned; not wanting to be with people, yet not happy with myself as I used to be. It was not exactly depression: it was just nowhere. Perhaps all recovery requires a period like this.

I did my exercises with discipline but with no joy. I wanted to sleep long hours, yet felt compelled to get up early.

I found myself arranging and rearranging my closet, the shoes, the handbags, the jackets, the slacks, as though I wanted to reorganize the contents of my life. But it added up to simply shuffling objects around.

Every friend I had was in some kind of personal crisis either with a marriage, a relationship, children, work, or health.

There were times when life had a dreamlike quality to it, as though I were moving through a landscape instead of being part of it, actually dreaming it rather than living it. The Buddhists would say that was the real reality.

Time seemed to bend and shimmer as though I could see it, past and future somehow melding into the present. I would dip into another "time" and place and be certain that it had actually occurred NOW. As long as I didn't allow myself to become anxious, it was actually rather nice, playful even.

When I spoke with my mother, she talked of not having heard from my father. She didn't know why he wasn't coming home. She feared he had left her because of a recent argument.

I had to remind her that Daddy had died several years ago. She was relieved that he had died rather than left her, because she was afraid she had driven him away. I reminded her that he had died at Johns Hopkins Hospital of leukemia.

She had wanted to know if she was helpful to him at the end. Had she been kind and attentive to him? I tried to reassure her that she had been wonderful, and there was nothing either she or anyone else could have done.

On a deeper level than I could touch, I identified with the state of being of my mother now. I could feel into her memory loss and understand it. I picked up her panic at being alone. Her best friend had died recently, so her solace every morning on the other end of the telephone would no longer be there. When I asked her how old Evie was when she died, Mother said, "Oh, she was only in her fifties."

I said, "Mother, *I'm* in my fifties. Evie must have been in her late seventies."

Mother was shocked. "*You* are in your fifties?" she asked, not remembering when she had given birth to me.

"Yes, I'm fifty-six," I answered.

"You're fifty-six? My God, you're old," she said.

"Yep," I answered, "and your baby son is fifty-three."

She gasped. "Warren is fifty-three?"

I laughed at the black humor involved with old age.

"Oh, Shirl," said Mother. "You can't imagine what it's like to get old." I reassured her that imagining it wasn't necessary. The real thing was rapidly approaching.

I wondered what my mother was thinking about death, and felt safe in asking. She had always been highly pragmatic about immediate realities.

"Death is a risky business," she said.

"Why?"

She pondered this one. Then, "Because you never know where you might end up."

"Well, are you afraid that you might go to hell?"

This thought was briskly dismissed. "Of course not," she said, "I've already been there!"

Trying to introduce a little comfort, I ventured, "Well, you know, you might meet up with some interesting people."

My mother's voice took on a lilt. "Oh, *yes*!" she said. "Wouldn't it be wonderful to be able to pick who you want to be with!"

As I waited for a revelation at my house in the mountains, I became more and more impatient and agitated. Sometimes I talked to friends but became quickly irritated and hung up.

I sat for days watching the rain. It fell on the bushes and trees, turning their leaves to shimmering emeralds. Why couldn't I make that kind of transformation? I was still disturbed by my conflict between performing and spirituality. Why couldn't I meld together my spiritual metaphysics and my love for entertaining? Why was there a schism in me? Why the separation?

Metaphysics and spirituality worked magic. So did the theater. Why couldn't I see that they were compatible? Why was one a trick to me, and the other real?

I felt somehow fraudulent, plying my theatrical tricks of the trade in a theater in order to elicit an emotional response. I felt manipulative, even though the audience knew going in that those were the ground rules in theater. It is the one safe place to discard reality and fall in love with fantasy. And the safety is in the collective that surrounds you. *Everyone* succumbs to the magic, because that's what they're there for.

But I found conflict and contradiction in that philosophy now. I didn't want to fool people anymore and call it good theater. I didn't want to be the trickster who wove an illusion that elevated people out of their bogged-down reality. I didn't want to be commissioned with that kind of responsibility anymore. I wanted them to be able to find the magic in themselves their own way. *They* were their own tricksters and capable of elevating themselves above the drudgery and despair they too often experienced.

We were each performers in our own lives, weaving our spells of entertainment in comedy and drama. We were our own producers and directors, casting our scripts the way we wanted, and indeed, insisting on starring in our creations.

I was having a hard time understanding my own script. For example, I enjoyed doing my seminars, because my intent was clear. I was the flint against which people could ignite the light within themselves. That to me had a contributive purpose.

What was the meaningful purpose in a stage show when so many human beings in the world were suffering? Suffering from sickness, poverty, and from lack of personal identity and esteem? At least in my seminars, they could perhaps get more in touch with who they were. In my shows, I was asking them, by definition, to forget about who they were. I was bedeviled now by the contradiction, and it was agonizing.

Then one day a thought struck me. As I was paddling around with my leg weights in the pool, it began to rain . . . a kind of cleansing rain it seemed to me. Then the rainbirds fell silent, and the drops of water falling on my head propelled my thoughts backward in time . . . to Greece and the purpose of the theater. I remembered reading that the Greeks, feeling cut off from the spirituality of the gods, needed a ritual by which to reestablish the divine connection. The identification with the godhead required a place in which people could congregate to collectively experience the regeneration of their connection to the gods. That place became the theater.

The theater offered people a place to rekindle and recapture their spiritual identity. The masked performer was a symbol, the magician who invoked the inspiration from the gods, sharing the spiritual myths and acting them out so that the myths became reality for the audience. The performer became the divine instrument that bonded the audience to the deity. Thus the audience and the performers and the deities became one, intertwined and inseparable.

The purpose of the theater and its performances then became one of creating uplifting spiritual illusion, which helped bond the human being with the divine. Such was its metaphysical purpose. The audience and the performers could then share in the divinity of each other.

When the truth of this concept hit me, I remembered something Picasso had said. When asked if art was truth, he answered, "Art is the lie that reveals the truth."

Suddenly I understood how to meld together my two worlds. The art of illusion was the exquisite lie that revealed the truth in any way the observer *chose* to see it. I, and everyone else, was choosing to perceive life, love, and the pursuit of happiness in a way that best served our growth. What might be one person's truth was not another's.

I could perform in one way and yet be perceived in the same evening three thousand different ways. And each perception was a metaphysical connection to a chosen illusion.

I was not "tricking" anyone. I was only a catalyst for their bonding with the missing magic in their lives. That made performing and acting an honorable profession, a gateway to realism. The expertise of illusion, which enabled another to recapture and bond with his or her own missing magic, was as profound a contribution to reality as I could ever hope to make.

I looked up and around me. I wondered what my Dad would think of my revelation. The tangy droplets of rain fell into my eyes, cooling the heat in my head. Suddenly the sun shone on the mountains in front of me, the raindrops immediately around me glistening like a curtain of polished diamonds. I heard myself gasp. Then slowly, as if directed by an all-knowing spiritual magician, an arched rainbow appeared over the mountains of snow. The theatrical illusion was complete.

I *chose* to perceive it as an omen, a beautiful ratification of my revelation that theater and metaphysical reality are one and the same. In other words, if one doesn't believe in illusion, one is not being realistic. I had finally had my revelation, and it had been there all along.

So I returned to the stage and resumed my tour. I opened in Pittsburgh, not far from where my mother and father had met, and it was a joy for me.

The show was sold out, the reviews fabulous, the audiences dreamily enthusiastic, and my knee was fine. I wore a bandage for each show to give me support. I knew I had attained a hard-earned wisdom, which had admittedly taken its toll but more than rewarded me with a sense of love for what I was doing.

Dr. Perry returned early from a trip to the Soviet Union where he had been invited to present a paper before the Leningrad Academy of Sportsmedicine and Science, to be with me on opening night. We sat in my dressing room afterward. He smiled with pride at my "comeback" and then leaned forward and said, "You know, you're not supposed to be able to dance."

"What do you mean?" I asked.

"Dr. Finerman and I didn't think you'd be able to get up there and do what you do ever again. Especially to this degree of excellence."

"Are you serious?" I asked.

"Dead serious," he answered.

"Then you're telling me that you didn't tell me the truth?"

"That's correct."

"I see."

He didn't editorialize, or apologize, or comment one way or the other. Then he said, "But your truth is different from other people's. And I knew that. So I believed you could do it, regardless of the physical limitations. And, you proved me right. So there's no sense in looking back."

He was more than right. I could have given up had he told me the truth, or I could have gotten up there on the stage and injured myself for life, believing that I could do anything. Either way it was a risk for him.

But he had psyched me out properly, because he was a man who had been through the same thing himself. He had been told by many doctors that he would never walk again, that he shouldn't live in a fool's paradise and expect a miracle. That was not a reality he wanted to accept.

He knew from experience that you make your own reality, and he had passed that on to me. I would be forever grateful for his astute insight into what I had been too naive to see myself. I had not been aware of what I had overcome. He had.

I went on to play five cities in Japan, four cities in Australia, London and Europe, and South America. The tour was a triumph personally and professionally.

Sachi came with me to Japan. We went to our old house—the house where Sachi had spent five years of her childhood. It was now a condominium apartment building. We stood on the street corner looking at what had replaced the home where so much of her formative years had occurred. "It's gone," said Sachi. "The past is really gone."

She wandered away from me, returning to some of her childhood secret places down small streets in the neighborhood. Her childhood friends were gone too. They were all adults now, attempting to keep pace with a world rushing headlong into the next millennium. I wondered if they were having the same confusions as we were.

I stood by the condominium apartment building remembering the house we had had for so long. The fish pond was gone, the tumbling waterfall, and the Japanese garden. All had been replaced by an apartment building—progress, they say.

I remembered the first time I had eaten sashimi and sushi, kneeling at a table in that garden thirty-five years ago. No one in America had heard of sushi then except in geography books. Now it was an American favorite. Women and men wore kimonos on the street, and the sound of geta (Japanese shoes) on the cobblestone streets heralded the arrival of a visitor.

I had had a husband then whom I lived with in that house, talked with in that garden, and shared Sachi with in the tatami rooms inside.

Today we didn't even know where he was. "He moves around a lot," I had heard from mutual friends. Yes, I thought. He certainly does. He moves around from country to country. I never asked where he was, because he was like a phantom. First you'd see him, then you wouldn't. But he had been an important teacher for me. Probably the most important in my life. He had taught me to be more discerning. It's one thing to have blind faith in someone. It's another to "know" within yourself who they are because you know yourself better. So eventually I divorced him. He didn't mind. He just disappeared . . . literally.

I stood in front of the house wondering where he was. No one knew, including Sachi. I wondered what it was like not to know where your father was. Only Sachi could feel that. I always knew where my father was. With all his stunted brilliance, he had been there for me. Even his broad-stroked cruelty had been honest. He was not a mystery. I could see that now.

And my father had warned me that my husband was dishonest thirty-five years ago in the living room of this very house which was no longer there. I had not listened. I accused him of being possessive and never daring to have an adventurous relationship of his own. He said, "You'll see, Monkey."

And I saw. Before my Dad died, I admitted that he was right and I thanked him. He nodded and smiled. But even after my divorce, Dad wouldn't let the matter drop. We were sitting at the kitchen table just before he went into the hospital for the last time.

"Look, Daddy," I said. "I've divorced the guy. Why can't you?"

"Because, Monkey," said Daddy, "the son of a bitch was smarter than I was."

Sachi came up behind me and tapped my shoulder.

"I understand so much more now," she said quietly. "I'm going to have dinner with Egouchi-san tonight and talk about my childhood."

Egouchi-san had been Sachi's governess when we lived in Japan. They too had a relationship I couldn't begin to fathom because it was traditional Japanese.

"Don't worry, Mom," she said. "I just need to hear about some things regarding Dad. It's got nothing to do with you. I need to figure out who I am now. I need to resolve the Japanese and the American parts of me."

We put our arms around each other and slowly walked away from the corner where so much of our love had gone unexpressed for years. We had taken it for granted and now it was time to talk.

And talk we did . . . for days in the hotel room in Tokyo, over Japanese meals in restaurants—sometimes with Egouchi-san, sometimes just the two of us. We talked about her childhood, her fears, her confusions about the two cultures, her concerns about being ready to bear children of her own. We talked about love, sex, work, and even death.

Then Sachi began to do interviews in Japanese—something she never wanted to do before. The cultural reminder had been too painful. And finally one night she told me to stay up and watch her on television. I did. There she was in her full-blown adult glory talking about her life for one hour in fluent Japanese. I didn't understand one word.

"Don't worry," she said. "I'll have it translated later."

"Sure," I said. "You know something, sweetheart. There are things I am never going to understand about you. By the same token, there's a lot you'll never understand about me. And there's stuff neither of us will ever understand about your father." Tears filled her eyes.

"I know," she said. "I realize now that I'm just going to have to let him go and get on with my own life."

"Yep," I said. "I had to do the same thing with him. My father and mother had to do the same thing with me—and I with them." She nodded and wiped her eyes.

"I guess we just have to let each other BE, huh?"

"I guess so," I said.

The trip to Japan had obviously been about very much more than performing. Both Sachi and I did some growing up and our relationship recognized a new dimension.

When I returned from my tour, I visited my mother in Virginia.

It was probably the last time I would visit her in the house where she and my father had lived for so many years, because she was going to move to California to be with Warren and me. Many treasures still lay sequestered in the dusty basement of that house on that weekend visit.

I waited until Mother had gone to bed before I made my way to the recreation room closet in the basement. It was as though I was guided to the drawer by a voice which, from somewhere within me, directed me to "the black folder" under a pile of papers. I didn't know what I was guided toward, I just knew I needed to listen.

I slid the black folder out from under the papers, running my fingers over the dust along its edge. Then I opened it and began to read. I could see it was about music. Suddenly I realized it was my father's Ph.D. dissertation on musical composition from Johns Hopkins. I had searched for this for years, finally concluding that it had gotten lost somewhere in the moving melee of the last twenty-five years.

I turned the pages carefully. There it was—all his research on the effect of musical composition on the human mind. He had explored the subject of sound and its metaphysical effects on human beings. He had discussed the subject many times with me as though he needed to prove that music healed and calmed.

Here was his thesis. This is what had been turned down by Dr. Bamberger. This had been the turning point in his life. Dr. Bamberger had failed him, and in doing so, had been responsible for nipping his "confidence" permanently in the bud. It had been an apocryphal story in our family—the cruel act perpetrated on the father of our household, which would serve to make him suspicious and distrustful, not only of *his* but of my talent, for the rest of his life. All because of her.

I continued to read. I turned the yellowed pages slowly so as not to damage their brittle edges. A piece of paper fell out. I picked it up. It was a letter—a letter addressed to Dr. Bamberger. I read it. It was from Dr. Stephen at the Johns Hopkins University School of Higher Studies in Education. The letter was polite and almost apologetic in what it said. Dr. Stephen was recommending that Dr. Bamberger not accept my father's dissertation because it had not been well enough researched, not well enough thought out, and indeed not well enough written and accounted for in relation to the theories he was proposing. He wished he could see his way clear to accept it, but it just wasn't thorough enough to pass.

I stared at the letter. So it hadn't been Dr. Bamberger after all?

I read through more of the dissertation. I saw it begin to disintegrate in what it was saying. Some of what he had presented wasn't even typewritten. It was still in longhand. My heart stopped. What had he expected?

Then in between the pages I saw notes and recommendations inserted and written by someone else. The notes implored him to research this or that more thoroughly, make the connections more clear and logical. The notes made sense. I looked closely at them. They had been written by my mother.

I was overcome by the realization of what this meant. Tears welled up in my eyes for all the years of living the frustrations, the fights, the accusations, the forgiveness, the love, represented in these dusty pages. This treasure I held in my hands was a metaphor for their life together, and indeed the catalyst for what Warren and I had become. Dad had been the harsh dreamer who couldn't follow through because of his own self-doubt. Mother had tried to influence him to be more thorough and, for whatever reasons, she had transferred her inspiration to us. Warren and I had both become overachievers of the first order, never to be accused of not being perfectionist in the realizations of our dreams.

I stood over the pages with tears splashing on the words, remembering the stories of my grandmother's brutal treatment of her son when he was young. His fear of the female authority figure had been played out in many ways, not the least of which emerged in that defective dissertation, his own thinly inspired attempt at innovative thought, resulting in the apocryphal story that Dr. Bamberger had failed *him*. My mother had tried to bail him out; but I suspected now that he preferred to fail so that he could prove that he would never have realized his dream, because he believed that somehow he didn't deserve to.

I sat down on a dusty chair. The air in the basement was dank. The brick walls chilly. But I sat there, going over the implications of this sad and revealing document. How had I translated it to my life?

Well, for one thing, no one was ever going to be in a position to fail me. *I* would decide whether *I'd* pass or not. *I* would follow through thoroughly enough with whatever it took. So would Warren. We would never be disappointments to ourselves like Daddy had been to himself and to Mother. And we had used Mother's insistence that perseverance was necessary to accomplishment. Neither of us ever gave up on anything until we had succeeded.

I wiped my tears. Why had I found this treasure now? It thoroughly exposed one of our family myths. Dad hadn't been failed unjustly. He had failed himself.

I thought of Warren's life, Warren's talent and brilliance. What were the motivating inspirations for him? He had not wanted to fail himself.

Just as the thought hit me, I found myself standing up and opening a drawer in a long-forgotten filing cabinet. There were old bills, tax forms, letters from bygone days.

Then my hand selected what looked like a homemade envelope, folded together by a child out of loose-leaf paper. Suddenly I recognized it. I had made this envelope for my father for Father's Day when I was about nine years old. I remembered having pasted it together. I remembered printing "Happy Father's Day" on the outside, with "Guess Who?" as the return address.

Inside was a card with a picture of a tree I had drawn.

The tree was full-blown with green leaves, and in the center of the leaves was a black bag.

The caption under the tree read in a childish scrawl: "If you read Dick Tracy today, the money is in the bag in the tree."

My breath left me. I felt the childish envelope with my fingertips. Why was I finding this *now*? Warren's picture, *Dick Tracy,* had just premiered across the Potomac in Washington a few days earlier as a benefit for Johns Hopkins Hospital, where my father had died, and which was attached to the University that had overlooked his dissertation.

I was overcome by the symbolism, although I couldn't quite piece it together. Did the tree I had drawn represent life? Was it the Family Tree? What did the money bag mean? Did it mean the riches in life are found within the family?

On the next page I had drawn my father's car with a flat tire on the way from Richmond, Virginia (where we lived at the time), to Arlington, Virginia, where he was seeking new employment, because he was fed up with the "peanut politics" of the teaching profession in Richmond. "Too many overpowering women I can't get along with," he had said. "They won't let me teach."

Had I unconsciously felt that his leaving the teaching profession, regardless of its trials and tribulations, would result in a flat tire (failure) for him on the way to a new profession (real estate), which wasn't really him?

Perhaps the seeds of my conflict had been present on that Sunday morning when I drew that picture. Perhaps I had taken my father's pain and lack of confidence onto my own shoulders so that I could do something about it. My mother, apparently, couldn't make a difference. I would try. And in doing so, his disheartenment would govern my life. Maybe that's the way it was with many parents and children; rare indeed is the child who has parents with love so wise, and understanding so objective, as to happily balance needed limits with the freedom to grow and develop the child's own talents, to allow realization of its full potential. Far more often the child is neglected, or overindulged, or limited beyond reason, only to reflect those problems in his or her own life, and project them upon others.

My mother had denied her creativity in order to nurture her children. She chose a family over career—and never let us forget it. I had chosen a career over family so that I wouldn't make the same mistake. What was my daughter seeing in me that I denied? What was I inspiring in her from the well of my own overachievement pattern? Had she, as a little girl, throttled her feelings, remaining immature for many years, in the knowledge that neither her mother nor her father was interested enough in her needs to always be there, on call daily, during her growing-up years?

Even in maturity, Sachi had been in some confusion, because she wanted a career *and* a family, and saw no reason why she couldn't make both work for her. But something had happened—seemingly insignificant. She had been given a puppy, which afforded her a dress rehearsal for what she could expect in the age-old conflict between motherhood and work. She couldn't handle it. If the puppy cried as she left her place to go to work, she was riddled with guilt.

At first she understood she was identifying the puppy's abandonment with her own. But then she realized that the most difficult thing for her to accept in herself was the fact that she could, and would, walk away from a living, needing creature in order to get on with her life. Her guilt had not been that of being unable to leave, but rather the guilt of discovering she could do so quite easily. It was a small but infinitely revealing step to recognizing that she could still be committed to a puppy, or a person, and leave for a while to pursue her own creativity. And from there to the realization that she was not going to allow herself to be colonized, put into *any* false position, by the demands and expectations of society, attitudes, family conditioning, and—last but far from least—herself.

My mother had "chosen" family. I had "chosen" career. Sachi would choose both, and make it work for herself.

And my father? It was as though he had never chosen at all. He had fallen between two images—that of being afraid to dare and that of wanting so much more—never venturing out because he felt so responsible as the "head of the house," but never really being that either. He simply didn't know how. He had never been inculcated with the values of self-esteem and a sense of positive worth. On the contrary, it had been the opposite for him. No wonder he did not dare to choose what to do with his life, his creativity, his aspirations, and his dreams.

Perhaps he had come to understand LOVE so deeply before he died because he didn't have anything else. His had been the ultimate victory—the surrender of self. He was finally liberated when he put himself into the emotional hands of LOVE—love of God, love of people, love of life, love of the trust in death. He had finally come to the most important trust and love of all—himself. He said so without shame or sentimentality. In fact, he winked at me when he said, "If I love myself, Monkey, I can love everything. Too bad it took me so long, eh? Do you really have to die to find this out?"

In the end his was the most courageous choice of all.

I placed the Dick Tracy envelope in my pocket. It belonged to Warren now. The film he had made could have been his own dissertation on his childhood, with his father as the leading character—the Tracy hero resplendent in his stylish yellow raincoat (Dad was very dapper), fighting crime and evil (Dad was black and white about good and bad), tempted by a wicked female figure (most of the shadow women of Dad's vivid imagination!): Ira Beaty, a man who, even though a husband and father, was never really fulfilled in that role, secretly longing for so much more from life if only . . . And Dick Tracy, never quite committing himself to the tie of marriage, because, in doing so, he might lose so much . . . Yet Tracy remained a hero-image, bringing laughter and adventure to his devoted fans. And the all-too-human person that my father had been still brought tears and cheers to the hearts of those who knew him.

I wiped my cheeks with dusty fingers. The dust of the past of our family would eventually pass away, just as we would. My mother did not have much longer: the treasures in the basement had come along for me just in time. I had needed clues to who we were—mother, father, brother, sister—how we really related to each other. We had been inextricably intertwined and would be until our children's children's children rummaged around in our own basements or attics, finding a fingerprinted locket here, an old script and box of crystals there, an old meditation tape or an even older, yellow-paged book I had written that could only begin to express the pent-up wellsprings of love that we had always felt for each other, the yearning creativity, the ideas unspoken: and somewhere beneath the surface, the profound certainty that each of us chose, above all, to be with one another in the branches of this particular Family Tree. That was how we chose to learn about love. No one knew us better than we knew each other. That knowledge would always translate to the larger family of the world we lived in. Learn to love and forgive and understand family, and the world could be our true playground. It was up to us.

As I turned out the light and climbed the basement stairs, I reached down and patted my knee. Without its having buckled under me, I would not have come to the understanding I now had. I would now be capable of walking with new strength for the rest of my life. If it had not "failed" me, I would not have understood how I had been subtly, but surely, failing and undermining myself.

I closed the door at the head of the stairs, leaving the rest of the unknown memorabilia in the darkness below. My mother had long since forgotten they were there. She and my father had saved them for fifty-five years, waiting, I suppose, for a time when one of us children might want to ferret gently through the collection, looking perhaps for a book of poems, photographs in black and white always taken alongside the family car, a game of jacks still kept with chipped marbles, a tattered diary, a rumpled favorite doll, a report card with comments on the side relating to our futures.

We would be searching for clues from times past that would help us to understand more of who we were today, never suspecting that one small Father's Day card drawn on a Sunday morning forty-seven years ago might lead to a flood of realization that we, the children, were indeed the product of dreams and nightmares—just as they had been of their parents.

I would return someday, to sift and savor other treasures, perhaps to glean new understanding, and to recognize that the world of our mom and dad, which looked so very different, was nevertheless inexorably Warren's world and my world, the passage of time only providing one of many links that would hold us together always.

Slowly, slowly the creative puzzle that was our family would come clear, and through the shifting shapes of our lives the harmonious pattern would emerge that would allow us to come to terms with the whole. . . .